Creation Stories of the Middle East

of related interest

The Social Symbolism of Grief and Mourning
Roger Grainger
ISBN 1 85302 480 5

Christian Symbols, Ancient Roots
Elizabeth Rees
ISBN 1 85302 179 2

Bulgarian Folk Customs
Mercia MacDermott
ISBN 1 85302 486 4

Rhythm and Timing of Movement in Performance
Drama, Dance and Ceremony
Janet Goodridge
ISBN 1 85302 548 8

Creation Stories
of the Middle East

Ewa Wasilewska

Jessica Kingsley Publishers
London and Philadelphia

First published in the United Kingdom in 2000
by Jessica Kingsley Publishers
116 Pentonville Road
London N1 9JB, UK
and
400 Market Street, Suite 400
Philadelphia, PA 19106, USA

www.jkp.com

Library of Congress Cataloging in Publication Data
A CIP catalogue record for this book is available from the Library of Congress

British Library Cataloguing in Publication Data
A CIP catalogue record for this book is available from the British Library

ISBN-13: 978 1 85302 681 2
ISBN-10: 1 85302 681 6

Printed and Bound in Great Britain by
Athenaeum Press, Gateshead, Tyne and Wear

Contents

In memory of my Mom,
Izabella Wasilewska

Acknowledgments

One of the old fables ascribed to Nasreddin Hoca, a Middle Eastern folk character, finishes with the line: 'Truth is relative. This is [always] your truth.' Nowhere else is this statement more true than in the discussion of various religions, especially of their core beliefs embodied by creation stories. While I have been interested in this topic for many years and have taught a 'Creation Stories of the Middle East' course at the University of Utah for the last few years, I did not seriously consider writing a book about it until my friend, Cathy Malchiodi, intervened. She found the answer to my complaint about not being able to find books which I could assign to my students as required material covering all the themes and texts of my lectures. Her solution was quite simple: 'write a book yourself.' Not only did Cathy initiate this project but she also helped me to find a publisher, Jessica Kingsley. I would like to offer my sincere thanks to Cathy for her involvement and friendship that survived long hours of ups and downs during the process of writing.

My deepest gratitude also goes to Jessica Kingsley not only for publishing this book but also for controlling its length. Once the idea was implanted in my mind I wanted to cover all possible issues involved in the treatment of creation stories of the Middle East and, before I knew it, my first draft included extended discussions of such concepts as religion and myth, as well as a lengthy introduction to the geography and history of the Middle East. With the help of Jessica Kingsley and Caroline Tingay I was able to shorten all of this to one reasonable Introduction, followed by the main topic of the book arranged in a chronological order of creation hoping that non-specialists will not get bored before reading the really 'fun' part of the book dealing with both deities and humans.

The person who 'suffered' the most through the creation of this book was Professor James Kelly, my mentor and friend, who edited all the drafts. After many hours of reading and discussing the topic I am absolutely sure that he must be shivering now every time he hears the word 'creation'. I extend my warmest thanks to him for always believing in me.

As with any long-term project this one would not be possible without the support of many friends and colleagues who contributed in many different ways to this book becoming a reality. I would like to thank (in alphabetical order) Margaret Brady, Kathie Dow, Jennifer Graves, Ursula Hanly, Tonya Hendrix, Peggy Kadir, Terri Khan, Karen Lupo, Paula Massey, Ewa Nalecz-Mrozowska, Gloria and Edward Skurzynski, Elaine Weis and many others, including my students, for their assistance. Special thanks go to Professor David Owen for his many suggestions, guidance, and friendship. I would also like to offer my gratitude to Stephen Osmond of 'The World and I' (a monthly magazine published by the Washington Times Corporation) who published a series of my articles on creation stories of the Middle East in 1994, long before the idea of this book was conceived.

Last, I would like to thank my aunt, Zofia Dziedzic-Godula, for her continuous love and support in each and every venture of my life. Without her this book could not have become a reality.

Although while writing this book I tried to remain as objective as possible and let the reader draw his or her own conclusions based on the material presented, I realize that occasionally I may have failed in my attempt to be just an impartial observer. All faults are mine, unless Sauvage and Squeak, my two adorable cats, are willing to share the blame for rearranging my papers and interfering with my computer system.

Introduction

Religion: In search of its origin

It is widely assumed that all human societies have some sort of religion whether 'primitive' or very complex. This assumption is based on the common belief that religion (or rather 'religiosity') and speech are among the intrinsic traits of humankind which distinguish us from all other animals. Usually humankind is defined as the species 'identified with the biological taxon *Homo sapiens*, one of an immense number of animal species inhabiting the Earth, connected synchronically in a complex web of ecological interdependencies, and diachronically in the all-encompassing genealogy of phylogenetic evolution' (Ingold 1988, p.5).

This definition, like many others, does not deny 'animality' – that is, a 'natural' state 'in which actions are impelled by innate emotional drives that are undisciplined by reason or responsibility' (Ingold 1988, p.5) – in each of us but it uses a qualifier in the form of *Homo sapiens* to exclude 'humanity' from all other beings. This is consistent with our present understanding of the concept of religion which requires the existence of language without which myths cannot exist and, consequently, without myths there is no system of beliefs. The key phrase here is 'present understanding' because our knowledge about emotions and thought processes in the animal kingdom (excluding *Homo sapiens sapiens*) is very limited. After all, according to various evolutionary theories the origin of humankind can be traced back in time as far as around 70 million years ago, to a small rat-like animal known as *Purgatorius* (Angela and Angela 1993). As cute as this animal may have been (its reconstruction is based only on the few remains of the teeth and the jaws) it is hard for us, the general public, to comprehend and, for some, to admit that this small creature was our ancestor and, consequently, that it had potential for the future development of both language and religion.

Since the ability to speak is a prerequisite for the development of myths it should be noted here that due to the fact that brains do not fossilize, it is very difficult to establish with certainty which of the human predecessors were capable of articulate speech (for discussion see Angela and Angela 1993). Furthermore, the presence of speech should not be equated with the 'invention' of religion itself, even with the presence of archaeological remains attesting to the special care taken of the dead as early as around 90,000 years ago (Angela and Angela 1993). Fixing the date for the 'beginning' of religion remains in the domain of speculation. Durkheim (1968) summarized this problem in very definite terms by simply saying:

> There was no given moment when religion began to exist, and there is consequently no need of finding a means of transporting ourselves thither in thought. Like every human

institution, religion did not commence anywhere. Therefore, all speculations of this sort are justly discredited; they can only consist in subjective and arbitrary constructions which are subject to no sort of control. (p.20)

The subject of prehistoric religion and hence of myths has been avoided by many scholars because 'in this field the gap between specialists and nonspecialists is narrower than in most… Some speculation is necessary at every junction' (Lippard 1983, p.3). Unfortunately, 'speculation' is the concept which dominates the study of prehistoric religion. This is the field in which each and every person interested in religion feels free to express his or her ideas without providing any hard or verifiable evidence. This, of course, does not mean that this subject cannot be treated scientifically. As I have argued before (Wasilewska 1991a) some 'hard facts' concerning the religion of prehistoric societies can be deduced when religious behavior is approached from a comparative, theoretical and cross-cultural perspective.

However, myths as well as names, actions, and functions of different divine forces worshipped by prehistoric people will never be known, regardless of how plausible some 'interpretations' might be. Unfortunately, myths of prehistoric societies are often 'created' by modern authors. For example, there is almost an obsession with the universality of 'Mother Goddess' (Gimbutas 1989) and/or fire/sun/fertility (Singh 1993) worship in prehistoric societies. Almost each and every prehistoric artifact which cannot be easily classified as domestic in its function is frequently interpreted in symbolic terms related to religion. Although I definitely believe in the concept of 'psychic unity' – that is, that there is no difference between the capability of the ancient and modern mind – I do have a problem with the rather haphazard assigning of the same values to different symbols in different cultures on the assumption that there is such a thing as symbolic unity and universality. As my research on the archaeology of religion and color symbolism (Wasilewska 1991a and 1991b) demonstrates, there is a tendency (but not a 'universality'!) to assign similar values to similar symbols in different cultures. But before we can assume the meaning of prehistoric symbols, many variables, often not related to religion, have to be taken into consideration.

In summary, our knowledge of prehistoric myths is very limited and likely to remain so. While eventually we will be able to ascertain when the ability to tell them (that is, speech) occurred for the first time, their content will continue to be a mystery. Only in sporadic cases can we make an educated guess as to the type of deities who were worshipped, but their names and their involvement with the human world will not be revealed to us until time travel becomes a reality. If there is a continuation of both cultural and archaeological patterns in societies that at some point produced a written language, we can safely assume that their religious traditions also survived into the literate period. Religion is a subject of continuous growth and transformation but this process, as with the case of language, is relatively slow as compared with, for example, the rapid development of science and technology in the twentieth century. Thus, the earliest solid information concerning the mythology of ancient societies can be acquired from the area where writing was invented for the first time in the history of humankind – the Middle East.

Creation myth: Toward its definition

Religion and myth are among those concepts that are being defined and redefined continuously by social scientists and humanists in order to address various components of these fundamental notions of each and every culture. What makes these concepts difficult to define is their common use in everyday language and instinctive understanding of their meaning by both the speaker and the receiver of the message. Since these are the terms that we 'feel,' we also tend to qualify their use depending on our personal background, education and constitution.

No matter what definition of religion is selected for any specific purpose of study, most scholars and non-scholars agree that religion as a concept can be divided into two major components: rituals and beliefs. While rituals can simply be described as 'religion in action' (Wallace 1966, p.102), the beliefs can be recognized as a state of thought (or 'states of opinion, and consist in representations'; for a discussion, see Durkheim 1968, pp.51–57), an ideological system of which myths are a part. This system should be believed in by the followers of any particular religion in spite of the lack of objective evidence for the factual basis of affiliated stories.

This is what each and every myth really is: it is a story. The word is derived from the Greek word *muthos* meaning word, story or fable. As with all other stories such as folk stories, fairy tales, legends, sagas and so forth, myths are narratives of various events perceived to be important because of their informative, moral, and/or entertaining values. However, in contrast to the others, religious myths are a part of a much bigger system of beliefs which they support, explain and promote.

Thus, in order to define myth one must focus on the type of information provided by its narrative which sets it in a very specific religious context. This is by no means an easy process. The first problem is with the term 'myth' itself, which in common understanding implies falsehood – that is, a story not substantiated by facts. In this sense 'myth' also has a secular meaning and is used as such quite frequently in English and other languages. While secular myths are not difficult to analyze because they are not connected with any specific ideological system, defining and evaluating religious myths is a much more difficult task. Since no objective evidence can be provided for or against the existence of supernatural beings (or forces), only specific components of each religious system can be analyzed in a scientific way. However, disproving part of an ideology does not mean that this ideology as a whole has no value. It must be remembered that religions are not to be proven; they are to be believed in, so they are all equal and should be treated as such.

But, as humans, we tend to label the religious stories of traditions other than our own as myths, implying their falsehood. This is in contrast to the 'true' messages carried by the stories of the religious system to which we ascribe, even if some of these stories can now be scientifically disproved (for example, the creation of humankind out of clay versus the evolution of hominids). This lack of objectivity interferes with our ability to develop a definition of the word 'myth' which is satisfactory for both believers and non-believers. Furthermore, one has to realize that religious myths have been created in a very specific reality, a reality that is foreign to us whether in relation to time (ancient societies) or to geography (technological/scientific and cultural isolation). These stories reflect reality as perceived by their messengers and as based on existing 'facts.' Although many of these 'facts' have been challenged or discredited with the development of modern science and technology, one must remember that many of our current 'truths' are likely to be challenged too.

In view of the above discussion I must agree with Strensky's (1987) definition of myth which states:

> Myth is everything and nothing at the same time. It is the true story or a false one, revelation or deception, sacred or vulgar, real or fictional, symbol or tool, archetype or stereotype. It is either strongly structured and logical or emotional and pre-logical, traditional and primitive or part of contemporary ideology. Myth is about the gods, but often also the ancestors and sometimes certain men... Such confusion indicates graphically enough that there is no such 'thing' as myth. (p.1)

Since there is no such 'thing' which can be objectively labeled as a religious 'myth' in the sense of implied falsehood, all religious stories should be treated simply as 'stories' in their ideological context, following the original meaning of the word *muthos*.

Like their secular counterparts religious stories can be read and analyzed in many different ways and have been since at least the sixth and fifth centuries B.C. until the present (for a presentation of different trends and contributors to this field see Frazer 1955; Georges 1968; Harrison 1903, 1912; Hicks 1999; Jung 1916; Jung and Kerényi 1963; Lessa and Vogt 1979; Mayerson 1971; Puhvel 1987; Stark and Bainbridge 1987; Strensky 1987, 1992; Toynbee 1956; Wallace 1966). They have also been divided into different categories, of which the most important for the understanding of human nature and the ever-changing perception of reality is the category of cosmic myths. The word 'cosmic' derives from the Greek word *kosmos*, meaning 'order.' This is the order in which the universe was created as seen by the followers of any given narration of a 'sacred history' (term developed by Mircea Eliade 1961, p.112). Thus, this category includes all myths which are concerned with an explanation of the beginning of the cosmos, earth, humankind and any other elements relevant to a given society. These stories establish our reason for existence as well as our significance within the universe.

These creation stories, which also include stories of destruction and rebirth, are the foundation of every religion. They provide us with information concerning not only the spiritual reality of a society which has been studied but also with a variety of other information ranging from technology, architecture and even the ideals of beauty. While for some cultures the creation of humankind is the central part of their stories, for others humans are so irrelevant that they are barely mentioned. For some, life on earth is important, for others the world beyond counts more. But no matter what perspective creation stories represent, they all reflect the reality of the time of their own creation, thus becoming invaluable sources of information on the life and culture of the peoples who have believed in them. Studying these stories brings us closer to other traditions as well as to a better understanding of our own culture. Nowhere else is this statement so true as in the case of the Middle Eastern traditions which have led to the development of three religious systems: Judaism, Christianity and Islam, whose believers can be found everywhere in the world.

The Middle East: Terminology

In the area where controversies abound and nothing, except for the ancient records, is written on stone anymore, the first problem that arises is the definition of the 'Middle East' itself. The land that it encompasses is defined differently depending on the field of study as well as on the personal perception of the scholar. While its northern border is widely recognized as delineated by the waters of the Black Sea and Caspian Sea (hence the most northern countries are Turkey and Iran), its other frontiers are 'moved' around depending on historical, cultural, linguistic, religious and political variables which are taken into consideration by scholars (for discussion and various definitions see Fickelman 1998; Longrigg 1967). I find Drysdale and Blake's (1985) definition of the area as covering 'large parts of northern and eastern Africa as well as Iran, Israel, Turkey and all the Arab states east of Suez Canal' (p.11) to be the most useful because it is an extended version of the term 'Near East' which is continuously employed by European educated speakers. The Near East as a term usually designates the area of the so-called great civilizations: that is, Egypt, Jordan, Palestine, Syria, Lebanon, Iraq – Arabic (Semitic group of languages) speaking countries using an Arabic script; Turkey – Turkish (Altaic group) and Latin script; Iran – Persian/Farsi/Iranian (Indo-European) and Arabic script; and Israel – Hebrew (Semitic) and Hebrew script. However, some scholars – for example, Dominique Collon (1995, p.7) – exclude Egypt from this term and add countries of the Arabian Peninsula. Thus, the term 'Middle East' allows one to overcome most differences of opinion regarding the Near East and includes all areas of the so-called great civilizations with any and all neighboring countries which in the past were under their influence.

But the trouble with terminology of the region does not end with the definitions of the Near East and the Middle East. Another common term used for the region by Europeans is 'Orient' (von Soden 1994, p.1). So, a typical American might have difficulty in understanding the route of the famous Orient Express train because for him or her, this term refers to 'East Asia' (more or less the 'Far East').

To this confusion one more general term might be added – 'Western Asia.' It covers more or less the same area as the above–defined Middle East, but sometimes with the exclusion of the western part of modern Turkey which is believed to belong to the classical – that is, European – world. This exclusion shall be ignored because the first inscription from the second millennium B.C. in Troy appeared to be written in the Luwian language (an Indo-European language, closely related to the Hittite language of Central Anatolia), not in Greek or Proto-Greek (Brandau 1998). This means that the western part of Turkey was too a part of the Middle Eastern cultural traditions. Therefore, the term 'Western Asia' should include all of Anatolia (that is, the Asiatic part of modern Turkey, also known as Asia Minor), not just a part of it.

In addition there are other terms, such as Mesopotamia, Persia, Syria–Palestine and Levant, that the reader should be familiar with in order to study ancient cultures of the Middle East. The first term, 'Mesopotamia,' is of Greek origin and refers literally to the '[the land] between the rivers' (Gr. *meso*, between, and *potamos*, river), that is, between the Euphrates and the Tigris (the land that is, more or less, modern Iraq). The term 'Persia' was used by the West until 1935 to designate the country known today as Iran which hosted one of the biggest empires in the history of the Middle East, the Persian Empire (that is, the Achaemenid Dynasty between around 550 to 331 B.C. and then the Sassanids Dynasty between A.D. 226 until the Arab conquest of A.D. 641) 'Syria–Palestine' and 'Levant' are used interchangeably to refer – in its most common sense – to the eastern shore of the Mediterranean Sea and include the modern countries of (from north to south) Syria, Lebanon, Israel, Palestine and Jordan which are dissected by various mountain ranges and rivers (see Appendix I for a topographical description of the region).

The ancient Middle East: The peoples

The last 200 years of exploration in the Middle East have brought to life ancient civilizations whose memories have been preserved, but only to a certain degree, by the most 'popular' book of all time, the Bible. A very limited number of European travelers who have visited the area since the Arab conquests of the seventh century have remarked on the magnificent structures and strange artifacts which they had seen in Egypt or Mesopotamia. Some of these (antiquities) even made it to Europe where very few people tried to understand their lost meaning while others exhibited them proudly in their collections of 'curios.'

Since their past remained unknown due to the limitations of treating the Bible as the most ancient written source of human knowledge, the antiquity of these civilizations was not recognized until the nineteenth century. Such great discoveries as the Rosetta Stone in Egypt or thousands of small clay tablets covered with cuneiform writing in Mesopotamia and elsewhere in the region (for a detailed description of the most important discoveries see Stiebing 1993) have led to the development of the Middle Eastern archaeology and other related disciplines focusing on ancient civilizations of the region (see Appendix I).

Egypt

Written records and archaeological discoveries have shown that Egyptian civilization (of Hamitic-Semitic origin) flourished between around 3150 B.C. (the unification of Lower [northern] Egypt and Upper [southern] Egypt by King Narmer) and 332 B.C. when Egypt was 'liberated' (or 'conquered,' depending on the point of view) from the Persians by Alexander the Great. During that period of time, also known as the Pharaonic Period, Egyptian civilization created – among other things – fabulous pyramids, thousands of less monumental but still very impressive tombs, excellent fortifications to protect its southern and northern borders, and marvelous, massive temples. The outside fascination with this civilization is probably mainly due to the Egyptian 'obsession' with death; that is, the strong belief in an after-life for which Egyptians spent their lifetime preparing. The uniqueness of this civilization is the result of its political and geographical isolation from the rest of the ancient Middle East, with whom Egyptians were in continuous contact but from whom they adopted only a very few ideas. One of them was thought to be writing, a concept that developed in the southern part of modern Iraq, in ancient Sumer, until an independent invention of writing by the Egyptians might be proven after more detailed studies of written records from the tomb of King Scorpion in southern Egypt.

Sumer

In spite of the great antiquity of the Egyptian civilization, this is not the most ancient historical culture that we know of. The Sumerians, whose origin is still enshrouded in mystery, used a writing system before the Egyptians. They probably invented it since they were the first ones to make a transition from 'before writing' to a written script (Schmandt-Besserat 1992). This script was more than a pictographic/ideographic system, for which the knowledge of a language is not necessary, because it involved phonemes. Their invention, the cuneiform script, was 'borrowed' and adjusted by many cultures of the Middle East, from the third to the first millennium B.C. The Sumerians referred to their land in southern Mesopotamia as Kengir, although the Babylonian designation for this southern land was Sumer. For more than 1000 years they dominated Mesopotamia, establishing most of the dogma and foundations for future civilizations of the area.

Among the 'firsts' that the Sumerians invented were many religious concepts, ideas, and traditions, which Western civilization inherited through several intermediaries. Their architecture, art, laws and so forth have survived long after the disappearance of the Sumerians at the beginning of the second millennium B.C.

The Semitic groups

The memory of the Sumerians lived on through the Semitic peoples who started to replace them in Mesopotamia from the third millennium B.C., although some may argue, on the basis of preserved vocabulary, that Semitic groups were present in the area even before that time. The Akkadians and the Assyrians were the first Semites who established their kingdoms north of Sumer land in the second part of this millennium. Although the Mesopotamians (a general term used for all cultures living in this area before Alexander the Great) referred to the Semitic migrations as 'people of the West' (MAR.TU in Sumerian), scholars are still discussing their 'cradle.' They were probably wandering nomads who eventually settled in Mesopotamia. Until the discovery of the ancient city of Ebla (modern Tell Mardikh) in northern Syria by Paolo Matthiae in the 1970s, the Akkadians were believed to represent the oldest Semitic group in the Middle East. While their empire was short-lived in spite of somewhat exaggerated claims made by its leading rulers such as Sargon of Akkad or his grandson, Naramsin, their language, written with the help of cuneiform, became a *lingua franca* of the Middle East for almost two thousand years. Even Egyptian rulers used it for international correspondence.

The second millennium B.C. witnessed the establishment of the Semitic kingdoms in Mesopotamia: the Assyrians to the north and the Babylonians to the south. They dominated the area until the second half of the following millennium. And, like the Akkadians before them, they adopted and/or incorporated into their traditions the important achievements of the Sumerians, including the cuneiform script and religion. Their power was replaced in the region by the Persians, the Indo-Europeans, who, in spite of great efforts by their rulers to continue traditions of the great kings of 'Sumer and Akkad,' failed effectively to control the Middle East and lost their empire to Alexander the Great who was welcomed as a liberator by many of their adversaries.

The Semitic people of Mesopotamia were not the only Semites in the Middle East. The others, known as Canaanites (Canaan – the Biblical designation for the land of Syria–Palestine) and as Aramaeans (both groups of north-western stock) lived to the west of the 'land between the rivers'. The North Semitic people such as the Eblaites had already established a powerful kingdom in the region by the second part of the third millennium B.C. By the second millennium B.C. the area was dissected into small political entities, sometimes completely independent, sometimes under the strong influence of foreign powers. The Canaanite communities, known as the Amurru ([people of] 'west') in Mesopotamian sources, which stretched from the north to the south of the Mediterranean coast, were very much involved in international trade and Canaanites became the 'middlemen' of the Middle East. One of the most famous and wealthy communities was the city of ancient Ugarit (modern Ras Shamra in northern Syria). The Ugaritians were truly cosmopolitan people who borrowed the idea of a cuneiform script but transformed it into a completely alphabetic script. They lost their prominence with the destruction of Ugarit by the Sea Peoples around 1200 B.C.

The Aramaeans were yet another Semitic group which established a number of small principalities both in Mesopotamia and in Syria by the end of the second millennium B.C. (first recorded in the Assyrian sources after the thirteenth century B.C.). Their language, sometimes referred to as 'Imperial Aramaic,' became the second *lingua franca* of the Middle East during the first millennium B.C. The Canaanites of this period are known as the Phoenicians (following the Greek tradition) and are famous for their 'colonization' efforts especially on the coast of North Africa. Both groups – as well as others, such as the Israelites, who arrived in the area during the so-called 'Dark Ages' following the invasion of the Sea Peoples – used a variety of quite similar linear alphabetic scripts whose beginnings can be traced back to the previous millennium.

The Hittites

The Sumerian invention of the cuneiform script attracted the attention not only of the Semitic peoples but also of others such as the Hittites and Persians. By the end of the third millennium and the beginning of the second millennium B.C. newcomers of Indo-European origin entered Anatolia, previously inhabited by wealthy communities without a writing system. They are known as the Hittites, although they called themselves the Nesians. They arrived with their linguistic relatives, the Luwians and the Palaians (or Paleans), and quickly began to dominate the local population of the Hattians or Proto-Hattians. While, again, the origin of these Indo-Europeans is a mystery, some scholars (including myself) look toward the eastern part of Eurasian steppes to the nomadic societies of Central Asia and Western China where yet another linguistically related group, the Tocharians, lived many centuries later.

Although the Hittites established a very powerful empire in Anatolia and beyond during the second millennium B.C., they then vanished from human memory only to be rediscovered at the beginning of the twentieth century. Only the Bible carried short references to the Hittites, presenting them as one of the tribes of Palestine in the first millennium B.C. It was a 'son of Heth,' a Hittite, who sold Abraham the land to bury his beloved Sarah.

Persia

Many people still do not realize that the south-western part of modern Iran was yet another cradle of early Middle Eastern civilization with writing. Here there existed the kingdom of Elam that survived longer than the Sumerian power and almost as long as Pharaonic Egypt. The Elamites were the third group of people who, at the end of the fourth millennium B.C., invented their own system of writing only to abandon it shortly afterwards in favor of the Sumerian cuneiform. Their language is not related to any other language and even today their culture remains quite mysterious due to the great difficulty in reading the ancient texts. Throughout their existence the Elamites focused on the Mesopotamian kingdoms to the west with whom they had ongoing and frequently warlike relationships.

With the exception of Elam, Iran did not have any literate cultures until the first millennium B.C. That was the time when Persia became dominated by the Indo-European peoples such as the Medes, the Cimmerians and finally the Persians. Of these three groups only the Persians left us with an impressive legacy of texts written with the help of – what else – a modified cuneiform script (also known as the Persian cuneiform alphabet). Beginning with Cyrus the Great (in the sixth century B.C.), the Persians established a huge empire stretching from Anatolia to Egypt and then beyond the northern and eastern borders of Iran. This power fell victim to Alexander the Great, a Macedonian, who commandeered the Greek forces against Persia, and claimed all these conquests for himself by 331 B.C. This was the beginning of a new era in the history of the Middle East – the Hellenistic Period. This was followed by the Roman Period (including the Byzantine empire) and finally by the Islamic Era beginning in A.D. 622.

The others

The above description is only a very brief summary of the land and the peoples of the Middle East with a chronological outline of its ancient history (see also Appendix II). It focuses only on the peoples whose creation stories will be discussed in this book. However, it must be noted that many others such as the Hurrians, the Urartians, the so-called Indo-Aryans, the Gutians, the Kassites, and the Philistines also contributed to the development of the Middle Eastern civilizations, although their accomplishments and/or languages remain mostly unknown. Only the Hurrians left literary evidence pertinent to the subject of this book and their contributions are discussed later.

PART 1

Written Sources

1

In Search of Foundation: The Sumerian Origin

The Sumerians and the origin of writing

In order to search for the origin of many different concepts one must always look to the most ancient written sources available at the time. While for centuries the Bible was a source of information about the beginning of the world and its institutions, the decipherment of ancient cuneiform tablets has led scholars toward the land to the east – to ancient Sumer. Here, in the most southern part of Mesopotamia, the Sumerian culture flourished for over a 1000 years of written history and, as some scholars suggest, even earlier. In spite of hundreds of thousands of Sumerian written sources, their origin still baffles many scholars, although more and more scholars agree that the Sumerians were already in the area long before writing was invented as indicated by continuity in the cultural development of southern Mesopotamia (Bielinski 1985).

The Sumerians' single most important contribution to the development of human civilization must be writing. As Denise Schmandt-Besserat's research (1992) has proven, tokens, both plain and complex, were used for recording quantitative messages since around 8000 B.C. by many varied cultural groups encompassing the area from Turkey and Syria–Palestine to the west and as far east as India and Central Asia. However, the transition from a clay token system to a writing system on clay tablets had occurred and continued only in the area of southern Mesopotamia in the second part of the fourth millennium B.C. It seems that the Sumerians were also the first ones to recognize the limitation of the pictographic/ideographic script and introduced phonemes to their writing system which is presently known as the cuneiform script.

According to the Sumerian tradition, writing – considered to be one of the most basic elements of civilization listed in the form of divine decrees in possession of the god of wisdom, Enki – had a mythical origin. It was 'invented' by a legendary ruler of Uruk (biblical Erech, modern Warka), Enmerkar, out of necessity when in his conflict with the lord of Aratta, he realized that the messenger, 'his mouth heavy,' could not repeat a complicated message word by word (Kramer 1959; Schmandt-Besserat 1992). 'Because the herald was heavy of mouth, could not repeat it–/The lord of Kullab patted (a lump of) clay, set up the words like a tablet –/Formerly there had been no one who sets words on clay –/Now as Utu is…it was so' (Kramer 1952, pp.37, 39).

In this epic, entitled by Kramer 'Enmerkar and the Lord of Aratta', Enmerkar is presented as a son of the Sumerian sun god Utu (Akkadian Šiamaš), although there are also references in the same epic to him being fathered by Enlil, another powerful deity in the Mesopotamian pantheon (Kramer 1952; see also Chapter 9). This reinforced the Sumerian belief in the divine origin of writing. The later traditions of Mesopotamia credited the gods themselves with this invention: for the Babylonians it was Enki, for the Assyrians Nabû, son of Marduk, and for Berossos (a priest of Bēl [Marduk] at Babylon in the fourth/third century B.C.) Oannes, a later version of Enki. This divine invention – which in reality can probably be credited to anonymous genius or a group of such geniuoes living at the time in Uruk or any other contemporaneous center of the Sumerian dominance – made it possible for us, over 5000 years later, to have a glimpse into the lives of the ancient people of the Middle East.

Oral, aural and written body of literature

The majority of written documents from ancient Sumer, and Mesopotamia in general, are administrative and economic in character, because the need to record various transactions was the main reason for the invention of writing. Among many other 'firsts' that the Sumerians invented they can also be credited with the establishment of a bureaucracy. However, once the system began to develop further other types of texts were written which provide information concerning the reality of life as perceived by the Sumerians and others in the area.

This reality is not always very easy to understand. Neither should it be considered to be the only one in existence at the time. The Sumerians never tried to organize their beliefs in such a way that it would be comprehensible for us, neither did they try to make sense and/or order of many conflicting traditions floating around at the same time. Others after them, like the Akkadians, Assyrians, and Babylonians, only added to the existing confusion by incorporating their beliefs into the already 'operating' Sumerian system. Numerous texts indicate that the scribes themselves were sometimes confused while recording ancient (already for them) stories often carried on through the oral tradition of the area.

As of today the earliest literary tablets can be dated to the first half of the third millennium B.C., around 2600 B.C. (Alster 1992; Biggs 1974). These earliest texts are considered by some to be somewhat 'defective'; that is, 'impossible for anyone to read …unless he was acquainted with it in advance' (Alster 1992, p.25). Since their comprehension depends on the knowledge of the sound of the text, the type of literature that we are dealing with is often aural in its character. These compositions are meant to be read or recited for an audience. This is quite understandable because the majority of people in the ancient Middle East was illiterate. However, the 'aural' character of the early Sumerian stories makes it very difficult for modern scholars to reveal their content fully (Vogelzang and Vanstiphout 1992), especially because many of these stories were transmitted in an oral form before being recorded with the help of writing. Furthermore, it must be remembered that oral tradition did not disappear once writing was invented, but how much of this tradition was ever transformed into the written form remains within the realm of educated guesswork.

The oral, aural and written characteristics of the ancient Mesopotamian literature make the task of interpreting texts quite challenging. This task is even more difficult when one realizes that many stories survived only in a fragmentary form. The irony is that frequently the most interesting or important part of the story is either missing or unintelligible. It is almost like reading an Agatha Christie mystery with the last few pages missing. Sometimes the missing or illegible parts can be reconstructed with the help of other copies or other related texts, but sometimes an interpreter has to fill in the gaps.

The learning and creating process

The process of interpretation had begun already thousands of years ago with the invention of writing and the emergence of a professional class of scribes. The highly sophisticated bureaucracy of the Sumerians and their successors required thousands of highly trained scribes for services requested by temples and palaces as well as private parties. Since education was neither compulsory nor universal, only those who could afford it, such as children of 'governors, "city fathers," ambassadors, temple administrators, military officers, sea captains, high tax officials, priests of various sorts, managers, supervisors, foremen, scribes, archivists, and accountants' (Kramer 1959, p.3), were able to spend an extended period of time in school. While the majority of students were definitely male, there were some Mesopotamian women who achieved the status of scribes and/or authors (Hallo 1996; Meier 1991).

However, in spite of the fact that the most famous divine scribes and/or patrons of scribes were the goddesses Nisaba, Geštinana and Akkadian Bēlet-seri (Hallo 1996), women as writers were not necessarily held in high esteem as King Assurbanipal (in the seventh century B.C.) stated in his letter to the gods: 'Disregard that a woman has written (this letter) and placed it before you' (after Hallo 1996, p.262 citing Meissner 1925, p.329). The irony is that the first confirmed 'non-anonymous, non-fictitious, author in the world history' (Hallo 1996, p.266) is Enheduanna, the daughter of Sargon of Akkad, the first 'emperor' in the Middle East (2334–2279 B.C.). She was the first creative writer in the history of literature whose compositions such as the *Exaltation of Inanna* represent a woman's point of view. However, most of the literary texts which survived were written by men presenting their perspective on life. This tradition of mostly male scribes throughout the history of the Middle East has affected the status of women and the role that they were assigned to play in the creation stories of many religions whose beginnings can be found in this region. Genesis is the best example of how one Biblical story has 'thrown' women into the abyss of inequality.

The main goal of the Sumerian and Akkadian (including Assyrian and Babylonian) schooling system was to train future scribes. Thus, the focus was on studying already existing texts and copying them. Thousands of so-called practice tablets written by students on each and every level of schooling have been discovered in Mesopotamia. 'Textbooks'– that is, tablets with 'groups of related words and phrases… [for] students [to] memorize and copy them until they could reproduce them with ease' (Kramer 1959, p.4) – were already prepared and standardized probably by the end of the third millennium B.C. These categorized lists of various objects, animals, trees, geographical names, minerals, grammar forms, and so on, provide modern scholars with a wealth of information about the level of science in ancient Mesopotamia.

In the twenty-fourth century B.C. Sargon of Akkad conquered the Sumerians and established an empire which extended far to the north claiming Anatolian Purushanda (Goodnick Westenholz 1997 ['King of Battle' – text 9]) and as far west as crossing the Amanus Mountains to 'the cedar forest,' the northern part of Syria–Palestine (Goodnick Westenholz 1997, ['Sargon in Foreign Lands' – text 7]). The Akkadians borrowed from the Sumerians not only their script but also an expressive body of literature developed by these 'black-headed' people. The use of both languages at the same time required fluency in both which was accomplished by the compilation of the first 'dictionaries' which have aided scholars so much in their decipherment of the Sumerian language and script.

The most common method of learning the art of writing was copying existing texts. According to Samuel Noah Kramer the favorite genres used for this purpose were 'myths and epic tales in the form of narrative poems celebrating deeds and exploits of the Sumerian gods and heroes; hymns to gods and kings; lamentations bewailing the destruction of Sumerian cities; wisdom compositions including proverbs, fables and essays' (1959, p.5). Thus, some literary creations copied by Sumerian and other students have survived to modern times. And since students in the past as in the present were not always so dedicated to their education – in spite of 'caning' as a proper method to keep them in line – many of these texts are full of mistakes which modern scholars have to discover and correct in order to interpret any given text properly. Furthermore, due to the variety of the existing sources, be it a 'professional' or 'student' edition, it is impossible to list most of them in this chapter. Thus, any specific stories which are relevant for concepts discussed in subsequent parts of this book are identified and referenced in appropriate sections.

Religion: The non-existent concept

Since the Sumerians were the first people to write, they are also credited with the invention of many other 'firsts,' some of which are beautifully recorded by one of the greatest and most dedicated Sumeriologists, the late Samuel Noah Kramer, in his book *History Begins at Sumer* (1959) which was first published in 1956. I am convinced that if not for this popular book which, with time, has become an archaeological bestseller, many people would have never heard about this great civilization. Kramer listed many 'firsts' and directed the general public's attention to 'Man's First Cosmogony and Cosmology,' which, as will be shown below, influenced most of the developing religions of the Middle East.

It must be noted that in the Sumerian language, as well as in other languages of the ancient Middle East, there is no specific word which is equivalent to the modern concept of 'religion.' The closest notion is expressed by 'the later Hebrew "fear of heaven" (yir at shamayim)' as indicated by Hallo (1996, p.212), which can hardly be applied to the

Mesopotamian – or in fact to the Egyptian, Anatolian, Canaanite and Persian – perception of the concept which did not exist and so did not require any definition.

The lack of such a term in the Sumerian and Akkadian languages (as well as in other languages of the Middle East before Greek influence) can easily be explained by a very different model of reality in which ancient people lived. While today we have an 'option' to choose our religion upon entering adulthood or even earlier, this option did not really exist in ancient Mesopotamia. The world of many gods and goddesses was so intermingled with the world of humans that their existence and actions were taken *a priori*. Since their number was never 'set,' addition of new deities to the existing pantheon and/or acknowledgment of their existence were never a problem. Depending on the time period, locale, situation and royal and personal preferences some gods and goddesses were revered more than others. But the presence of others was rarely if ever forgotten.

Those who were the most popular over the millennia we know the best due to the number of texts in which their names, functions, and actions were preserved. The others are sometimes only known from their names on somewhat obscure texts and are difficult

Figure 1.1 The national leading god of Assyria, Aššur. From a glazed brick panel

to place in the overall pantheon of deities. Even at the time of military conflicts between Assyria and Babylonia in the first half of the first millennium B.C. neither side denied the existence of gods worshipped by their opponents. Their 'national' gods – Aššur for the Assyrians and Marduk for the Babylonians – were leading a symbolic fight for supremacy over the area with the full recognition of their respective powers.

Around 1300 B.C. attempts were made to assimilate Aššur (whose origins are quite obscure – he was possibly a local god of the Assyrians who personified the city of the same name) into Sumero-Babylonian tradition by identifying him with Sumerian Enlil (Black and Green 1997), one of the 'creators' of the Sumerian origin. Later on, in the eighth century B.C., Anšar, one of the 'old' gods of the Babylonian account of creation (Enûma Eliš), became identified with Aššur possibly in order to place this Assyrian god at the time of the origin of the universe, chronologically before Marduk. Eventually under Sennaherib (704–681 B.C.) the whole Babylonian Epic of Creation, originally written to elevate the position of the national god of Babylon, Marduk, over much older Sumerian deities, was 'claimed' with accompanying rituals by Aššur himself (Black and Green 1997).

In spite of these 'borrowings' from the Sumero-Babylonian tradition and of the very unclear iconography of Aššur, he remained the god of all Assyrians symbolizing their political entity and national identity. His connection with the state is well attested by his name being incorporated into the names of powerful Assyrian rulers of the first half of the first millennium B.C. such as Aššur-nadin-šumi (Assurnasirpal), Aššur-banipal (Assurbanipal), Ašš ur-ahhé-iddina (Esarhaddon). His Babylonian counterpart, Marduk (whose origins are also obscure although he can be dated to the first part of the third millennium B.C. (Black and Green 1997)), was closely associated with the city of Babylon and Babylonian supremacy in southern Mesopotamia since the second millennium B.C. He was also worshipped in Assyria in spite of many of his attributes being 'copied' by Aššur.

Marduk of Babylonia and Aššur of Assyria were the leading gods of their national pantheons, but not the only ones who were worshipped by all Mesopotamians and others (for a discussion of the monotheistic concept of the god Aššur see Parpola 1997a). The original Sumerian deities were still very popular and stories about them were continuously told and retold, sometimes with a new twist. Although names of ancient Sumerian gods, goddesses and heroes were sometimes changed into their Semitic equivalent, their attributes and iconography 'borrowed' for newer deities whom they also represented, they were still revered and recognized for their greatness and their role in the universe. (For a history of Mesopotamian religion see Jacobsen 1976.) In this sense the ancient people of the Middle East were much more tolerant of other religious systems than we are today. This changed enormously with the introduction of the only god of the Israelites: in order to revere this god all others had to die. However, this does not mean that the stories associated with them died too. They were adjusted, transformed, recalled and attributed to the one god of the Pentateuch (Old Testament).

There is no doubt that Genesis and other parts of the Pentateuch borrowed heavily from the polytheistic traditions of the region. Since the Sumerians were the people with the earliest form of writing, many concepts and symbols which have come to be associated with the monotheistic god of the Judaic, Christian and even Islamic traditions can be traced back to them. However, it must be remembered that at least one thousand years passed between the last texts written by the Sumerians themselves and the earliest composition of the Pentateuch account known as Yahwistic. During this period of time, and even before, Sumerian writing traveled with its body of literature through the Middle East from Mesopotamia to Persia, to Anatolia, to Syria–Palestine and even to Egypt. Some of the Sumerian stories such as the Epic of Gilgamesh and/or story of the Flood became 'bestsellers' everywhere. The others were adjusted to other realities and incorporated into the literary works of any given region. The process of adaptation of ancient stories and symbols is quite visible for those who are studying the subject. Sometimes 'borrowers' put little or no effort into disguising the original stories. Other times they used only their own symbolism, not being sure how the original was really told. Many tales were transmitted orally so those who finally put them in writing often used their imagination to adapt them for their purposes.

Currently it is quite obvious that the Sumerian contributions to the continuous development of the Middle Eastern religious systems cannot be overlooked by anyone who wants to be an objective researcher of truth. They include, among others, such important concepts and symbols as watery birth, order and means of creation of the universe and humankind, universal deluge, existence of a paradise, a sacral tree, special relationship between snakes and women, and so forth. However, it must be understood that the continuous process of adaptation and incorporation of ancient traditions to newly developing religious systems in no way undermines the importance of these religions or the validity of claims made by their followers. Again, religions are to be believed in, not to prove their superiority or supremacy over the others.

2

In Search of Control:
The Egyptian Theologies

The Egyptian idea of sacred writing

As in the case of ancient Mesopotamia, the Egyptian stories of creation have been preserved thanks to extensive written records whose beginnings can be found at the end of the fourth millennium B.C. Although there is no agreement among scholars whether the Egyptian system of writing known as hieroglyphs developed independently in the valley of the Nile or if the idea (at least) was borrowed from the Sumerians, the fact is that by the beginning of the third millennium B.C. this system was already well developed and in use.

However, for the Egyptians, writing was much more than just a way to record a spoken language. They believed that the hieroglyphs were 'divine words' and each and every one of them was a powerful, divine entity containing 'the trace of a being, a thing, or the world the gods wished to bring into existence' (Meeks and Favard-Meeks 1996, p.5). Names particularly – whether divine, human or animal in their origin – were thought to carry so much power that sometimes writing them down was perceived to be dangerous for the people involved. For this reason some signs, especially in religious texts such as the Pyramid Texts and Coffin Texts, were altered to 'neutralize any potential dangers within the royal tomb' (Shaw and Nicholson 1995, p.129). However, it was all writing which was perceived to be of divine inspiration, allowing people to reveal the world and to understand it better. Since hieroglyphic writing was pictorial in its appearance, its images were comparable to the sacrality of art which was believed to reveal the stories about divine actions, character and involvement through images.

Thus, all writing was considered to be sacred and in this sense all written records carried, to different degrees, the divinity of the Egyptian deities. But the most sacred of them all were texts focusing on religious themes such as the creation and evolution of the universe and concepts associated with death and eternal life. Quite frequently the above concepts were intertwined together in one 'edition' because they were part of the same ongoing cycle of birth, death and rebirth. Occasionally their author was presented as being one of the gods himself, such as, for example, the god Thoth to whom the Book of Breathings was attributed (Morenz 1973).

The Funeral Texts: The most sacred of them all

In spite of their perceived divine authorship, the Egyptian religious texts do not present either unity or uniformity of ideas and formulas. Often texts contradict each other as a result of numerous alterations, changes in perception of reality, the passage of time causing some stories to be forgotten or their meaning becoming unclear, and so forth. This obviously did not bother the ancient Egyptians, although occasionally they would strongly recommend the correct copying of the old texts as reflected by the last part of the Instruction of Ptah-hotep (Morenz 1973).

Often these texts would be recited, especially during official ritualistic ceremonies, but some texts were not destined to be even read. They were considered to be secret as a part of the sacred writings accessible only to those who were chosen to be the intermediary between the world of the sacred and that of the profane – namely, priests. This secrecy particularly surrounded funerary texts which were designed to be used by the dead on their journey to the after-life and especially that of the pharaoh whose existence and being had to be immortalized through magical spells. These texts contain a wealth of information concerning not only the Egyptian perception of achieving divine existence with the deities after death but also the origin of the universe, theological doctrines, and various myths and rituals.

The Pyramid Texts

The earliest of the texts are the so-called Pyramid Texts which were found carved on the walls of the burial chambers and corridors in the royal pyramids (that is, those housing only kings and queens) dated to the late Old Kingdom and First Intermediate Period. They consist of spells, utterances or incantations, the earliest of which, 228 in number, were written in columns by the last ruler of the Fifth Dynasty, Unas (2375–2345 B.C.), at Saqqara. The total number is around 800 texts (most sources cite 759) although no pyramid contains all of them. The highest number, 675 spells, was recorded in the pyramid of Pepy II of the Sixth Dynasty (Shaw and Nicholson 1995). Modern scholars have assigned numbers to the Pyramid Texts following the order of their appearance, counting from the burial chambers onwards, but some scholars believe that the reverse order would be more appropriate.

The Pyramid Texts were written in order to ensure the king's safe passage to the other world and his well-being in the next life with deities. The majority of them focus on the importance of the syncretic sun-god, Re-Atum, suggesting their compilation by the priests of Re at Heliopolis. Thus, the theological doctrine concerning the creation of the world and its order is known as the Heliopolitan or Solar Theology of the Fifth Dynasty. This doctrine also establishes clearly Osiris' position as the king of the dead, of the after-life. Furthermore, it seems that many of these utterances must have been composed long ago, even in the Prehistoric Period (before 3200/3100 B.C.), before they were written down. They must have been transmitted in an oral form through hundreds if not thousands of years since they are written in the archaic form of the Egyptian language and sometimes refer to customs which were definitely no longer performed during the Old Kingdom. The most famous of these utterances is the so-called 'Cannibal Hymn' (No. 273–274) recorded only in the pyramids of Unas and Teti. They refer to Unas as, for example, '...the bull of heaven/Who rages in his heart,/Who lives on the being of every god,/Who eats their entrails/When they come, their bodies full of magic from the Isle of Flame' (Lichtheim 1975, p.36).

According to some investigators this and other paragraphs from the Utterance 273–274 may refer to the abandoned custom of human sacrifice and cannibalism. However, this type of description may be just metaphorical and refer only to the act of acquiring powers from other beings through a symbolic act of devouring him, her or it. It could be similar to the ritual of Holy Communion in the Catholic Church where the 'body' of Jesus Christ is symbolically consumed by his followers.

The Coffin Texts

With the process of decentralization of royal power during the First Intermediate Period and 'democratization' of the Egyptian religion in general the spells originally intended only for kings and queens began to be used by private parties such as other members of the royal family, high officials and nomarchs (local rulers of administrative districts known as nomes). While during the Old Kingdom officials wanted to be buried as close as possible to the king, hoping that through this proximity they too would somehow be included in his after-life existence, now they could secure their own after-life without being a direct part of the royal cult. The original collection of the funerary utterances was expanded to around 1100 spells (Silverman 1997) and was written in cursive hieroglyphs mostly on the interior surfaces of the wooden coffins, but sometimes also on tomb walls or ceilings. These texts – dated to the First Intermediate Period and the Middle Kingdom – are known as the Coffin Texts. In addition to original spells, some of which were omitted since they could not be understood anymore (Aldred 1963), new texts, non-royal in their origin, appeared. These included incantations and even maps, termed as 'guide books,' such as the Book of Two Ways, assuring the safe passage of the deceased to the other world: either to the underworld, the kingdom of Osiris, or to the sky for travel with the sun-god Re. They represent the belief that non-royal persons, if they were wealthy enough to perform all necessary rituals, expected to have an after-life similar to that of the divine king. However, these people were also aware of many dangers on the way to immortality which are well illustrated by titles of spells such as 'Not to rot and not to do work in the kingdom of the dead' or 'Spell for not dying a second death' (Shaw and Nicholson 1995). Furthermore, reaching the other world did not mean automatically that the life of the dead would be easy since some incantations are concerned with such 'petty' issues as fear of hunger and thirst (Lichtheim 1975). On the other hand the Coffin Texts also addressed very serious issues such as the creation of winds, great inundations and people as equals.

The Book of the Dead

By the end of the Second Intermediate Period and the beginning of the New Kingdom, an even larger group of people gained access to eternal existence thanks to a less costly and more accessible production of old and new funerary spells and prayers mainly on papyri, but also (rarely) on coffins, amulets, walls, bandaging linen, and statues. This collection, which consists of slightly less than 200 'chapters,' has a modern name – the 'Book of the Dead' – although the Egyptians referred to it as the 'Book of Going Forth by Day' (Silverman 1997, p.136). However, it was not a book in the modern sense, since the number of 'chapters' – that is, spells – and their sequence in any one copy varied from that of any other and their choice was a matter of an individual's need and preference, local custom, and the copyist. Some of the spells were more popular than others so they were copied more frequently – for example, Chapter 6 which was described on shabti/ushabti/shawabti figures (small mummiform figurines placed in the tomb of the deceased) 'for making a ushabti work for a man in the God's domain' (Lurker 1984, p.35). Although the number of chapters is smaller than of utterances of the Pyramid and Coffin Texts, many of the earlier spells were simply combined. The chapters were written in hieroglyphic, hieratic and demotic scripts and frequently illustrated with painted vignettes representing such popular scenes as the Ceremony of the Opening of the Mouth. The Egyptians made attempts later to provide the Book of the Dead with a uniform character and even composed new compilations such as the 'Book of Breathings' (possibly the Saite Period) and the 'Book of Traversing Eternity' of the Ptolemaic Period.

Other creation-related sources

The fourth important source of information concerning the Egyptian perception of creation is the so-called 'Shabaqo [Shabaka] Stone' dated to the end of the eighth century B.C. (the Twenty Fifth Dynasty). The so-called Memphis Theology or Doctrine which it contains was copied on a basalt or granite stone from an earlier text, already half-eaten by worms, on the orders of king Shabaqo. The original text was for many years believed to be of the Old Kingdom Period, but more detailed research indicates that this doctrine focusing on Ptah as a creator is of a much later date, and that it was composed after 1325 B.C. (Hornung 1992, pp.43–44) or in the Nineteenth Dynasty.

The above sources, although the most crucial for the understanding of the Egyptian ideas on creation, are not the only ones. There is an additional body of literature which refers to this topic in a somewhat 'incidental' manner which will be used in the discussion. However, it must be remembered that the Egyptian writings (as we know them today) did not produce 'creation texts' comparable to the ones of the Mesopotamian tradition until a very late period, after the fourth century B.C. (Ptolemaic and Roman Periods' temple inscriptions). Thus, the interpretation of their view on creation always remains rather incomplete and confusing.

3

In Search of Tolerance: Anatolian, Canaanite, and Persian Sources

Although Mesopotamian and Egyptian sources concerning the subject of creation can be at times very confusing and contradictory, at least there is a relative abundance of textual information accessible to modern scholars. Unfortunately, such sources are very limited in other regions of the Middle East, such as Anatolia and pre-Biblical Syria–Palestine, and/or they represent a great mixture of traditions which developed outside of this region as, for example, in the case of Persia. For this reason the discussion concerning these cultures is very inconclusive and often quite speculative. However, as incomplete as these sources are for the reconstruction of the ancient creation stories of these particular regions, they still provide complementary material for the subject in general.

The following sections focus on the presentation of available sources in their cultural and linguistic context. Thus, the chronological line of the development of various ideas is somewhat 'adjusted,' since the traditions of the Hittite Anatolia (the second millennium B.C.) and Persia (the first millennium B.C) as 'connected' through their Indo-European roots are discussed first, and then the second millennium B.C. Syria–Palestine. This arrangement also allows for a smooth transition to Genesis and the Quran whose roots can be found in the land occupied previously by the Canaanites.

The country of thousands of gods: The Hittite Anatolia

The arrival of the Indo-Europeans to the Middle East at the end of the third millennium B.C. and at the beginning of the second millennium B.C. and later during this millennium changed not only the political map of the region but also brought some ideas whose origins can be sought as far as the western border of modern China. While the topic of the original homeland of the Indo-Europeans is still one of the most discussed and controversial issues in archaeological and linguistic studies (Bower 1995; Lincoln 1991; Mair 1995; Mallory 1996; Renfrew 1987), the fact remains that during the second millennium B.C. the first Indo-European 'empire,' the Hittite Kingdom, was established in the heart of Anatolia. Furthermore, the Hittites can be credited with being the first Indo-Europeans with written records since they adapted the cuneiform system of writing, so prevalent at this period in the Middle East, to express their own language.

However, the Hittite Kingdom, whether at the peak of its power (the sixteenth and the thirteenth centuries B.C.) or during the transitional times, was not a homogeneous state (for its history see Bryce 1998; Gurney 1990; Loon 1985; Macqueen 1996). The Hittites ruled over the older population stratum of the Anatolian plateau known as the Hattians, whose language, known as hattili, still remains a mystery due to the scarcity of written (in cuneiforms) material preserved. Modern scholars refer to this possibly non-Indo-European language as 'Hattic' to distinguish it from the Hittite, an Indo-European language, which in the written sources of Anatolia is identified as nesili (Nesian). While Hittite was an official language of Anatolia during the second millennium B.C. and the language in which official texts were most commonly produced, there were also other groups of Indo-European people such as Luwians (south) and Palaians (north) who arrived in Anatolia at the same time as the Hittites and under whose influence they remained. The Luwians even developed their own script known as the Hittite hieroglyphic which was in use at the same time as the cuneiform script. Finally, one must mention the presence of a still linguistically non-identified group of people, the Hurrians, who arrived about the same time to the Middle East and spread mainly in north Mesopotamia and north Syria. The Hurrians played a very important role in the Hittite empire, especially during the second part of the second millennium B.C. and many stories of their origin are recorded in writing. Furthermore, due to a very extensive international policy (including frequent military expeditions) the Hittite kings and their subjects were very familiar with the religious themes of both Mesopotamia and Syria–Palestine.

Thus, one can see that discussing the mythology of Anatolia is quite a difficult task since it involves so many different, although sometimes connected, traditions. The Hittites were in the habit of welcoming each and every deity into their pantheon and believing that their worship should be performed in their native languages. This tolerance, openness or political wisdom led to the development of an enormous pantheon of Anatolian gods and goddesses (for the most complete list see Gessel 1998). The very high number of these deities indicates clearly that many of them were worshipped only locally (so-called Little Traditions) while a fixed number of them constituted the official deities of the state (so-called the Great Tradition) which were 'present,' for example, during the signing of any important treaty between Hittite kings and their foreign counterparts.

It seems that even the Hittites themselves were somewhat confused about 'the thousand gods of Hatti' in their attempts to establish the official pantheon of the state. The open-air rock sanctuary at Yazılıkaya of the second part of the second millennium B.C. is the best example of the Hittite willingness to incorporate various divine forces into their list. This natural rock formation located about a kilometer from the capital of Hittites, Hattussas, consists of two galleries, the bigger of which (Chamber A) is carved with two processions of walking gods and goddesses. Although all these deities are Hittite in the sense that they were all worshipped in the Imperial Anatolia, many of them are identified by the Hurrian names written in the hieroglyphic Luwian.

The result was that only foreign myths (mostly Hurrian, but also Babylonian and Canaanite) appear to be written as literary compositions while the Hittite and Luwian texts are mostly ritualistic; that is, associated with rituals, cult inventories, magic spells and incantations (Gurney 1977; Güterbock 1961). There are guidelines for performance of proper ceremonies so the reality perceived would continue as the reality lived. It is interesting to note that many compositions of the Indo-Iranian (Aryan) tradition – which was an offshoot of the original Indo-European traditions – are also very ritualistic (for Zoroastrian ritualistic prescriptions see Kotwal and Boyd 1982; for the Vedic tradition see Frawley 1993; Rajaram and Frawley 1995).

While there is not much doubt that literary compositions of the Hittites and the Luwians must have existed, their scarcity among the documentation from Anatolia can be explained either by the accidental nature of archaeological discoveries or by the existence of these compositions in the oral form where it was felt unnecessary to write down what everyone else knew. This would be quite consistent with the nomadic Indo-European traditions of Eurasia whose numerous groups such as the Saka and the Scythians have relied on their memory to carry on their beliefs. However, their practices were facilitated by the presence of open sanctuaries – rock, spring, and so on (as, for example, in Iranian tradition: see Hinnells 1975) – which were marked with the signs assuring proper performance of the ritual at any given place, such as, for example, the great nomadic sanctuary of the second millennium B.C. (and later) at Tamgaly, Kazakhstan.

The same idea could have been employed by the Indo-European groups of Anatolia whose origins were also nomadic. Although most of the surviving evidence refers to the official cult of the state, the Hittite cult inventories allow us to catch a glimpse of the religious customs outside of the main temples. It seems that the principal objects in open-air sanctuaries or other small sacral enclosures included such items as a ḫuwasi-stone (an upright stela), a weapon, or an animal. The relatively small size of these objects indicates that at least some sacral places in Anatolia could be portable and used in the same fashion as the ones from their likely homeland on the steppes of Eurasia.

The nomadic Indo-European stratum was intertwined with the native Anatolian (Hattic) beliefs with their focus on the mother-goddess as the life-giving force. Her numerous images were found at different prehistoric sites of Asia Minor and her worship was doubtless the strongest factor in the religious life of people from Çatal Hüyük, probably the most famous Neolithic site in the Middle East. While at the beginning she must have been the single most recognized divine force of the 'native' Anatolian pantheon she still could not conceive without her consort, a male deity associated with 'the fertilizing power of water' (Macqueen 1996, p.110). These two deities preserved their power under the Hittite rule as the Sun-Goddess of Arinna and the Weather-God of Hatti. However, their mutual relationship and their standing among other deities with regard to the creation process are unknown. As of today there are simply no Hittite, Luwian or Hattic stories found which refer to the subject of creation of either universe or humankind.

The stories which can be considered a part of 'extended' creation themes are the ones which deal with accounts describing the battles between the Storm (Weather)-God and the serpent, Illuyanka. These particular compositions might be considered to be variations on the Indo-European 'final battle' tradition as referred to by Mallory (1996). In addition, the Hittite myths of 'vanishing' gods, be it the storm-god or the sun-god, provide us with information concerning their effect on nature and misery falling on earth with their disappearance.

Finally, the most important source on creation process in Anatolia is the Hurrian group of myths known as the Kumarbi cycle which represents the competition for kingship between different gods. Because of their themes, the above stories are discussed in the chapter focusing on the divine kingship.

Currently there are no stories found which narrate or even refer to the creation of humankind. However, since some of the Hittite compositions discuss the concept of sin and the role of humans on the earth they are also included in appropriate sections of this book.

Indo-Iranian traditions of ancient Persia

In order to understand the ancient Iranian mythology focusing on the origin of the universe and humankind, one must realize first that this mythology is a combination of at least two great traditions: of the Indian 'Rigveda' (the Vedic body of literature in general) and of the Iranian 'Avesta,' a collection of sacred scriptures. Together they are known as the Indo-Iranian tradition (a part of the Indo-European tradition) whose origin and mutual relationship are very obscure (Malandra 1983).

Although there is linguistic evidence for the presence of Indo-Iranians in the Middle East during the second millennium B.C. (for example, in the Hittite texts), and their presence in Iran is confirmed at the beginning of the first millennium B.C. in the Assyrian sources (Curtis 1993), their homeland and routes of their migrations are still a subject of many discussions (Rajaram and Frawley 1995). Although there is no doubt in my mind that they were originally nomadic groups, many of whom inhabited the Eurasian steppe as far east as western China (for example, Caucasoid mummies of Tarim Basin), the evidence for their origins and chronology will probably remain disputed for many years to come.

While discussion of the Indian tradition known also as the Vedic tradition of the Hindu religion (for this topic see Frawley 1993; Rajaram and Frawley 1995) is beyond the scope of this book, specific references to relevant topics will be made with regard to Iranian tradition based on the Avesta which is the most important source of our knowledge on religion of ancient Iran. However, one must also mention Achaemenid inscriptions written in the Old Persian language which occasionally provide additional information, especially with the reference to godly attributes and rituals.

The collection of sacred scriptures known as the 'Avesta' is attributed to Zaratuštra, a prophet who is believed by some to have lived as early as the second millennium B.C. (Curtis 1993), while the majority of scholars ascribes him a date some time during the seventh or sixth centuries B.C. (Dresden 1961; Malandra 1983). Although many legends are associated with Zaratuštra (later known as Zoroaster – Curtis 1993; Hinnells 1975) in reality only a small part of the Avesta readings – such as Gāthā of Yasna (Zaratuštra's meditations and preaching; 17 hymns – Hinnells 1975); that is, 'worship, adoration' texts – can be assigned to him while the rest is of a later edition. The Gāthā are believed to be closely connected with the oldest holy book of the Vedic tradition known as the 'Rigveda', the composition of which is dated to the second millennium B.C. (either to its beginning or to the end). The movement that focused on these texts is known as Zaratuštrianism and its main orientation is toward 'an ethical dualism between "Truth" (Aša) and "Falsehood" (Drug) which is regulated and topped off by a monotheism expressed by Ahura Mazdā' (Dresden 1961, p.334). While the use of the term 'monotheism' is inappropriate in reference to Zaratuštrianism since Ahura Mazdā, although the leading divine entity, was not the only one recognized, this particular stratum of Iranian religion is probably closer to the original religion of Indo-Iranians (Indo-European) than is its second form, Zoroastrianism, also known as Mazdeism.

In addition to 'Zaratuštrian texts' of the Avesta, Zoroastrianism is based on the remaining corpus of Yašt ('sacrifice'), Vendīdād ('law against the demons'), and also recommends worship of Indo-Iranian gods such as Mithra and Haoma (Indian Soma) and the goddess Anāhīta (Dresden 1961). This is the tradition that was immortalized in the Pahlavi books known as Bundahišn (Zandágāhīh), the Dēnkart (the version of the Avesta) and the famous Sāh-nāma written by Firdausi around A.D. 1000 (for tales from this famous composition see Picard 1993). Elements of both traditions were incorporated into the ideas of other religions such as Manicheism (the third century A.D.) but since they were later compilations of various religious movements, they are excluded from the discussion. All the above texts are very difficult to translate and to interpret due to their antiquity, linguistic problems, and overall limited understanding of Indo-Iranian tradition (Malandra 1983).

Owing to the fact that the above traditions are clearly not of Middle Eastern origin – although their final forms were influenced by the native religions of the area – Iranian creation stories are not treated as separate topics for analysis in the following chapters but rather incorporated into the text whenever necessary. This way the reader can become acquainted with its main themes without losing focus on the evolution of religious concepts in the Middle East.

Canaan: Before the god took over

For many years the Bible was considered to be the main source of information concerning mythology and beliefs of Canaan; that is, Syria – Palestine. Unfortunately the information provided by this source was significantly biased and quite unclear in spite of some additional sources of the Phoenician corpus of inscriptions and references in classical sources. This situation was changed in 1929 when the ancient city of Ugarit (modern Ras Shamra in northern Syria) was discovered and produced thousands of inscriptions in a modified (alphabetic) cuneiform form (Ugaritic) as well as in the Akkadian, Hurrian, and Sumerian languages. Thus today scholars rely heavily on these texts in the interpretation of the ancient beliefs of Canaan.

As usual, the majority of inscriptions from Ugarit are economic in their character. However, many religious texts from the fourteenth and thirteenth centuries B.C. have also been discovered (for discussion of these and other related texts see Handy 1994). Unfortunately, among them there are no specific texts focusing on the creation of universe and/or humankind although they are sometimes alluded to. It is clear that the focus of Ugarit mythology (and probably of Canaanite mythology in general) was on the theme of fertility and the struggle for kingship. Since many texts were found near the main temple of Baal in Ugarit it is not surprising that they are ritualistic in their nature, written often as 'librettos for actual rituals.'

The longest and the best known-texts are the ones which belong to the so-called Baal fertility cycle and these are also the ones which provide the most information concerning the principle of the existence and organization of the world. Since the myths which are part of this cycle have been translated and discussed by many (Coogan 1978; Smith 1994), only a short narrative of the main story and discussion of its most relevant parts for the topic of this book are provided in the appropriate sections. The other supportive texts from Ugarit which are referred to are the stories of Aqhat, of Kirta, and some others.

The Canaanite stories as presented by the Ugaritic texts reflect the reality of a seasonal nature of Syria–Palestine. As Gordon explains, the fertility to which the ancient aspired 'was within the framework of nature; they wanted each manifestation of fertility in its due season. They wanted nothing (not even blessings such as rain and crops) out of season. What they dreaded was the failure of rain and crops in season' (1961, p.184). In this respect the ancient Canaanites and their mythology differ from the Egyptian and Mesopotamian concepts, since the existence and prosperity of these two civilizations depended on the beneficial or disastrous flooding of their main rivers. The Canaanite dependence on rain and dew for their crops is reflected in their worship of Baal, a god responsible for both, whose characteristics can be compared to the weather gods of Anatolia. However, in contrast to Anatolian deities whose disappearance or vanishing act without any particular reason was the one to cause the misery on earth, the Canaanites perceived the seasonality of their reality in terms of the struggle between forces of life (fertility) and death (sterility). This cycle was not annual but rather sabbatical; that is, there was a seven year season of prosperity, followed by seven years of misery. For example, Danel, a father of a hero known as Aqhat, curses Baal by using this seven year formula: 'For seven years let Baal fail,/Eight, the Rider on the Clouds:/No dew, no showers,/No surging of the two seas,/No benefit of Baal's voice' (Coogan 1978, p.41). This seven year/day formula was of a great importance for the ancient Canaanites and was transplanted also to the Pentateuch (for example, seven days of creation, seven years of famine). Unfortunately, its 'magical' meaning will remain unknown in spite of various explanations provided both by serious scholars and by eloquent numerologists.

In view of the lack of other literary compositions which refer to creation and mainte-nance of the universe the main focus of all researchers is on the Baal cycle. Since the focus of analysis on the fertility theme and the 'dying-god' image in this cycle has been already criticized by others (Walls 1992), these topics are addressed in the following chapters only with regard to its main theme: the battle for divine kingship.

Finally, one must realize that Ugaritic texts are most certainly copies of narratives (the fourteenth or the thirteenth century B.C. – for discussion see Handy 1994), original editions of which could have been much older and preserved only in the oral tradition among people whose records are presently lost. Furthermore two important works on Baal from Ugarit were written by one 'author,' Ilimilku, who worked for King Niqmaddu as a scribe and as a priest (Handy 1994). The following question arises then:

How much of what we learn from these texts is Ilimilku's own perception or his interpretation of existing traditions? Thus, a certain amount of speculative interpretation has to be included in the efforts to reconstruct beliefs of the ancient Canaan.

The interpretation of Ugaritic texts is aided by other supportive texts such as available inscriptions from Syria–Palestine, the Hittite narrative known as the 'Elkunirša Myth,' the Pentateuch, the account of the Phoenician history written by Philo of Byblos in the first century A.D., and some later sources. However, their usefulness for the subject of creation stories is rather limited because of numerous problems involved in their interpretation and reliability of the texts themselves (Handy 1994). Thus, they are only occasionally used in relevant parts of discussion.

4

In Search of One God: Biblical and Quranic Attempts on Reconciling Realities

There is no creation story more famous in the world than the account, or rather accounts, recorded in Genesis. It is not only that the narratives of the Old Testament are recognized as the basis of belief systems of Judaic, Christian and Quranic traditions but also because their dramatic qualities translate so well into artistic visions. However, it is not that commonly known among the general public that Genesis and the Pentateuch (in Judaic tradition referred to as the Torah [Law]) in general are the product of more than one author, and none of them seems to be the god. The term 'Bible,' used commonly to describe the sacred book of both Judaism and Christianity, is derived from the word 'byblos' for papyrus or paper, which was one of trading items in the city of Byblos (also known as Gubla, on the coast of modern Lebanon). In Greek this word was known as its diminutive 'biblia,' meaning 'books.'

The Holy Bible which is considered to be the sacred scriptures of Judaism and of Christianity is not exactly the same book with regard to these two main religious groups as well as with regard to divisions within. The Hebrew scriptures consist of 39 books which were originally written in Hebrew, with the exception of a very few sections which were written in Aramaic. The Christian Bible includes both the Old Testament and the New Testament, but the two parts are structured slightly differently depending on the group of Christians who are using it.

The part of this Holy Book which is of interest for the work on creation stories is known as the Pentateuch (from Greek *penta* – five– and *teuch* – book). These are the first five books – Genesis, Exodus, Leviticus, Numbers, and Deuteronomy – of the Christian Old Testament. The same five books are known as the Torah in the Judaic tradition. Because of limited space, the discussion concerning the creation narratives of Judaic-Christian traditions is confined to Genesis (unless indicated otherwise, all textual quotes are from *The Jerusalem Bible*, 1968) with occasional references to other sources which are too numerous even to be listed in this section.

The Pentateuch is not a uniform collection of writings. Most scholars agree that at least four major sources were used for compilation of this part of the Holy Book. They are known as the Yahwistic tradition (J – from Jehowah), the Elohist (E – from Elohim) tradition, the Deuteronomic (D) tradition, and the Priestly tradition (P). Although a final agreement has not been reached in the scholarly world, the Yahwistic and Elohist accounts are dated to the beginning of the first millennium B.C. and are often treated, for the sake of the flow of discussion, as one source; that is, as 'variant forms in prose of an older, largely poetic Epic cycle of the era of the Judges' (Cross 1973, p.293). The Deuteronomic tradition is dated most commonly to the seventh century B.C. and its inclusions did not seem to affect the first books of the Pentateuch. Finally, the Priestly account is agreed to be based on a document dated to the Exilic or Post-Exilic Period, the sixth or the fifth century B.C.

In order to provide the reader with the background information necessary for under-standing creation accounts as presented by Genesis and later on by the Quranic tradition (since the seventh century A.D.), the following sections focus on the discussion of the authorship and main features of the combined version of the J and E traditions under the heading of the Yahwistic account (for convenience), and of the Priestly account. This chapter finishes with the basic information concerning the Quran and its organization to explain difficulties involved in 'pulling out' necessary information from this Holy Book of the Islamic religion.

Yahwistic account (J)

long view

The author or authors of the Yahwistic version of creation set up their work with an obvious goal in mind, to present the history of mankind from the beginning of time to the settlement of the chosen people of Israel in their promised land. Thus, the chrono-logical order of the events is quite evident: the primeval history (from the creation to the dispersion of humankind), the ancestry (the patriarchal sagas until the arrival to Egypt), and the final establishment of the nation in Syria–Palestine with the great assistance of Yahweh. In this sense the writer(s) of the Yahwistic version actually was (were) doing exactly the same thing that their Babylonian counterparts did a few hundred years earlier with Marduk: they wrote a story to elevate the position of their god, the only god, Yahweh, over all other existing traditions and deities.

However, before the Yahwistic narrative was put down in its written form as it is available to us today, its composition must have been preceded by its oral history or histories which contributed to inconsistencies in the text. The development and careful analysis of this tradition (from each and every possible angle) have been a subject of many studies starting in the nineteenth century. The most notable publication of this early period of studies concerning the whole book of Genesis was by Gunkel (1901, republished 1997). Although the review of the long history of studies and various methodologies is beyond the scope of this book (for major trends see Wallace 1985), it is necessary at least to highlight some issues which are relevant for textual interpretation of the creation stories.

The Yahwistic source on creation stories is a product of traditional literature (for discussion of this term with regard to the J and E sources see Wallace 1985) whether in its oral, aural or written form. As such it represents the ideas which were part of at least a few generations of people who shared common beliefs, traits, and modes of subsistence in the most general meaning of the term 'culture.' However, as in the case of any other culture, the Yahwistic one did not develop in a vacuum. The influence of the Canaanite and other Near Eastern traditions is very visible in some parts of the JE source, while in others it is more veiled. For example, the motif of divine intervention for the benefit of infertile marriages of some patriarchs (both Mesopotamian and Canaanite stories), the divine epithets for the only god of Genesis as repetition of the ones used by El and Baal in pre-Biblical Syria–Palestine, and finally the story of the Deluge so popular already two millennia before are the best examples of 'traditional themes' woven intricately into the JE narrative.

While the contextual similarities and differences in the JE source can be more or less successfully discussed, analyzed and compared both on the external and internal levels, the composition of the text itself causes numerous discussions as to its poetic or prose origins in the oral tradition (see Wallace 1985). Although, in my view, the detailed knowledge of this subject is not absolutely necessary for the interpretation of creation stories, one must be aware that some poetic parallelism, expressions and so forth might have influenced the language used for description of various actions and/or personalities, especially the one of Yahweh.

Unfortunately, in spite of being able to analyze successfully many aspects of the Yahwistic and Elohist accounts, it seems rather unlikely that it will ever be known how much of this combined narrative is a creative interpretation of a writer or writers or how many oral narratives of the same episode were incorporated into a written version and why these selections were made. The point on which many scholars agree is the fact that this version is 'one of the earliest written literary works in Israel' (Wallace 1985, p.46). But its exact dating is still a subject of debate. The majority of scholars oscillates between the mid-tenth century B.C. to the eighth century B.C., while some others date this text as late as the sixth century B.C., almost overlapping with the Priestly account (for discussion see Cross 1973 and Wallace 1985).

The focus of the Yahwistic account on presentation of the traditional history of the chosen nation to its establishment in the Promised Land and on the elevation of Yahweh into a victorious god of the people in continuous hardship and distress are another widely recognized aspect of this narrative. However, it must be noted that the Yahwistic version of creation (Genesis 2:4b–3:24) is more 'specialized' than other creation stories of the Middle East. While it refers only briefly to the creation of the universe (including earth), the center of the narrative is without any doubt the creation and 'development' of humankind. It almost seems that the writer or writers were not only interested in presenting what was considered to be a 'factual account' of events as the response to the eternal questions – where did we come from and what is our purpose on earth – but that he or they tried to establish once and forever the 'truth' about gender roles and the concept of an 'inborn evil' in all of us. He or they were very successful in this attempt. There is no other single story in all the creation myths of the Middle Eastern and Indo-European traditions which so skillfully stripped women from even a chance to achieve status equal to men. Today only specialists and very careful readers can actually narrate the introductory passage concerning the beginning of the world, while almost anyone in the Western hemisphere can recall the story of Adam and Eve. The image of Eve created from Adam's body as the helper to the man, which developed so many thousands years ago, still haunts modern society.

Priestly account (P)

Since the Priestly tradition is of a later date than the Yahwistic account it is logical to assume that its writer or writers should also be considered to be the editors of the final text. On the other hand one might wonder why he or they did not try any harder to avoid not only numerous inconsistencies between both narratives but especially contradictory statements which are so visible in stories dealing with the creation of humankind and the Flood. The evidence of the editing efforts of the P source can be found at the beginning of Genesis, since it is the Priestly version which begins the Pentateuch. In view of the fact that the Yahwistic account almost ignored the creation of the universe, it seems that the Priestly source intended to 'fill' this gap. Its focus was on the 'chronological' presentation of events from the state of non-being to the creation of humankind. Then, after its introduction finishes on 2:3 (or 2:4a), the details of the Yahwistic version of the creation of mankind follow. The P narrative can also be distinguished in other parts of Genesis such as those concerned with the flood (both J and P are combined), the covenant with Abraham, and the description of purchasing of the Cave of Machpela, but is not limited to them. However, its redactor(s) had never tried to change the existing 'plot' of the JE tradition and utilized this main source for its own purpose, the reconstruction and clarification of religious institutions. For this reason many scholars believe that the Priestly account was not a product of an independent oral literary composition but rather a compilation of known sources (mainly onomasticons – lists) to promote the religious unity of the people of Israel.

Although there is no general agreement on whether the Priestly narrative was ever an independent account (see Cross 1973), the common understanding is that this version was very much concerned with the establishment and/or promotion of laws and formulas in addition to its narrative qualities. The significant part of these laws was the focus on covenants which distinguishably divide the history into four periods, of Adam, Noah, Abraham, and Moses – each finishing with the covenant (Cross 1973). In this sense, the P editor or editors were less interested in details of the 'historical' process and more in ritualistic aspects of the Yahwistic religion. Although it might be easily assumed that the Priestly author(s) agreed with his or their Yahwistic predecessors as to the social reality created – or confirmed – by the story of paradise and expulsion of Adam and Eve from it, one may still ask the question whether the introductory part of Genesis was intended to 'soften' the drastic inequality of genders as presented by the JE edition. Even if not, the Priestly version of creation still confirms that the leading trend in cosmic mythology of the Middle East in the middle of the first millennium B.C. was continuously based on much more lenient and 'objective', older traditions of the Middle East.

The Quran

It is interesting to note that this 'objectivity' is also preserved by the Quran, the Holy Book of Islam (unless indicated otherwise all textual quotes are from Irving's 1985 translation of the Quran). While the story of paradise is a cornerstone of the creation narrative, the first woman is never presented as a creation from Adam's rib. On the contrary, in the best tradition of the Middle East, people were created equal and from the same substance. Although the story of the rib still exists among the many Hadiths (exemplary conduct of the Prophet – also known as the Sunna) which, in contrast to the Quran, are not considered to be infallible sources of knowledge, its impact is rather minimal.

The Quran is the sacred Muslim scripture which is believed to be revealed to the only true prophet, Muhammad, by the god, Allah himself, at the beginning of the seventh century A.D. All revelations were immediately written down and memorized by his followers, to be compiled after Muhammad's death in A.D. 632. Since the Quran is considered to be the word of Allah – there was only one messenger involved – its content is believed to be infallible. For this reason the true Muslim is required to know its content in the original language of revelation, Arabic of the seventh century, because editions and translations are suspected of disturbing the true message of Allah. In contrast to the Holy Book of Judaic and Christian traditions, the Quran is not organized in a chronological order with regard to presentation of history. It is divided into 114 chapters (suras) of various sizes and information concerning the creation accounts is spread out throughout many of them.

As will be demonstrated in the next chapters, Muhammad's revelations, especially with regard to the subject of creation, were very much based on the Pentateuch tradition. It is not surprising because both Mecca and Medina, two cities where the revelations were received by the prophet, were at the time very cosmopolitan cities with a sizable population of Jewish and Christian merchants. Having the 'advantage' of becoming the later 'editor' of holy scriptures focusing on one god only, Muhammad's revelations managed in many cases to avoid criticism expressed by the followers of other religions (for example, Zoroastrians) of the 'ungodly' character of the only god of the Bible (for the text see Neusner 1986, pp.178–179).

The result is that Allah of the Quran is much more consistent in his behavior and actions than his 'predecessor' Yahweh. The stories which would contradict his recognized 'goodness' were removed from the Quranic text and appear only among numerous Hadiths. The teachings of the Quran only emphasize the leading role of Allah as having four main functions: creation, sustenance, guidance and judgment. Thus, the older traditions of the Middle East, at least with regard to the subject of creation, were combined successfully in the Quran to provide more or less consistent explanations for the existence of only one god, dualism of the universe, the order and purpose of everything, and the very positive nature of Allah as a creator and protector of mankind. In this sense, the creation account and the creator of the Quranic tradition reflect the certain 'objectivity' of the first Sumerian and Egyptian accounts.

PART 2
Creation of the Universe

5

Out of the Watery Abyss

The origin of the universe and its *modus operandi* are probably the most universal mysteries that humans have tried to comprehend, explore and explain from time immemorial. Depending on technological and scientific advancement different models of perceived reality have been developed and 'offered' to the general public as the leading, or sometimes even the only, truth. Since there was no concept of 'religion' among the ancient people of the Middle East, early explanations concerning the beginning of the universe and its continuous evolution were not in conflict with the existing scientific theories on the subject. In this sense the reality perceived was also the reality lived.

Both realities, or rather the one ruling reality, had to be and were adjusted depending on the ever-changing (but not necessarily progressing) social, political, and cultural conditions of any given area and time period. However, some elements of what we can call early cosmogony and cosmology remained constant from the earliest historical period until the Hellenistic Period (beginning in the fourth century B.C.) in Mesopotamia and Egypt. Some of these elements were adopted by others, including both Genesis and the Quran, which developed their own ideologies, borrowing heavily from a mixture of available traditions.

In order to present a complicated pattern of the evolution, expansion, diffusion and adjustment of the ideas concerning the origin of universe the following discussion begins with ancient Mesopotamia, proceeds with ancient Egypt and finishes with the Old Testament and the Quran. Whenever possible appropriate references are made to other cultures.

Mesopotamia

One of the most important problems with the subject is the fact that the Sumerians did not leave one consistent text which explains their concept of the evolution of the universe from the beginning until the time of their reality. This does not mean that such a text did not exist. Repetitions of similar lines in different compositions may indicate that such a text once existed but it could have been carried on only in the form of an oral tradition (Lyczkowska and Szarzynska 1981). Hence modern scholars are forced to piece together the Sumerian cosmology and cosmogony from shorter or longer references to these events which serve as a sort of 'introduction' to the main subject of an otherwise unrelated text. For example, the important information concerning a partial order of the creation of the universe has been found in the text dealing with the origin of a toothache worm which received permission from the deities to enjoy our teeth and gums. The modern title of this text is 'Toothache Incantation' and its late copies of the Old Babylonian and Neo-Babylonian periods have survived. This text establishes the position or place of the worm in the universe as follows: 'After Anu [had created heaven],/Heaven had created [the earth],/The earth had created the rivers,/The rivers had created the canals,/The canals had created the marsh,/(And) the marsh had created the worm' (Speiser 1973, p.75).

Most of the sources on the subject of the Sumerian religion are from the second millennium B.C. They are either copies of the original Sumerian texts or their later renditions. Many of them were found in Nippur where the cult center of the god Enlil was located at the temple known as *E-kur* (the 'Mountain House'). Others were scattered throughout Mesopotamia, Anatolia and even Syria. The echo of the early beliefs of the Sumerians can be found in texts as late as the third century B.C. By that time they were quite 'twisted' and mixed but still recognizable. Thus the task of systematizing the creation beliefs of ancient Mesopotamia is quite challenging, but nevertheless possible.

The Sumerian prima materia

There is no life, as we know it, without water. Sweet waters are necessary to sustain human, animal and plant life, while salt waters often set visible boundaries beyond which nothing seems to exist. Thus, it is not surprising that many societies around the world have referred to the watery birth of the universe. The Sumerians were no exception. In their view, water, which can be described as some sort of cosmic sea or ocean, was believed to exist forever. They did not try to understand how it came into being or when. Its existence was accepted *a priori* as the *prima materia* of each and every element that was to be created. This type of understanding required the assumption that there was only one element from which everything, whether of divine or of profane nature, came into being, each and every one in its proper time. Hence, the creation process was perceived as a continuum of the emergence of various elements in the fixed order. In modern terms, this order together with other 'laws' of nature was encoded in the *prima materia* allowing only for the limited flexibility of choices and actions to be made by all created out of it. In this sense, then, the whole universe consisted of invisible connections (the principle of magic) which were capable of being weakened or even broken, but which had to be restored in order to assure the continuance of the existence. There was always a reason for the existence of different things, even if they were as annoying as a toothache, since they were divine creations at the proper time; that is, at the time when they were 'allowed' to emerge according to the encoded laws.

The Sumerian *prima materia* was personified in the form of a deity as were all other elements of nature. The Sumerian list of deities gives this honor to the goddess Nammu 'written with the pictograph for primeval "sea,"' described [as] 'the mother, who gave birth to heaven and earth' (Kramer 1959, p.83). The other texts call her 'mother, first one, who gave birth to the gods of the universe' or as 'Mother of Everything' (Leick

Figure 5.1 The god Ea (Sumerian Enki) in his dominion of the sweet waters of apsû. Another god, possibly Šamaš (Sumerian Utu), is approaching him by climbing a symbolically presented zikkurat. From a cylinder seal

1994, p.13). The Sumerian sign used to describe her is *ENGUR*. The same sign was used as a synonym for *abzu (apzû)* which can be translated as 'the sweet water sea/ocean' and 'the watery deep,' strongly suggesting the subterranean ocean. However, the *abzu* itself, as sweet waters located below the earth, is associated with the realm of a male god Enki (Semitic Ea), and in the Babylonian tradition of *Enûma Eliš* is personified by the god of the same name, Apsû. This apparent contradiction can be explained by Enki's association with the goddess Nammu. Enki, whose full name is Enkig, was her son who was believed to occupy the abzu together with his wife, Damgalnuna (Damkina), and his mother. Thus, it is possible that the defined part of the *prima materia*, the sweet waters, which was essential for the sustenance of creation, was 'transferred' to him by Nammu. The symbol *ENGUR*/abzu associated with both of them also symbolized Enki's main temple, *E.engura (E.-abzu)*, in the city of Eridu (modern Abu Shahrain). According to the Sumerian King List it was the oldest and most important city of the Sumerian tradition. The WB/Ashmolean Museum 1923.444 text of this list refers to it in the following words:

> When the kingship was lowered from heaven
> The kingship was in Eridu(g).
> (In) Eridu(g) A-lulim(ak) (became) king
> And reigned 28,800 years;

Alalar reigned 36,000 years
    2 kings
Reigned its 64,800 years.
I drop (the topic) Eridu(g);
Its kingship to Bad-tibira(k)
    was carried.

(Jacobsen 1966, p.71)

It is quite reasonable then to argue that the first city of the Sumerian tradition could have been entrusted to Enki by his mother Nammu who somehow transferred at least part of her powers to him.

According to Leick (1994) only the 'southern,' Eridu model, was focused on the watery birth in the Sumerian mythology while the 'northern,' Nippur model, was more concerned with heaven and earth as primary movers. She bases her argument on the geographical conditions of both areas which emphasize the importance of two different although connected elements. However, another explanation might be that the Eridu model was the underlying notion of all Sumerians, since it seems to be the oldest. Furthermore, the temple of Enki in Eridu was one of the most important cult centers throughout the history of Mesopotamia. Here, at the temple courtyard, a tank of holy water, also known as *abzu*, was located. *E.engura* was visited not only by worshippers but also by the deities themselves. Their cult statues were transported by a boat or a chariot to Eridu (the other frequently visited site was Nippur) to receive blessings from Enki, the god of wisdom, who was also a keeper and distributor of *me*.

The concept of the Sumerian *me* (Akkadian 'parṣū') is extremely difficult to understand for modern readers. It seems that its idea was also a mystery for ancient people since they did not adapt it to their system. The Sumerian *me* is a plural, animate noun which expresses what one can term, using anthropological jargon, as 'cultural traits' (Kramer's (1959) 'culture traits and complexes,' p.99) of the Sumerian civilization. They represent laws and rules as well as 'offices' which governed and maintained the universe since its creation. Kramer listed 68 of them in his 1959 book *History Begins at Sumer*. Among them are lordship, godship and kingship but also sexual intercourse, prostitution, power, the destruction of cities, wisdom and even four musical instruments. Such a variety of concepts collected under one name is a rather unusual notion in itself. Many years ago when researching a subject not related to Middle Eastern studies, I came across a similar concept among the Toda of India who called their 'cultural traits' *ma*. Since some scholars look to the east in search of the origin of the Sumerians (it is possible that Sumerian is related to the Dravidian languages of India), it might be worth pursuing this idea.

Definitely the Sumerian *me* are part of the law and natural order as encoded in Nammu, the primeval matter. She herself is rarely mentioned in the texts which have survived. Leick (1994) explains her possible absence from the corpus of texts as follows:

She may either belong to an older stratum of Sumerian or pre-Sumerian deities who did not become subjects of literary compositions, or owe her appearance in the hymns and god-lists to a tendency to anthropomorphize general concepts such as abzu or ENGUR and thereby integrate it into the Sumerian pantheon but without really becoming a 'character.' (p.14)

Another explanation might be that the scarcity of texts relating to Nammu is rather a matter of the Sumerian belief system than anything else. Her existence as the *prima materia* was acknowledged but not dealt with since no amount of offerings, sacrifices and prayers could have changed the encoded laws. The other deities could have been influenced by these actions within the limits of their powers, but Nammu has remained a constant force outside of anybody's reach. A similar concept might be found in Anatolia where the position of the mother-goddess of many names seems to remain unchallenged through thousands of years, although there are no literary compositions regarding the specifics of her character and functions.

Figure 5.2 The 'national' leading god of Babylon, Marduk, accompanied by his snake-dragon. From a cylinder seal

Nammu then herself represented the cosmic sea or ocean as the order that exists *a priori*. This is quite an interesting concept since in many religions water is associated with the opposite of order – with chaos, inconsistency, instability and change (Kopalinski 1990), and with the state of chaotic non-being as in ancient Egypt.

Lost battle of the Babylonian mother of all

This element of watery chaos can be seen in the Babylonian Epic of Creation. Its Babylonian title is *Enûma Eliš* ('When above' or 'When on high') in accordance with the Mesopotamian tradition of naming any given composition with the first few words of its opening. The Epic of Creation was recorded on seven tablets and its fragments were discovered in the great library of King Assurbanipal at Nineveh, at Assur (with some 'adjustments' to accommodate the god Aššur's involvement), at Kish, and at Uruk. It has been 'put together,' translated and published by various scholars since the first 'modern' edition by George Smith in 1875.

Although all fragments are copies from the first millennium B.C., the overwhelming majority of scholars have agreed that this great epic was composed during the second millennium B.C., either in its early part during the Old Babylonian Period or at its end during 'the nationalistic revival at the time of Nebuchadnezzar I (twelfth century B.C.)' (Foster 1995, p.9). It was considered to be of great importance in both Babylonia and Assyria and was recited on the fourth day of the New Year's festival (Speiser 1973, p.31), 'akītu', in Babylon. Here, at Babylon, Marduk had his most impressive cult center and since the epic was written in order to elevate his position over the more ancient Sumerian deities, the most lavish New Year ceremonies were performed in his honor in the same city. The last recorded akītu in honor of Marduk took place in 538 B.C. under the rule of Cambyses, king of Persia (Black and Green 1997).

In spite of its popularity this poem does not necessarily reflect the idea of creation as perceived by all Mesopotamians. It is a clearly political endeavor to justify the highest position of Marduk, 'national' god of the Babylonians, among the pantheon of much older Sumerian deities. This seems to be quite a common practice among the Semitic 'palace' writers whose rulers felt it necessary to 'include' themselves and their ideas or beliefs into an already established Sumerian reality. For example, Sargon of Akkad justified his power and rule over the Sumerians in his 'Birth Legend' which is quite similar to the story of Moses, although much older. Only the first fourteen lines of an incomplete seventy are cited below:

> Sargon, the mighty king, king of Akkade, am I.
> My mother was an en-priestess (?), my father I never knew.
> My father's brother inhabits the highlands.
> My city is Azupirānu, which lies on the bank of the Euphrates.
> She conceived me, my en-priestess mother, in concealment she gave me birth.
> She set me in a wicker basket, with bitumen she made my opening water-tight,
> She cast me down into the river from which I could not ascend.
> The river bore me, to Aqqi the water-drawer it brought me.
> Aqqi the water-drawer, when lowering his bucket, did lift me up.

> Aqqi the water-drawer did raise me as his adopted son,
> Aqqi the water-drawer did set me to his gardening.
> While I was (still) a gardener, Ištar did grow fond of me,
> And so for [...] years I did reign as king,
> The black-headed people, I did rule and govern. (Goodnick Westenholz 1997, pp. 37, 39)

Enûma Eliš seems to be the creation of one poet who was not well versed but rather confused about Sumerian mythology. For example, the Sumerian god Enki who had different names is presented here as more than one being despite the fact that he is the same entity. Nevertheless, the author succeeded in his goal – Marduk was elevated to the role of the leading god. In order to do so, he had to 'kill' the female principle, Tiāmat, the mother of all, personification of the salt waters.

While in the Sumerian tradition the waters of Nammu represented the order and law, the Babylonian epic represents the state of pre-existence as chaos.

> When above the heaven had not (yet) been named,
> (And) below the earth had not (yet) been called by a name;
> When) Apsû primeval, their begetter,
> Mummu, (and) Ti-âmat, she who gave birth to them all,
> (Still) mingled their waters together,
> And no pasture land had been formed (and) not (even) a reed marsh was to be seen;
> When none of the (other) gods had been brought into being,
> (When) they had not (yet) been called by (their) name(s, and their) destinies had not (yet) been fixed,
> At that time) were the gods created within them. (Heidel 1951, p.18)

Although other translations are similar to the one cited above, it must be noted that 'Mummu' can be translated as 'primal' (Held 1976, p.231) or as 'matrix' (Foster 1995, p.11), or simply as a name. In fact this is an Akkadian 'play on words between Mummu-Tiāmat and Mummu the vizier' (Foster 1995, p.12) which might be somewhat confusing in the process of interpretation.

Tiāmat, the progenitress in the *Enûma Eliš* tradition and in this sense a counterpart of the Sumerian Nammu, is no longer the only 'cause' of the process of creation. Although she still remains the most powerful of the two, her aspect of 'life-giving' waters has been transferred to Apsû and she is left only with the salt waters, the ones which set boundaries and provide fish but otherwise represent negative forces later in the epic as personified by her rage. The conclusion that she represents only the salt water is quite easy to make even without the specific references to her attributes. Not only is she presented as the opposite of Apsû personifying the sweet waters, but also her name, Tiāmat, is a variation of the word 'tiamtum' meaning 'sea' (Black and Green 1997, p.177). In addition, the metaphor used by the poet with regard to splitting her body by Marduk can be translated as 'He [Marduk] split her [Tiāmat] open like a mussel (?) into two (parts)' (Heidel 1951, p.42) or 'He split her in two, like a fish for drying' (Foster 1995, p.32). Tiāmat cannot bring forward the universe because she alone cannot sustain it. Her title 'Mother-Tiāmat' or 'Mummu-Tiāmat' ('Mummy-Tiāmat' if we continue playing the game of words) is stripped of the Sumerian importance as the *prima materia* in which everything is encoded. Instead she is recognized as a female element necessary for procreation in partnership with a male. Thus, the primordial state of *Enûma Eliš* is the one in which 'mingling' of the waters is essential since it connects female and male elements, allowing other beings to emerge through this union. Both Lambert and Leick pointed out the possible interpretation of this 'mingling' as 'a metaphor for sexual procreation' (Leick 1994, p.15). This is quite possible, especially when one takes into consideration that the later deities also emerge in pairs. It is quite ironic that, chronologically speaking, the perception of the origin of the universe has gone through transition from the female element as the only mover (Nammu), then to male and female as a couple (Tiāmat and Apsû), and finally to the presence of the only mover – a male (Marduk). Actually the act of stripping the woman of her role in providing life is well reflected by the *Enûma Eliš* in which Marduk kills Tiāmat to assume his position as the leader god and continues the act of creation (which began with Tiāmat) and the ordering of the universe which was not possible in the chaotic world of pre-existence. The echo of this struggle between the creator god and the water-monster can also be seen in the Biblical tradition (Brandon 1963).

Neutral waters of pre-existence and the 'outside' god

Yet another version of creation out of water is presented by the Neo-Babylonian account (sixth century B.C.) which was recorded both in Sumerian and Babylonian and discovered in the city of Sippar by Hormuz Rassam in 1882. According to Heidel (1951) the story of creation as presented in this bilingual account is 'a rather elaborate introduction to an incantation which was recited for the purification of Ezida, the temple of Nabû at Borsippa' (p.61). As in the case of the *Enûma Eliš* this composition was written in order to elevate the position of Marduk above all other deities. The stage of 'nothingness' is described as follows:

> A holy house, a house of the gods in a holy place, had not been made;
> A reed had not come forth, a tree had not been created;
> A brick had not been laid, a brick mold had not been built;
> A house had not been made, a city had not been built;
> A city had not been made, a living creature had not been placed (therein);
> Nippur had not been made, Ekur [Enlil's temple at Nippur] had not been built;
> Uruk had not been made, Eanna ['House of Heaven'] had not been built;
> The Apsû had not been made, Eridu had not been built;
> A holy house, a house of the gods, its dwelling, had not been made;
> All the lands were sea;
> The spring which is in the sea was a water pipe. (Heidel 1951, p.62)

This rather lengthy description of what was not there (note similarities with the Yahwistic account discussed later – see p.68) refers to the existence of waters only: the sea and the spring (sweet waters). However, they are not personified with the names of any particular divine forces, but are presented as a reality, probably the reflection of the landscape near Bahrain where sweet water springs come out of the sea. The importance of this location is shown later in the discussion of the Sumerian paradise, but it should be mentioned here that the name for Bahrain, an island on the Persian Gulf, is interpreted as 'two seas' which are 'the salt waters and the sweet, the latter bubbling so surprisingly out of the very sea-bed, to the north of Bahrain' (Rice 1984, p.167).

It is interesting that the above text does not elaborate at all on the origin and attributes of these waters; neither does it refer to their role in the process of creation. After making the statement concerning non-existence or pre-existence, the text follows with the emergence of Eridu, Esagil (the 'Lofty House,' Marduk's temple in Babylon), and Babylon itself. How they were built and/or completed is not explained, with the exception of the foundations of Esagil being laid by Lugaldukuga and finished after Babylon was founded (Heidel 1951). Then the text proceeds to the description of the creation of the world by Marduk as one would build a dam. First Marduk made a 'reed frame' on the water and after creating dirt he used it to fill out the frame. Having made the earth he proceeded with the creation of mankind whom he needed to help him out with the construction and maintenance of other things and beings that were created in no special order.

This text is so interesting because it does not present Marduk himself as a part of creation. He seems to exist, as well as other deities, outside of what used to be *prima materia* in older traditions. In this sense, he is more like the only god of Genesis. Furthermore, the Sumerian tradition of creation must have been quite strong at the time of the recording of this incantation because the first city that somehow emerged is Eridu, the home of Nammu and Enki. However, the second city is Babylon whose political rise is closely connected with the spreading of Marduk's popularity in Mesopotamia.

Among things created and named by Marduk were two important rivers: the Tigris and the Euphrates. While the concept of naming is addressed later, it is necessary to note here that according to yet another text republished by Heidel (1951), 'An address to the river,' the Euphrates itself is called 'the creator of all things' (pp.74–75). This incantation talks about this river being dug out by great gods and to which both Ea (Enki) and Marduk were presented.

 This contradiction was obviously not of much concern for the ancient authors. It seems that they were able to select the elements of older traditions and incorporated them into texts which were composed to suit a new situation and/or a ritual.

Greek accounts of the Mesopotamian watery birth

There are two Greek accounts referring to the Babylonian tradition of creation as it was accessible to their authors through existing texts. The younger one, recorded around A.D. 500 or a little later, was mentioned by Damascius in his treatise entitled 'Difficulties and solutions of first principles.' His short account simply lists the origin of deities in their order of appearance. He starts with Tauthe and Apason who are obviously Tiamat and Apsû. Interestingly enough he makes a point of calling Tauthe 'mother of the gods' and diminishes the importance of Apason by identifying him simply as 'her lover' (Doria and Lenowitz 1976, p.136) or 'her husband' (Heidel 1951, p.76). Furthermore, the names of female deities are listed before the names of their male companions with whom they emerged in pairs, the reverse order of the tradition of the *Enûma Eliš* as noted by Heidel (1951). Unfortunately, we can only speculate whether Damascius was simply courteous toward women or believed that their role in creation was of greater importance than those of male deities.

The listing proceeds with the presentation of Moymis (Mummu) as the only son of Tauthe and Apason. According to the translation provided by Heidel (1951), Damascius refers to him as 'the mental world...proceeding from the two principles' which suggests to him the existence of the world 'in the mind of the creator before it becomes an external reality' reflecting the Platonian concept of *logos* (p.76). On the other hand, Doria and Lenowitz's edition of the text refers to Moymis as 'who is everything we see' (1976, p.136); that is, more of the external world than the mental one. The listing of the next generations of deities is in accordance with the *Enûma Eliš* tradition and finishes with Bēl (Marduk) presented as 'the Maker' (Doria and Lenowitz 1976, p.136) or 'the fabricator of the world' (Heidel 1951, p.76). Again, although Tauthe is referred to as the mother of gods, she is not the ultimate creator, Bēl is.

The earlier source, 'Babyloniaka,' was written by Berossos in the third century B.C. He was a priest of Bēl (Marduk) in Babylon who presented the history and culture of Babylonia from the time of creation to his own time in three volumes. His work, now lost, survived in fragments in references of other classical authors such as Josephus (A.D. 37/38–around 100), and Eusebius (died A.D. 342). Berossos, as narrated by other authors, claimed that he based his work on 'the public records of Babylon which had been carefully preserved for 150 myriad years' (Doria and Lenowitz 1976, p.237). In the first volume, which focused on the origins of the world, he refers to 'darkness and water' from which strange creatures came into being. They were described as various combinations of humans and animals, 'borrowing [different body parts] from each other/pictures of them/in Baal's [Bēl's] Temple/Babylon/they all lived inside a woman/she was their mistress/Omorka/ Um-ruk/in Chaldean Thalath/Tiāmat /In Greek Thalatta (sea)/equaling in number Selené (moon)' (Doria and Lenowitz 1976, p.239).

The story proceeds with Bēl killing Omorka and splitting her body into two halves for the purpose of creating heaven and earth. The similarity of the account to the *Enûma Eliš* is quite noticeable. Omorka, like Tiāmat, is identified with the salt-water sea and darkness which are presented as a primordial state of pre-existence. However, since Apsû is missing from this account one might speculate that Omorka, like the Sumerian Nammu, symbolized all waters. Thus she, whether alive or dead, was able to have all living creatures born from her as the text goes on to explain. However, Omorka still represents primordial chaos, which is changed into order with her death credited to Bēl.

It is remarkable that the Sumerian tradition of the watery birth has survived in the mythology of Mesopotamia for thousands of years although its presentation or interpretation has changed and/or adjusted in the process. It is even more remarkable that the echo of this tradition can be seen in other mythologies of the Middle East which have been carried out outside the region and are subscribed to by many in modern times.

The formation of heaven and earth

The emergence of heaven and earth in the Sumerian tradition is a somewhat compli-cated matter. The orderly emergence of the universe from the waters of Nammu called for these two elements to develop first before everything else could come into being. The respective words for 'heaven' (and 'sky' – many languages do not make the distinction between these two) and 'earth' in the Sumerian language are *AN* and *KI*, and, as Kramer noted, the Sumerian term for the universe is a combination of both – *AN-KI* (Kramer 1959). The disputation, one of the most popular genres in the Sumerian literature, between Cattle and Grain includes a reference to the appearance of the universe itself as 'the mountain of heaven and earth' (Kramer 1986, p.65). Thus, one can assume that the Sumerian universe emerged as a mountain, a primordial hill, which in many cultures symbolizes the meeting place between heaven and earth.

Thus, the next logical step would be the separation of these two. This act is poetically described by the epic entitled 'Gilgamesh, Enkidu and the Nether World':

> In days of yore, in distant days of yore
> In nights of yore, in distant nights of yore,
> In years of yore, in distant years of yore...
> After heaven had been moved away from earth,
> After earth had been separated from heaven,
> After the name of man had been fixed,
> After An had carried off heaven,
> After Enlil had carried off earth. (Kramer 1986, p.65)

Since the Sumerian mythology or rather its authors had a tendency to personify and to anthropomorphize elements which were not human, both heaven and earth were presented as two separate deities, respectively An and Ki. The Sumerian sky/heaven god An, whose Babylonian name was Anu (Damascius' Anos), was perceived to be father of all the gods. His emergence from Nammu would suggest her to be his mother, although in the Babylonian tradition of the *Enûma Eliš* his parents are described as Kišar (mother) and Anšar (father), Damascius' Kissaré and Assoros. They emerged as the second pair, after Lahmu and Lahamu, from the original deities of the watery chaos of Tiāmat and Apsû. Some scholars suggest that they were children of Lahmu (Damascius' Daché) and Lahamu (Damascius' Dachos) who in turn are very confusing creatures. If we follow the list in Damascius' account, Lahmu should be female, but in Mesopotamian iconography Lahmu was presented as a male deity with a beard and long hair. Lahmu and Lahamu as well as *lahama* (one of the creatures associated with Enki) seem to be derived 'from the Old Akkadian *lahmum* (probably meaning "hairy")' (Black and Green 1997, pp.114–115). These 'hairy' beings are responsible for giving birth not only to Anu of the *Enûma Eliš* but also to Illinois (Enlil) and Aos (Ea/Enki) in Damascius' account.

To complicate matters further, Anšar and Kišar might be representing An and Ki as heaven and earth (Black and Green 1997). The *Enûma Eliš* refers to Anu as their first born who is equal to Anšar (Heidel 1951). To top it all, An has also been regarded as a son of Uraš who as a male deity was a local god of the city of Dilbat in northern

Babylonia (the Prologue to the Laws of Hammurabi of Babylon, Black and Green 1997; for the laws see Roth 1997). Thus, it seems that by the time the Babylonian Epic of Creation was written the author was already confused as to the Sumerian order of creation and relationships between older deities.

An's lineage is as confusing as his marriages. Since he emerged together with the goddess Ki, they were considered to be married and to have produced a variety of plants as their offspring. She was also a daughter of Nammu whose subterranean waters she represented. On the other hand An(u) was also associated with the female deity Uraš whose name also was explained as 'earth,' as well as with Antu, and even Inana/Ištar (the most popular goddess not only of Mesopotamia but even of the whole Middle East).

The union of An and Ki is especially interesting when other texts are taken into consideration. The account of creation from Nippur, which was the center of Enlil's worship, states: 'Heaven was born of its own accord, Earth was born of its own accord./Heaven was abyss (= ENGUR), Earth was abyss' (Leick 1994, p.16). For Leick this particular passage represents the local tradition of Nippur which regards the physical entities of heaven and earth as *prima materia*, not the waters either of order or of chaos. In my view, the reference to both elements being the *ENGUR* indicates their emergence from the waters and the main element of their entity. Leick (1994) also points out the fact that although the above account refers to the emergence of heaven and earth at the same time, the other texts list either earth before heaven, or *vice versa*. Thus it seems that, at least in the case of this pair, who was first was not essential.

The union between An and Ki was sexual, as demonstrated by both Van Dijk (1964) and Leick (1994). They both refer to the small fragment of a text from the middle of the third millennium B.C. which mentions the vulva of earth and 'a hole in the earth ... to be filled with water. An, the Sky, "stood up like a young man (and) An and Ki roared together"' (Leick 1994, p.17). Another disputation, this time between Wood and Reed, describes this union in the following words:

> The pure young woman (Earth) showed herself [after adorning herself
>   with metals, gems and even diamonds] to the pure Sky,
> The vast Sky [after presenting himself to her] copulated with the wide
>   Earth,
> The seed of the heroes Wood and Reed he ejaculated into her womb,
> The Earth, the good cow, received the good seeds of Sky in her womb,
> The Earth, for the happy birth of the plants of Life, presented herself.
> (Leick 1994, p.18)

It is obvious that Sky's sperm represents rain waters which irrigated the earth well enough to provide favorable conditions for the birth of plants. This is the motif seen more frequently in Anatolia and in Syria–Palestine than in Mesopotamia as previously noted by Lambert, and Leick (1994). However, the equation between water and male semen as represented by the same sign suggests that the Nammu waters of life began to be replaced by the male's fluid, reducing the role of the goddess to the carrier of the seed, here explicitly stated to be a cow. The motif of bull, the Neolithic symbol of virility and strength, is then 'reintroduced' into Sumerian mythology in connection with the father of all the gods, not just in connection with the typical weather or storm gods usually represented and/or identified with this animal. Since An was rarely represented in art, his iconography remains obscure except for presentations from the later periods when his symbol was a horned cap (Black and Green 1997). His sacred animal was believed to be the heavenly bull and his sacred number was 60 (Hooke 1953).

In the *Enûma Eliš* tradition Tiāmat was presented as the original material from which heaven and earth were created by Marduk. A series of events, summarized briefly here, led to this act. After young deities such as Anu and Nudimmud (Enki/Ea) were born, following the older generation of gods coming directly from the line of Tiāmat and Apsû, they became so noisy that they irritated Apsû. He and Mummu, the vizier, asked Tiāmat to 'do way with them' so they could get some sleep. Tiāmat, having strong motherly feelings for her noisome offspring, was outraged by such a suggestion. But Mummu and Apsû decided to go ahead with their plans of eliminating the overactive younger generation. Unfortunately for them, the young gods were in the habit of eaves-dropping, so upon learning about the deadly plans concerning them, Ea, their leader, designed a plan which resulted in the killing of Apsû and the imprisoning of Mummu. Ea assumed Apsû as his dwelling where he lived with his wife Damkina. Together they begot their son, Marduk, who soon grew to be quite powerful and a nuisance to others by playing with the four winds created for him by his grandfather, Anu. The other deities, sleep-deprived again, complained to Tiāmat, reminding her of Apsû's and Mummu's fate in the hands of Ea. This time Tiāmat decided to punish these arrogant young deities. She created an army of monsters and made the greatest of them, Qingu, to be her lovely husband. She entrusted the Tablet of Destinies (discussed later, see p.78) into his hands and was ready to start the battle. The young generation of troublesome deities became quite worried about what could happen to them but none of them was brave enough to stand against Tiāmat. This was the time for Marduk to offer his conditions to the horror-struck young gods: he would fight Tiāmat but if he won and saved them, he will become the unquestionable leader forever. Not having much choice, the gods made the deal. After many preparations worthy of his royal persona, Marduk went against Tiāmat, and after a horrifying battle, he captured her.

> The Lord [Marduk] trampled upon the frame of Tiāmat
> With his merciless mace he crushed her skull.
> He cut open the arteries of her blood.
> He let the North Wind bear (it) away as glad tidings.
> When his fathers saw, they rejoiced and were glad,
> They brought him gifts and presents.
> He calmed down. Then the Lord was inspecting her carcass,
> That he might divide (?) the monstrous lump and fashion artful things.
> He split her in two, like a fish for drying. (Foster 1995, p.32)

And the result of splitting Tiāmat's carcass was creation of heaven and earth by Marduk. These two were physical entities which were not personified but used as dwellings for deities whom Marduk assigned to the newly created holy places. Thus, Marduk was honored with the title of creator, while Tiāmat was reduced to the role of the substance from which the creation of heaven and earth was possible.

The motif of splitting an original heaven–earth entity can also be found in the Anatolian tradition, represented by the Hurrian 'Song of Ullikummi,' in which this act was performed by the Primaeval Deities with the help of a copper cutting tool. In the Quranic tradition, heaven and earth are presented as being once a solid mass which Allah ripped apart (Prophets XVII, 21:30 (III)).

There is yet another text from Babylon which refers to the creation process in its introduction to the ritual concerning the restoration of a temple (Heidel 1951). The god credited with the creation of the heavens is Anu. However, the text does not mention the creator of the earth although it refers to Ea as a creator of reed marshes, forests, mountains, seas, and vegetation among other things. Although it is unclear what material he used in the process (if any), it seems that it may have been clay, based on line 26, which in Heidel's translation is 'Ea nipped off clay in the Apsû' (1951, p.65). If so, the sweet waters of Apsû are still indirectly the prime mover.

The above Babylonian accounts refer to the creation of heaven and earth as separate physical bodies which came to being through different actions of leading gods. In the case of the Sumerian account in which heaven and earth are presented as the mountain or universe and are personified, the act of copulation between An and Ki as described above did not necessarily require their separation. However, in order to incorporate them into the visible model of physical reality, these two lovers or consorts had to be separated. This led to the emergence of other deities who personified both cosmic and natural forces of order necessary for the existence and maintenance of the universe (discussed in the next chapter).

Egypt

Main elements and themes of creation

Although the Egyptian *Enûma Eliš* or 'Genesis' has not yet been found and was probably never composed during the Pharaonic Period, there are four principal accounts of creation which can be reconstructed today. All four originated in different locations and different time periods as the result of priestly efforts to elevate local gods over the rest of the existing deities. They are known as Heliopolitan, Hermopolitan, Memphite and Theban theologies or doctrines. The focus of each doctrine is different but they share common elements which were very much rooted in Egyptian ideology. That does not mean that they can or should be combined into one linear, 'chronological,' sequence of events as has been done by a few authors (Clark 1959). However, they can be presented in a somewhat chronological fashion with regard to the process of creation.

One of the most interesting themes in Egyptian creation stories and others is the understanding that creation was a continuous series of frequently repetitious acts, not an isolated event in the remote past. This concept was connected with the perception of the role of the pharaoh as the link between the worlds of the sacred and the profane and as the continuous reincarnation of Horus, the divine ruler of Egypt after the death of his father, Osiris, who became the lord of the after-life (more about him later). This way even the act of building a temple was a repetition of the construction of the first temple brought into being by the divine forces for themselves (this motif was possibly borrowed by the Canaanites and then through them carried on to the Biblical tradition). While the origin of this concept is simply unknown, it might be speculated that it was associated with the observance of the regularity of the Nile's inundations. It appeared around the same time every year and then when the waters recessed the land emerged from them. No wonder then that the Egyptians believed in the emergence of the world from the flood waters and the continuous repetition of this act.

This watery chaos was personified by a male deity known as Nun and was associated with the primeval darkness, *keku semau* (Hornung 1992). As the state of non-existence *per se* it was frequently perceived quite negatively since this state lacked all the elements connected with the perception of time, space and life itself. Nun, as was believed, never ceased to exist, and after the first act of creation he was 'relocated' to the edges of the universe (for a discussion of this outer universe see Allen 1988). This was the dimension which threatened the existence of the universe with its opposite, chaos, disorder and non-life. Nun represented not only the primordial ocean but also the watery depths of the underworld through which the sun was to travel during the night, tunneling through the body of the crocodile, only to be reborn on the horizon (Hornung 1992). A very similar concept of the duality of cosmos (order) and chaos exists also in the Indo-Aryan tradition, although this tradition focuses more on ethical and moral dualism (for description see Malandra 1983).

Out of these waters of non-existence the primordial hill was believed to emerge in most of the Egyptian accounts. This mound was like an island in the middle of the ocean, on which the creator was to stand. Sometimes the creator himself was identified with the primeval mound. According to the Pyramid Text No. 1587, the sun-god Atum was addressed as the 'hill' (Lurker 1984, p. 96), while the Memphite doctrine identifies Ta-tenen (Tatjenen), which means 'elevated land,'– often portrayed as a bearded man with a complicated crown (ram's horns, sun-disc and two plumes) – with Ptah, one of the most ancient gods in Egyptian mythology. 'And he [Ptah] is Ta-tenen, who gave birth to the gods, and from whom every thing came forth, foods, provisions, divine offerings, all good things' (Lichtheim 1975, p.55).

This primordial hill was symbolized by the *benben* stone at Heliopolis which could have also represented 'the petrified semen of the sun-god Re-Atum' (Shaw and Nicholson 1995, p.52). Its name seems to derive from the ancient Egyptian word *weben*, 'to rise,' and its appearance could be a prototype for the later obelisks and pyramids (Shaw and Nicholson 1995). The concept of the primeval hill was so important that even sanctuaries were built over a small sand hill, and some tombs and cenotaphs had a representation of a symbolic island in the center. In addition to Heliopolis and Memphis other cities too, such as Thebes, claimed to possess the primeval hill in order to establish their antiquity over the others. In yet another tradition this mound was believed to be Osiris' tomb whose many earthly re-creations were often set on an island. Thus, the rising and retreating waters of the Nile over the island alluded to his death and resurrection.

Although most Egyptologists agree that the tradition of the emergence of the primeval hill from the waters of Nun is a metaphorical, conceptual image of the beginning of the world as seen and thought of by the Egyptians, there is also the possibility that this image might have referred to possible historical events of the very remote past. This possibility is discussed by Rice (1986) who points out that some Egyptian texts describing the original mound may refer to the Sumerian Dilmun, or modern Bahrain. The tradition of Dilmun and the Egyptian primordial mound as being a 'place of reeds,' 'a pure land,' 'place of ancestors,' 'place of sunrise' and so on may be 'a direct inheritance or was handed on to the Egyptians by the third party' (Rice 1986, p.123). Although Rice's unusual idea that the Dilmunites were the connection between two great civilizations of the Middle East, the Sumerian and the Egyptian (without even mentioning the Indus valley), needs much more joint research with various specialists, it is also very appealing for those in search of the origin

Finally, one has to mention the connection between the primordial mound and one of the most popular objects of ancient Egypt – a scarab whose design is based on a common dung beetle. The picture of this insect symbolized the idea 'to come into existence' (Ward 1994, p.186). While this little creature is considered by most of us to be just a pest, the Egyptians were fascinated with its perceived ability to come out of the round ball, a 'hill' made out of dung, pushed around by a male beetle. Although the Egyptian perception of a beetle's biological process was faulty (Ward 1994), the appearance of a new beetle (only male beetles were thought to exist) out of the hill was thought to represent the rebirth of the sun and thus was associated with such sun-gods as Khepri (also a form of Re) and Atum.

However, in some traditions the primeval hill was replaced by a lotus flower emerging from the flood waters of Nun. The physical properties of this waterlily made it a natural choice for the representation of the Egyptian cycle of life and death. The lotus flower opens up every morning toward the east when the light shines, only to disappear deep into the water, closing its petals, when darkness comes. Thus, even the deceased would express their wish to be transformed into a lotus so they would be reborn, as Spells 81A and 81B of the Book of the Dead indicate (Faulkner 1997, p.79, for example, Spell 81A: 'I am this pure lotus which went forth from the sunshine, which is at the nose of Re; / I have descended that I may seek it for Horus, for I am the pure one who issued from the fen'). On this lotus the creator was to appear, sometimes depicted as a sun child but most frequently as a ram-headed god (Hornung 1992), which was yet another way to represent Amun (the leading god of Thebes) as connected with the absorption of attributes belonging to the original ram-headed god, Khnum.

Since the Egyptian imagination seems to be limitless, the celestial cow was yet another being which emerged from the deep waters of Nun. The cow was considered to be the sacred animal mainly associated with the heaven or sky goddess Hathor who was frequently worshipped in its form. The sun disc was placed between her horns to affirm her importance as the daughter of Re, although the celestial cow was also believed to be his mother bringing him to life every day. Hathor's name can be translated as 'house of Horus' (Shaw and Nicholson 1995, p. 119) and she was considered to be the mother of each and every king, many of whom used the title 'son of Hathor.' Her attributes, especially her headdress with the sun disc, were frequently assumed by Isis, thus the king was also described as Isis' son.

In spite of contradictions concerning the identity of the entity which emerged from the state of non-being represented by a watery chaos, the process of creation seemed to have started in most cases with the appearance of one of the sun-gods. While the main themes of creation stories and perceptions of the cosmic forces and their imagery in Egypt were more or less consistent throughout the Pharaonic Period, the modes or means of creation and its sequence differed depending on the religious center which produced them. The following sections present the most popular theologies concerning the origin of the universe.

The Hermopolitan Doctrine of Creation

The earliest account of the Hermopolitan Theology dates back to the Middle Kingdom (2055–1765 B.C. or 1650 B.C. if the Thirteenth and the Fourteenth Dynasties are included). Although this is not the earliest creation story that has been discovered, it is discussed here first because it refers to the state of non-being from which various forces emerged in an arranged and orderly fashion.

This account was composed in the city of Hermopolis Magna (ancient Egyptian *Hmnw*), Middle Egypt. It focuses on eight deities and is known as the Ogdoad. During the Pharaonic Period the name of the city, *Khmun*, was derived from the word for eight and its original name is preserved even today in the locality known as el-Ashmunein (Shaw and Nicholson 1995 p. 210), 'the two eights.'

I like to refer to this creation story as the 'scientific' one, because these first four divine couples were often represented in Egyptian art as frogs (male deities) and snakes (female deities), amphibian animals which ruled the earth well before any other living forms emerged. This visual perception of the first Ogdoad was probably a result of yet another Hermopolitan tradition reflecting the reality of the landscape and its animals 'playing' in mud after the flood waters receded (Ions 1983). But they were also sometimes presented as eight apes welcoming the sunrise as the symbolic creation or rather re-creation of the world (Lurker 1984).

However, it is not their visual appearance which is important but the names and their meaning (male names are given first): Nun and Naunet as 'watery depths'; Huh and Hauhet as 'unendingness'; Kuk and Kauket as 'darkness'; and Amon and Amaunet as 'that which is unseen' (after Ions 1983, p.29). These four pairs as uncreated forces are presented by Hornung as 'primeval flood, hiddenness, endlessness and the undifferentiated ones' (1992, p.41) and by Lesko (1991) as watery abyss, hiddenness, darkness, formlessness (p.95). Actually these forces, although not fully named at the time, were mentioned for the first time by the Coffin Texts, Spell 76, referring to the emergence of Heliopolitan Atum: 'On the day that Atum evolved –/Out of the Flood, out of the Waters,/Out of darkness, out of lostness' (Allen 1997b, p.10).

It seems that the names of goddesses are simply the feminine form of their male consorts and thus they can be treated as doublets. Out of the deities of the Ogdoad only Amun (Amon) and Nun are part of the mainstream cosmogony of ancient Egypt, together representing an image of the watery depths through which the unseen forces of Amun were moving. These gods together with their consorts were already known from the Pyramid Texts of the Old Kingdom. 'Your offering-cake belongs to you, Niu and Nenet, who protect the gods, who guard the gods with your shadows./Your offering-cake belongs to you, Amun and Amaunet, who protect the gods, who guard the gods with your shadows' (No. 301, after Lesko 1991, p.94).

These four couples of the non-being state created the world which they inhabited during the so-called golden age, and then they died. However, even in the other world their powers still influenced the world's affairs since they were responsible for the flooding of the river Nile and the daily sunrise. Although this was the main theme of the Hermopolitan cosmogony, there were at least four versions of this story as told in Egypt. Each of them was strictly connected with Hermopolis as being built on the primeval hill represented by a temple near which there was a sacred lake known as the Sea [Lake] of the Two Knives. These two knives were possibly represented by two sycamore trees which are mentioned in other Egyptian texts, and illustrated the battle between the sun-god and the Nether World. Spell 15 of the Book of the Dead refers to this event in the following words:

> How beautiful are your [Re] rising and your shining on the back of your mother Nut, you having appeared as King of the Gods. The Lower Sky has greeted you, Justice embraces you at all times. You traverse the sky happily, and the Lake of the Two Knives is in contentment. The rebel has fallen, his arms are bound, a knife has severed his spine, but Re will have a fair wind, the Night-bark has destroyed those who would attack him. (Faulkner 1997, p.40)

Thus, the sun as Re could be seen as rising on the horizon in the frame of the two knives as sycamores. The 'Isle of Flames' was believed to emerge as a symbolic presentation of this primordial mound from the Sea or Lake of the Two Knives.

One variant was associated with the god of moon and wisdom, Thoth. Although the dating of each version is highly debatable it seems that Thoth was incorporated into the already existing tradition of the Ogdoad after his cult was established in Hermopolis Magna. Thoth, in his form of an ibis, was believed to lay an egg on the primeval hill whose existence was caused by the Ogdoad. It was his 'gift' from which a young sun-god hatched and immediately appeared on the horizon. At the same time the Ogdoad was perceived to be his souls while Thoth himself was self-creation.

Three other variants are connected with the emergence of the sun-god Re. According to the first one an egg was laid by the 'Great Cackler,' the celestial goose. This cackler was often connected with Amun, although in the Graeco-Roman period it was associated with Horus (Lurker 1984). If Amun were to be the 'Great Cackler,' thus his role as a transitional force from the non-existence to the existence state was intended to be stressed as a very positive force in contrast to the remaining pairs of the Ogdoad. This situation is even more complicated since some sources indicate that the egg carried an air (Ions 1983) which in the Ogdoad was represented by Amun himself and his wife Amaunet. More commonly, it was believed that the egg contained the sun-god Re, the future creator of the world.

The birth of Re is also referred to in the third version of this theology. This time he was born as a divine child out of a lotus flower which emerged from the Sea of Two Knives (Ions 1983). According to Lurker (1984) it was Horus, not Re, who was carried by the flower.

In the fourth account it was a scarab beetle contained in the lotus who transformed himself into a boy child and probably represented Re or his aspect too.

The Hermopolitan Theology was clearly not concerned with the events which must have occurred after the creator was brought into being as a part of the existence created by the non-beings of the Ogdoad. These events were addressed by other doctrines, especially by the one from Heliopolis.

The Heliopolitan Ennead

Probably the most influential account of creation was the so-called Heliopolitan Theology or Doctrine which was already known during the Old Kingdom. The compilers of the Pyramid Texts – which are our best source of information concerning this variant – obviously assumed that its main principles were already widely popular when they included references to this theology. While the Hermopolitan doctrine tried to deal with the question of pre-existence, the Heliopolitan account refers to the events which occurred with and after the self-emergence of Atum, the god of Heliopolis (ancient Egyptian *Iwnw* which is the Biblical city of On – Lesko 1991), from the watery abyss of Nun. It is traditionally called Ennead; that is, group of the first nine deities (in Egyptian, *pesedjet* – after Shaw and Nicholson 1995, p.93), although the number of divine beings included differed (the Egyptian term *Ennead* was also used to indicate the gods in general; see Allen 1988, p.8). For example, Horus was always a part of this Ennead and he was the tenth god. Other texts refer to Enneads which included between five and twenty deities (Silverman 1997).

The god creator of the Heliopolitan account was Atum who, by the time of the Pyramid Texts, became identified with Re as Re-Atum. This identification is quite clear in the Book of the Dead, Chapter 17:

> 'Now come into being all the words of the Lord of All: I was Atum when I was alone in the Abyss; I was Re in his glorious appearings when he began to rule what he had made.'
>
> *What does it mean?* It means Re when he began to rule what he had made, when he began to appear as king, before the Supports of Shu had come into being, when he was upon the hill which is in Hermopolis... (Faulkner 1997, p.44)

One can also see that by the time of this 'edition' of the Book of the Dead not only is Atum represented as Re but also as many other deities of various traditions which are mentioned by the text. Furthermore the above text also refers to an important role of Shu, 'dry air' or 'void,' whose birth and functions as related to Atum's self-realization are thoroughly discussed by Allen (1988).

Atum's name can be translated as 'the all,' 'lord of all' or 'completed one' since he created himself out of the primeval chaos which he also personified (for full etymology of his name see Allen 1988). He was able to do it with the help of magic or 'divine energy' (*Heka*) which included or connected with 'perception' (*Sia* – translated as 'divine knowledge') and 'annunciation' (*Hu* – also translated as 'divine utterance'); that is, conceptualization of what was to be created and pronunciation or the 'divine word' to bring the concept into realization (for more information concerning Egyptian magic see Ritner 1993).

Atum was perceived to be 'the all' because he came into being before even heaven and earth were separated. Papyrus Bremner-Rhind, which was compiled at the beginning of the Ptolemaic Period (305–30 B.C.) but was based on the earlier sources, includes a description of Atum as:

> I [Atum] am the one who evolved as Evolver.
> When I evolved, evolution evolved.
> All evolution evolved after I evolved,
> Evolutions becoming many In emerging from my mouth,
> Without the sky having evolved,
> Without the earth having evolved,
> Without the ground or snakes having been created in that place. (Allen 1997e, p.14)

Atum's beginnings are not very clear since there are various allusions to his emergence. He either appeared as a primordial hill himself or as a being in need of a place to stand which he then created as a mound, or as the sun Re-Atum on the hill risen from the waters of Nun. Most of the time he was portrayed in an anthropomorphic form wearing the double crown of Egypt in order to stress his protective role over the kingship itself.

However, depending on the aspects which his believers wished to stress at any particular time, Atum – in combination with Re – was symbolized by the Ben(n)u bird which was possibly a prototype for the Greek Phoenix, or as the scarab beetle which was associated with yet another of his divine forms, Khepri. Both of these aspects are addressed by the Pyramid Texts, Spell 600: 'Atum Scarab!/When you became high, as the high ground,/When you rose, as the benben in the Phoenix' (Allen 1997c, p.7).

In contrast to the Hermopolitan Theology, Atum was the only one who existed so he had to 'design' the way to bring other deities, other elements of the universe, into being for the world to appear. Without having a partner, Atum used his hand to produce his offspring who in turn had more children leading to the population of Atum's world with new elements of nature and cosmos. Since the heaven/sky and the earth were not the first forces who emerged from Atum, the rest of the process is narrated in the next chapter.

The many within the one: The Memphite Theology

This account is probably the most consistent and philosophical of the stories of creation from ancient Egypt. It is a dedicatory inscription which was written down from an older copy for the celebrations associated with the erection of the Ptah temple at Memphis by the Nubian pharaoh of the Twenty Fifth Dynasty, Shabaqo. 'His Incarnation [as ruling pharaoh] copied this writing anew in the house of his father Ptah South of His Wall, when his Incarnation found it as something that the predecessors had made, worm-eaten and unknown from the beginning to end' (Allen 1997a, p.22).

Although for many years it was believed that the original was composed some time during the Old Kingdom, recent studies indicate that this text is probably not earlier than the thirteenth century B.C. In some ways the Memphite Theology is like an unintended continuation of the story of creation which began with non-existence, followed by the birth of deities (and the accidental creation of people – see Part 4, pp.38–41), to reach its apogee with the creation of all the principles of life 'encoded' in the only creator, Ptah (for discussion of the most-known texts concerning Ptah see Allen 1988).

While the issue of the monotheistic character of Egyptian religion is addressed elsewhere (see pp.67, 90-93) – demonstrating that the Egyptians believed in a multiplicity of deities – the account of the Memphis priests illustrates perfectly the ancient ability to combine the idea of many (gods) and one. In this specific text it is Ptah, the ruling god of one of the most ancient cities of Pharaonic Egypt, Memphis, who is the creator of everything. The name Memphis was probably derived from Men-nefer ('established and beautiful'; after Shaw and Nicholson 1995, p.180), a name of the pyramid town near the pyramid of Pepy I (2321–2287 B.C.). However, the city's original name was Ineb-hedj, 'White Walls,' and was built by the legendary King Menes of the Manetho tradition who is frequently identified either with Narmer or with Aha (Lesko 1991). In Memphis the king erected a great temple dedicated to Ptah.

Thus, the Memphite doctrine declares Ptah to be the king of Upper and Lower Egypt, unifier, and '"self-begotten," so says Atum: "who created the Nine Gods"' (Lichtheim 1975, p.52). He is also addressed as the creator who brought everything into being through his thought (heart) and word (tongue), meaning that this was creation out of nothing (*ex nihilo*), only through the words of the god (the so-called Logos doctrine, comparable to the idea of creation from the New Testament). His actions are described in the following words:

> There was evolution into Atum's image through both the heart and the tongue. And great and important is Ptah, who gave life to all the [gods] and their ka's [sic] as well as through his heart and this tongue, as which Horus and Thoth have both evolved by means of Ptah. (Allen 1997a, p.22)

This idea of creation through conceptualization and then pronunciation was known in Egypt already from Spell No. 261 of the Coffin Texts where references were made to Atum's mode of creation as coming from 'his mouth' – 'when he took Annunciation in his mouth' (Allen 1997f, p.17). However, in the Memphite Theology Ptah not only creates everything but also establishes the principles of existence and maintenance of everything. 'Thus all the faculties were made and all the qualities determined... <Thus justice is done> to him who does what is loved, <and punishment> to him who does what is hated. Thus life is given to the peaceful, death is given to the criminal' (Lichtheim 1975, p.55).

His role is summarized by Allen (1997a) as follows:

> It has evolved that Ptah is called 'He who made totality and caused the gods to evolve,' since he is Ta-tenen, who gave birth to the gods, from whom everything has emerged – offerings and food, god's offerings, and every good thing. So is it found understood that his physical strength is greater than the gods'. So has Ptah come to rest after his making everything and every divine speech as well, having given birth to the gods, have made their towns, having founded their nomes, having set the gods in their cult-places, having made sure their bread-offerings, having founded their shrines, having modeled their

bodies to what contents them. Do have the gods entered their bodies – of everything of wood, every kind of mineral, every kind of fruit, everything that grows all over him, in which they have evolved. (p.23)

Ptah was able to take on such a tremendous task of creating and organizing the state of existence because in him all divine forces were encoded. He was the Supreme God in whom the other deities came into being. 'Ptah-Nun, the father who [made] Atum./Ptah-Naunet, the mother who bore Atum./Ptah-The Great is heart and tongue of the Nine [Gods]' (Lichtheim 1975, p.54).

Horus was explained as his heart, while Thoth was his tongue. The Ennead was his teeth and lips and only thanks to Ptah did Atum come into being to create the rest of the universe in the traditional way, through masturbation. But even then it was Ptah who 'pronounced the name of every thing, from which Shu and Tefnut came forth and which gave birth to the Ennead' (Lichtheim 1975, p.54). As can be seen, once again the Egyptians were not bothered not only by obvious inconsistencies of this account in comparison to others, but also within the text itself. For example, if Horus was Ptah's heart why had he to be created again as the part of the Ennead, Ptah's teeth and lips?

But the genius of the Memphite Theology whose extensive fragments in translation I quoted above is in the sophistication of its creators. By ignoring any physical or biological aspects of creation the theologians of Memphis were able to offer a brand new mode of creation which was not only very comprehensible but also capable of incorporating other well-rooted ideas of the Egyptian cosmogony and cosmology. Ptah was the only, although not one but many. He was 'who begot himself by himself, without any evolving having evolved;/Who [craf]ted the world in the design of his heart;/Evolution of his evolutions,/Model who gave birth to all that is,/Begetter who created what exists' ('Hymn to Ptah'– after Allen 1997g, p.20).

The beginning at the end: The Theban Theology as the summary

The above accounts of creation were the most popular ones in ancient Egypt. However, this does not mean that other deities were not honored with the title of creator. Since the concept of creation was closely associated with the Egyptian ideas of kingship, birth, death and rebirth, various deities were evoked at the time of writing a text or reciting it. Among them are Khnum, Neith, Hathor, Nefertem, Khepri, and especially Amun.

The center of Amun worship was the capital of the New Kingdom, Thebes. Although this god was already mentioned by the Pyramid Texts and then as Amun-Re who ruled Egypt since the Middle Kingdom almost continuously, only in the second part of the second millennium B.C. was he pronounced not only the king of Egypt, 'the king of the gods,' but also the creator.

According to the Leiden Papyrus composed during the reign of Rameses II (1279–1213 B.C.) it was Amun, 'the hidden one,' who was the origin of everything and everyone. Chapter 100 states:

Who began evolution on the first occasion.
Amun, who evolved in the beginning, with his emanation unknown,
No god evolving prior to him,

No other god with him to tell of his appearance,
There being no mother of his for whom his name was made,
And no father of his who ejaculated him so as to say 'It is I.' (Allen 1997h, pp.24–25)

Since nobody knew his name, he was 'the hidden one,' nobody existed before Amun. It must be remembered that names were extremely important in Egyptian religion with regard to both birth and death. The being existed because he, she or it was recognized and identified by name among other spiritual and physical components. Once the name was destroyed, the being ceased to exist since it was incomplete. The act of naming was also the act of creation as clearly illustrated by the Memphite Theology in which Ptah was the one who named everyone and everything: 'To know the name of an individual was to have some control over him or her' (Silverman 1991, p.28). Thus, since there was no-one who named Amun, he must have been the first one and nobody had any control over him (a similar idea was applied to Yahweh of Genesis). His mystery was stressed by Chapter 200 of the Leiden Papyrus:

> He is hidden from the gods, and his aspect is unknown. He is farther than the sky, he is deeper than the Duat [the underworld]. No god knows his true appearance...no one testifies to him accurately. He is too secret to uncover his awesomeness, he is too great to investigate, too powerful to know. (Silverman 1997, p.126)

Obviously the theologians from Thebes who made this version of creation were very much aware of the existence of the leading accounts from Heliopolis, Hermopolis Magna, and Memphis. Quite skillfully they incorporated all three accounts into Amun's creation process, setting up the chronological order of these theologies following the 'common' logic of emergence of different elements. 'The Hermopolitans were your first evolution.../You made your evolution into Ta-tenen [the Memphite account]... The Ennead is combined in your body;/Your image is every god, joined in your person... (Allen 1997h, p.24).

In the Khonsu Cosmogony which was preserved by the Ptolemaic text the order is different and not as logical as on the Leiden Papyrus since it 'begins' with the Memphite Theology.

> ...Amun in that name of his called Ptah created the egg that came forth from Nun...as Ptah of the Heh gods and the Nenu goddesses who created heaven and earth. He ejaculated and made [it] at this place in the lake, which was created in Tjenene, it flowed out under him, like that which happens, in its name of 'grain of seed.' He fertilized the egg and the eight came into existence from it in the district around the Ogdoad. He languished there in Nun, in the Great Flood. He knew them; his neck received them... He traveled (hns) to Thebes in his form of Khonsu... (Lesko 1991, p.105).

The final result of this theology was that Amun was presented as 'father of the fathers,' the one but not the only (similar to Ptah) because all other deities were his aspects. His being was summarized in Chapter 300 as follows: 'All the gods are three:/Amun, the Sun [Atum-Re], and Ptah, without their seconds./His identity is hidden in Amun,/His is the Sun as face, his body is Ptah' (Allen 1997h, p.25).

Thus, in the Theban account all important components of pre-existence and existence, order and disorder come together. Since the gods of the Amun 'Trinity' assimilated in themselves many other divine forces and manifestations of the ancient Egyptian religion before Theban cosmogony was composed, it was only natural that Amun would become the 'Only' according to this account through the assimilation of these three. But again, the textual 'speculations' concerning the identity and the origin of the divine power or powers are no evidence for the monotheistic character of the Egyptian religion. It must be remembered that in order to have monotheism all the other deities except the 'one and only' must be annihilated in each and every form. The Egyptian deities were simply assimilated and linked together through philosophical creations, but their physical worship in their original and/or syncretic forms continued in Egypt almost without interruption. Thus there were many gods who, through fusion, became the One of this only one of a kind philosophical thought of the ancient Egypt (gods became one through syncretization: for example, take five gods, hyphenate their names and then you have one). 'When I had come into being, being came into being, and all beings came into being, after I came into being' (papyrus of the Early Ptolemaic Period – after Lesko 1991, p.115).

The only god and his creation: Traditions of Genesis and the Quran

There is no doubt that there was more than one deity involved in the creation process in Mesopotamia and Egypt, in spite of the Egyptian concept of assimilation or fusion of various gods into one. A similar concept is known in ancient Iran where, according to the Zaratuštrian tradition, Ahura Mazdā is a 'projection' of himself 'and the six "Augmentative Immortals" (Ameša Spenta)' (Dresden 1961, p.335) who can be translated to English as 'Good Mind' (connected with cattle), 'Truth' (fire), 'Power' (metal), 'Devotion' (earth), 'Wholeness' (water), and 'Immortality' (vegetation), and presented as his sons and daughters. But in this tradition there is also his opponent, the twin brother, Angra Mainyu (Zoroastrian Ahriman), who represents the evil forces, the 'non-life,' as well as many other deities whose presence should erase the term 'monotheism' from any references to this religion. But can this term be even used in reference to religious systems based on Genesis or the Quran? This is the question that needs to be thoroughly examined in view of existing creation stories.

The authors of Genesis seemed to be quite inconsistent in their attempts to present Yahweh as the only god. While the Priestly account was quite careful to not even use words 'sun' and 'moon' to describe new creations referred to only as the Greater and Lesser Luminaries in fear of evoking the names of 'pagan' deities (Gordon 1996, p.24), the Yahwistic account keeps referring to many deities under the common noun Elohim. Even the Quran did not avoid references to Allah as 'we.' Thus, either the redactors of the Holy Books of Judaic, Christian, and Islamic traditions were sloppy editors or they recognized the necessity of the existence of other divine forces whom they would not honor with a term 'deity' but instead fused into the character of the 'one and only' and/or set up as independent spiritual entities with both negative and positive qualities (for example, army of angels, satans and so forth).

But, in both the Quran and Genesis, only one god, referred to in both the singular and the plural, was responsible for the creation, without assistance from other spirits. The following are the versions of creation of the universe in chronological order of their recording. Since the Bible is probably the most accessible book in the world, the direct quotations from Genesis are kept to a minimum. It must also be noted that in addition to the creation stories of Genesis there are other Biblical texts referring to this process (Graves and Patai 1964) or supplementary sources such as Pseudoepigrapha (see Charlesworth and Evans 1993; Platt 1980; Ullendorff 1968) which cannot be discussed here due to the limited focus of this book.

The Yahwistic tradition

As mentioned in Chapter 4, the JE authors were not much interested in the creation of the universe since their focus was on mankind. Thus only passage 2:4b–7 is concerned with this event, which is described as the action of Yahweh Elohim (gods). It starts with the statement similar to *Enûma Eliš* referring to the non-existence of elements of the earth such as flora at the time when god made heaven and earth. This non-existence was caused by the lack of water because the rain had not yet been created and Yahweh was about to bring waters from the earth to cover all grounds. The use of a temporal clause 'when…' and negative statements concerning the conditions of earth are very typical of Sumero-Akkadian-Babylonian tradition as pointed by many authors (Wallace 1985) and referred to above. The means of creation can only be assumed as the god's command.

The picture of the non-existence state here is of the desert which needs rain to fertilize it. This reflects the situation of the Canaanite land, the productivity of which depends more on the waters provided from heaven or the sky than on the flooding of local rivers. On the other hand, Yahweh was able to fructify the land by providing the waters from the ground. However, it is not clear whether the passage refers to flooding which would be consistent with the Mesopotamian and/or Egyptian traditions, or to the underground waters which were so celebrated in the Anatolian tradition. Furthermore, this short description of the beginning of the universe implies only one day was needed for the whole process (in contrast to the P account) which led to the establishment of conditions necessary for the ultimate creation of Yahweh – the first man. Thus, the order of creation as established by the JE account is desert, water, first man, trees, animals, and finally the first woman. This order is not only inconsistent with other Middle Eastern accounts discussed above but also with the Priestly version which precedes it in Genesis but was written down later. It is also not very logical from the point of view of envisioning creation in which earth comes into being after the desert is already described. It indicates either sloppiness on the part of the Yahwistic redactor(s), or a lack of interest in any origins before the creation of humankind. Finally, in contrast to the Priestly account and other Middle Eastern stories in which waters are associated with chaos and darkness which must be fought or overcome to create order, the Yahwists present water as a friendly element, as was noticed many years ago by Gunkel (1901– reprinted 1997). This echoes the Sumerian tradition of an 'orderly' Nammu.

The Priestly account

In the best tradition of *Enûma Eliš* and other Middle Eastern accounts the Priestly narrative (1:1 to 2:3; the superscription 2:4a is omitted here since it only introduces the Yahwistic account) refers to the creation of all elements from the state of non-existence as represented by the watery depth ('deep') enclosed in the darkness. It is commonly recognized that the Hebrew word for deep, *tehom*, is a close relative of the Babylonian Tiāmat (Brandon 1963; for opposite view see Heidel 1951). Thus again the beginning is envisioned as a watery chaos which seems to be independent of god's spirit hovering over it. This brings into mind not only the Mesopotamian tradition but also the Egyptian beginning in which Atum is the very first mover existing independently of the forces of non-existence even if he is its part.

The first element which was commanded to its existence on the first day was light. It was the light (see common motif of the Egyptian traditions) which allowed for the division of time into day and night (see the Zoroastrian and Zurvanistic accounts below, p.73). The creation of light was also implied by *Enûma Eliš* where the first generations of deities born to the watery chaos, Tiāmat and Apsû, emanated light. What is very interesting is that the light is created before bodies of light and is treated as an independent creation which is 'good' according to the god himself. There is no evaluation of darkness but instead there is a clear separation of those two which allows for naming; that is, 'official' establishment of the existence of two measures of time which by itself had to exist before in the watery beginning because darkness was its part.

The second day takes us back to the Mesopotamian traditions of creating both the vault of heaven and the flat disc of earth out of waters. In the Babylonian account Marduk was the one who created both at the same time from the carcass of Tiāmat. In the Priestly account the vault of heaven was created first out of waters. The remaining waters under this vault were left for the next day's creation – the earth with its seas. The question then arises, why couldn't Yahweh create both at the same time? Is it possible that the Priestly editor(s) tried to stay within the gender-oriented framework of thought as represented by the JE tradition by first producing the male element of Mesopotamian tradition, the heaven, only to be followed by its inferior female counterpart, the earth? Or was the creation of the earth with all its immobile living things – that is, plants – was believed to be more time-consuming?

The fourth day was the time to create the illuminaries which are nameless, as noted above. They were created in order to have a division of time, 'to divide day from night, and let them indicate festivals, days and years' (1:14–15). The problem is that days and nights were already established on the first day and there were no festivals to celebrate since there was no history yet. Thus, it looks like the Priestly redactor(s) made a kind of summary of the long account in the *Enûma Eliš* of the creation of the same things (replacing sanctuaries with festivals) by Marduk (for the text see Foster 1993; for outlines of both accounts see Heidel 1951) and adjusted it, rather sloppily, to the existing reality.

The fifth day was spent on the creation of all living creatures of the waters and of the heaven or sky. These creatures were blessed with the following words: 'Be fruitful, multiply, and fill the waters of the seas; and let the birds multiply upon the earth' (1:22–23). It is interesting that this blessing was only given to these creatures and later to humankind, but was denied to other creatures of the earth which were created on the sixth day. But why? Is it possible that the water and sky creatures needed to be blessed because in the other accounts of the Middle East they had a very special meaning or role to fulfill? For example, in the *Enûma Eliš* it was Tiāmat who created water-monsters (great sea-serpents of the P account), and the birds were traditionally associated with the realm of the dead in various traditions of the area. Thus, one might speculate that by offering them a special blessing the only god of Genesis claimed his power over elements associated strongly with the pagan traditions of the older deities of the region. This one blessing would then give Yahweh the control over the domain of waters and the Nether World. His final creation on the sixth day, humankind, would take care of earth in his name so all three realms would be connected in the 'one and only' god of the Priestly account.

While Mesopotamian deities usually celebrated the creation of any important elements with a divine banquet where beer and wine flowed freely, Yahweh could not finish the act of his creation with a similar celebration for two reasons: lack of company and lack of alcohol. Since neither of them existed at the time, the only logical choice for the Priestly writer(s) was to give the god a day of rest on the seventh day. However, he or they never explained why someone as powerful as Yahweh needed it. Unless, of course, even the only god of the Bible and the Quran was still perceived in human terms so popular in polytheistic religions of the region.

The Quran

Since the organization of the Quran is very different than that of the Pentateuch, the information gathered from its different chapters is somewhat incomplete. Some events of the creation process are mentioned a few times in a similar form while others are completely omitted. Thus, the reconstruction of this process as based on the Quran is only partially possible.

According to this holy book, Allah is the creator of everything, because there is no other deity besides him. The sura from Livestock addresses this point in a very specific way, asking the question 'How can He have a son while he has no consort?' and answering it 'He created everything and is Aware of everything!' (VII, 6:101 (XIII)). Although there is no straight description of the state of non-existence it might be assumed that it consisted of water since in the Prophets one can find the following passage: 'Have not those who disbelieve seen how Heaven and Earth were once one solid mass which We ripped apart? We have made every living thing out of water' (XVII, 21:30 (III)).

Thus, the solid mass, possibly the echo of the Sumerian tradition of the universe (heaven–earth) as a cosmic mountain, emerged somehow or was commanded by the god to appear from the watery non-being. Once visible it was divided by Allah into two parts: heaven and earth. This was the beginning of the creation process which took six days, similar to the Priestly account. During this time a lot of specific things were created but their order is almost impossible to establish. It seems that the time or light spoken of as 'the alternation between night and daylight' was commanded about the same time according to the House of Imran (IV, 3:190 (XX)) since it is mentioned in parallel with the creation of heaven and earth in this sura. The next step appears to be placing headlands and mountain passes on the earth (Prophets; XVII, 21:30 (III)). Over them the heavens (possibly all seven of them) were raised (Thunder; XIII, 13:Intro. (I)), and the sky was spread over the earth. This set up the scene for such creations as 'the sun for radiance and the moon for (reflected) light, and measured it out in phases so you may know how to count out the years and [to make other such] reckoning' (Jonah; XI, 10:Intro. (I)), and then stars. On earth, rivers and 'two pairs of every kind of fruit' were placed (Thunder; XIII, 13:Intro. (I)) to be watered by god with the help of rain, which is also his creation. Then, finally, Adam and his wife were created and the story of the Yahwistic paradise follows.

From the above description it should be obvious that the Quranic account is very much based on the combination of both Biblical traditions with some additional information, origin of which can be found in older stories of the Middle East. Furthermore it seems that the Quran tried to avoid the inconsistencies of Genesis by rewriting the story of the Priestly account to suit the needs of the Yahwistic version of the creation of mankind. This can be seen in the lack of references to animals being created before humankind. It seems that, similar to the Yahwistic account, animals were created after Adam, for both food and transportation (Bees; XIV,16: Intro. (I)). Thus, the Quranic account can be considered to be a conscious attempt of Muhammad to 'solve' problems occurring in the existing and most popular versions of creation (of Judaic and Christian traditions) in order to make his teachings more accessible and comprehensible to his future followers. His 'editing' of the story of the paradise is discussed in Chapter 10.

The seventh day was also the day of rest for Allah. On this day he sat down on his throne in order to maintain, command, protect and guide his creations. As in the case of the god of Genesis, he had nobody else to celebrate with.

Conclusions

A careful examination of the Middle Eastern stories of the creation of the universe reveals many similarities and some differences. These differences are particularly obvious when one attempts to connect all available traditions of cultures in contact in one more or less logical whole. The Indo-European (including Indo-Iranian) traditions concerning the creation are especially difficult to understand because they encompass so many different cultural strata and religious traditions. The creation themes in these stories are numerous, representing a wide range of commonly used explanations for the origins of the cosmos. Malandra (1983) lists them as:

(1) creation through the dismemberment of a primordial giant, the cosmic man; (2) the incubation and hatching of the embryonic world from the cosmic egg; (3) the fashioning of the cosmos by an artisan or carpenter god; (4) creation by a hero who drives or holds apart heaven and earth; (5) creation by a powerful being (d(h)ātar) who literally 'places' (d(h)ā-) the cosmos in the void. (pp.10–11)

As can be seen from the above discussion, these are not 'native' traditions of the Middle East and for this reason they were not discussed above. However, some ideas from nomadic traditions of Eurasia were transplanted to the Middle East and incorporated into the ruling concepts at the time.

Even when the stories, themes, and concepts were borrowed by others, they were always adjusted to fit into the already established reality of the borrowers. These Middle Eastern realities were sometimes quite different in their perception of the existence of the world. In ancient Mesopotamia the process of creation was perceived as a continuum in which all elements emerged at their proper time in accordance with the encoded order of existence. In Egypt, it was also a continuum but a cyclical one which called for the repetitions of various actions in order to avoid the threat of chaos and darkness. In Genesis it was a one-time sequence of creation acts which set up foundations for the future development in which the god rarely interfered. The principle of continuous creation was revived to a certain degree with the Quran in which Allah is presented as being constantly involved in the creation of living things, especially of humans, as will be demonstrated in Part 4 (see p.155).

Another interesting point that should be made is the 'gender' change of the creator-deity in the overall evolution of religious concepts in the Middle East. The Mesopotamian transition (from a female element, through a couple, to the main male god and finally to the only god of Genesis) might reflect the level of knowledge about conception and birth and the diminishing role of women in Middle Eastern societies as this knowledge progressed. In other words, this transition has gone from the goddess who alone possessed the secret of life, to the equality of both sexes as necessary for procreation, and finally to the male alone who does not need a house to store his seed. The example of such a god in Mesopotamia is Marduk while in Iran this is Ahura Mazdā of the Zaratuštrian tradition, also known as Ohrmazd by followers of Zoroastrianism. While the details of Marduk's creation are known, the Gāthīc passages of the Avesta only inform us about the existence of twin primordial spirits, 'the "better" and the "evil" one, a basic theme of Zaratuštra's philosophy, as engaged in the creation of "life" and "non-life"' (Dresden 1961, p.337), with Ahura-Mazdā emerging as a creator of everything. The details of this creation are referred to in Zoroastrian tradition in which Ohrmazd (Ahura Mazdā) 'first created the Amahraspandas [the later form of the Ameša Spenta], six originally...and the seventh Ohrmazd himself... Of material creation (he created) first the sky, second water, third the earth, fourth plants, fifth cattle, sixth man; the seventh was Ohrmazd himself' (Dresden 1961, p.339).

It should be noted here that in contrast to typical creation stories of the Middle East which focused on the first element as being water, the Iranian tradition selected sky as the foremost important element of the universe. This can be explained by the agricultural character of the 'water-focused' mythology as opposed to the tradition of Indo-Iranian (Indo-European) nomads with their focus on sky and mountain deities (see Hittite gods, pp.103–108). In Iran there were the Alburz Mountains (Mount Hara/Harburz) which were closely associated with the creation as the first mountain to emerge and connect the deep below with the sky (Curtis 1993). Furthermore, one must also pay attention to the 'reinvention' of Ohrmazd who, from the account cited above, emerges as the only god. Thus, the event of creation made him into the only essential divinity of the origins, a sort of father of everything in the best style of the Greek Zeus of Hesiod's *Theogony* of the eighth century B.C.

A similar concept could have been at work in Canaan. Since both El and Asherah, his wife, are presented as creators and owners of all, they could be assumed to be the beginning of everything. However, it seems that there were other deities before them from whom they won their leading position in the pantheon. Since that time it is El whose abode is on high mountain and he himself is 'the source of the rivers, / The midst of the springs of the oceans' (Handy 1994, p.90).

Since Asherah is not living with him (she has her own temple), so El alone is in control of life (rivers) and possibly of the chaotic cosmic ocean from which, one might assume, the first elements of creation derived. This means that although preserving the title of creatress and owner of all, Asherah is also somewhat stripped of her original powers.

This reassurance of Ahura Mazdā's role could have been needed due to the tradition of so-called Zoroastrian heresy known as Zurvanism which is recorded in both Iranian (Pahlavi) and non-Iranian sources (Syriac and Armenian). In my view, Zurvanism is probably one of a very few ideological systems which can be incorporated into each and every religion, providing the comprehension of existing concepts as a very acceptable approach for any believer. Dresden (1961), after Zaehner, summarized the beginning of the story of Zurvān (Time) in the following words:

> When nothing at all existed, neither heaven nor earth nor any other creature which is in heaven or on earth, there existed one, Zurvān by name... For a thousand years he sacrificed that perchance he might have a son whose name should be Ohrmazd, who should create heaven and earth and all that is in them. (pp.355–356)

Thus, before the emergence of other elements there was only one hermaphrodite god, Zurvān, Time, whose existence no-one can challenge or deny. This original 'high god' could have been already known in the Middle East at the end of the second millennium B.C. since the name 'Za-ar-wa-an' seems to be found among the Nuzi (cuneiform) tablets of the Hurrian origin (Brandon 1963 p.197). The appeal of Zurvān as the primordial god personifying the concept of time and possibly of space can be seen by the interest in the concept itself as shown by the Greek scholars of the fourth century B.C. (Eudemus of Rhodes, after Brandon 1963).

The idea of time (and space) as the ruling matter can be compared to the Sumerian concept of Nammu. In both cases the rest of the world emerged as a logical chain of events – in evolutionary manner, somewhat independent of its 'creator' in whom/which all the elements were encoded. This way each and every 'creation' had or has his, her or its predetermined destiny which is outside of his, her or its own control. Thus, in both ideologies there is no place for the final judgment and determination of immortality for humans since death is the ultimate end for mortals.

However, the concept of Nammu was based on the waters of pre-existence and existence *per se*. In contrast to the later traditions of Mesopotamia, Egypt, Canaan, and the Pentateuch, this 'cosmic ocean' was not a chaotic state of non-being, just the opposite. This was a pre-organized form *a priori* from which everything emerged; thus every living thing was perceived to carry in itself the element of water. This concept of the original water as being the main component of living organisms was carried on by the Quranic tradition without passing any judgment on its positive or negative qualities.

6

Divine Order and Its Creators

The process of creation was not finished with the emergence of the universe – be it one or more deities – from the watery abyss. In the polytheistic religions of the ancient Middle East it proceeded with the creation of other forces personified by both male and female deities. The order in which they came into being also often established their hierarchy within the divine society and their actions, both positive and negative, were to affect all matters of the existing world. In other cases it seems that the battle or competition for the divine kingship was responsible for the proper functioning of the universe. Thus, it is necessary to discuss the most important deities associated with creation and/or the establishment of power in order to understand not only the process of the world formation but also the maintenance of what was already in existence.

However, in monotheistic religions of the Middle East the only deity – be it the male god of Genesis or the somewhat androgynous Allah of the Quran – was 'forced' to assume all functions, which were previously divided among the many, in one being. This caused inconsistencies in the character of the monotheistic god whose actions have sometimes been difficult for believers to explain or to justify. Thus the divine conflict survived but its form has changed and sometimes its consequences.

Mesopotamia

In Sumerian theology, in contrast to many religions – including the leading beliefs of the modern Western world – gods and goddesses were not only a significant part of the process of creation, but they themselves were coming from the 'inside' of *prima materia* in the order that was already pre-destined for them. They were believed to be the part of a concept larger than the universe itself, not the independent beings who created it. Such an understanding allowed for the Sumerian and then Akkadian deities to exist as immortal, powerful, spiritual and knowledgeable supernatural beings who, at the same time, were held responsible for their actions. Breaking the *prima materia* rules called for punishment – such as losing one of the above 'godly' attributes – to restore law and order.

The third element of creation – Enlil and the Tablet of Destinies

After An and Ki emerged from the Sumerian waters of order as the universe (presented in the form of the mountain – see Chapter 5), they needed to be separated to fulfill their encoded functions. This job was performed by Enlil, the air or atmosphere god. Enlil, whose name in Akkadian was Ellil, was considered by the Mesopotamians to be one of the most important deities in the whole pantheon throughout thousands of years. According to a text which describes the creation and dedication of the pick-axe, 'in order to bring forth what was useful,/The lord whose decisions are unalterable,/Enlil, who brings up the see of the "land" from the earth,/Planned to move away heaven from earth,/Planned to move earth from heaven' (Kramer 1959, p.83).

Not only did he plan the move but he also carried out his actions as described above in Gilgamesh, Enkidu, and the Nether World (see p.54). Then it seems that he filled up the space left with the substance *LIL*, translated from Sumerian by Kramer (1959) as wind, air, breath, spirit, atmosphere (p.77). Thus his name can be translated as Lord of Air (EN – LIL), allowing for a wider interpretation of him as a wind or storm god (Hooke 1953). According to Black and Green (1997) the reference to Enlil (sometimes also known as Nunamnir) in one text as East Wind and North Wind is no evidence that he was ever connected with the *lila/lilû* and its female equivalents 'lilītu' and 'ardat-lilî' who were demons of the desert (sometimes connected with Lilith of the folk tradition of the Middle East). His sacred number was 50 and he was believed to reside in the part of heaven 'north of Anu's way' (Hooke 1953, p.26).

Since at the beginning of creation there was no-one else to be his parents it can be assumed that Enlil is the offspring of An and Ki. The fact that he himself 'had carried off the earth,' his mother, Ki, may also indicate the existence of a very special union between them, which might have even involved a sexual relationship (Kramer 1986, p.65). This would not be unusual or 'sick' but rather a logical solution because the number of divine beings available for procreation was quite limited at the time, if the main chronology of the creation events is to be followed. This may explain also why in some texts Enlil is presented as a son of An and brother of Aruru who also represented 'mother earth.' In fact since the second millennium B.C. this 'mother/earth goddess' has been identified and appeared under different names such as: 'Mami or Mama (clearly "mother"); Dingirmah ("exalted deity"); Ninmah ("exalted lady"); Nintu ("lady of birth"); Ninmena ("lady of the crown"); Bēlet-ilī ("lady of the gods" in Akkadian); Nammu' (Black and Green 1997, p.133).

However, as in the case of many other Mesopotamian deities, Enlil's parentage is not that certain since he is also described as a son of Enki (Lord of Earth; a different deity than Enki of the sweet waters) and Ninki (Lady of Earth) (Black and Green 1997). He fathered a number of children including Inana, Utu (Šamaš), Nergal, and his own minister Nusku who, beside his functions associated with Enlil, became quite popular and an independent deity to whom many hymns and prayers were directed as, for example, those translated by Foster (1993, 1995).

Ninlil was Enlil's wife, whether in Sumero-Babylonian tradition or in Assyrian tradition under the name of Mullissu – a wife of Aššur who was frequently equated with Enlil. She might have been a kind of artificial deity in the Sumerian pantheon as a female counterpart of her husband's name, NIN-LIL (Lady of Air), but not necessarily of his powers. One of the most interesting stories recorded by the Sumerians is the myth of Enlil's banishment to the Nether World for raping Ninlil. This event occurred when mankind was not yet created and the deities were the only 'inhabitants' of the universe, including Enlil's city, Nippur. He was a young man, and she was a young maid, probably a virgin. Her mother, 'old woman of Nippur,' Nunbaršegunu, obviously realized that Enlil would be a good choice as a husband for her daughter, so she instructed Ninlil how to get his attention: 'In the pure stream, woman, bathe in the pure stream,/Ninlil, walk along the bank of the stream Nunbirdu,/The bright-eyed, the lord, the bright-eyed,/The "great mountain," mountain father Enlil, the bright-eyed, will see you' (Kramer 1961, p.97).

She was right. Enlil saw her but he also wanted more than a kiss. 'The lord speaks to her of intercourse (?), she is unwilling,/Enlil speaks to her of intercourse (?), she is unwilling;/"My vagina is too little, it knows not to copulate,/My lips are too small, they know not to kiss"' (Kramer 1961, p.97). Unfortunately, Enlil did not take 'no' for an answer and raped Ninlil on a boat that was brought to him by Nusku. This act enraged all the deities since it was obviously against all established laws. In spite of Enlil's extremely high status in the Sumerian pantheon and his great powers which allowed him to be called 'the father of the gods' and 'the king of heaven and earth,' he deserved a punishment worthy of his crime. The punishment was death, a one-way trip to the Nether World from which – in theory at least – there is no return.

But there is an unexpected twist to the story. Ninlil is pregnant and possibly for that reason she considers herself to be 'married' to Enlil. Thus, she makes a decision to follow him to *Kur* (the underworld). Enlil is not pleased about this turn of events since he is aware of Ninlil's pregnancy with his son, the moon god Sîn (also known under the names of Nanna, Suen, Nannar and others). He does not want his son to be born in the land of no-return where he would have to remain if Ninlil were to give birth there. Thus, Enlil designs a rather diabolical plan worthy of his divine powers. On his way to *Kur*, he assumes the forms of three minor gods who are identified by Kramer (1959) as 'the gatekeeper,' ' the man of the nether-world river' and 'the ferryman' (p.86). Then, in his assumed 'bodies,' Enlil asks Ninlil to have sex with him so she could continue her way to *Kur*. The result is Ninlil's pregnancy with three more deities who become a part of the Nether World as the substitute for their brother, Sîn (as a goddess she could have carried four different pregnancies at the same time).

The idea of substitutions was very popular in ancient Mesopotamia. Since the laws of nature (Nammu) were perceived to be constant and already encoded, whatever actions threatened the existing order the results had to be 'repaired.' For example, if death were to occur as the result of some event, somebody had to die even if it was not the individual who committed the 'crime' but a substitute for him or her. In the story of Enlil, the birth of the new deities of *Kur* was a substitute for the moon god's birth outside of the underworld. The order was thus restored.

As mentioned above, the sacred city of Enlil was Nippur where his most important temple *E-kur* (the 'Mountain House') was erected. One might get confused with the double meaning of the Sumerian word *kur* which refers both to 'mountain/s' and to the 'Nether World.' While this word may have had two different origins, linguistically speaking (Black and Green 1997), its double meaning could have easily been connected. As 'the mountain/s' it seems to refer to the Zagros Mountains, extending its meaning to 'foreign country'; that is, lands with which the Sumerians were in contact but did not inhabit. Black and Green (1997) suggest that the Sumerians located their underworld in the east mountains where the entrance to *Kur* was believed to exist (p.114). Thus, through the triple use of the word *kur*, three attributes, concepts or events were combined in the most powerful deity of them all, Enlil. He himself was the 'Great Mountain' which may refer to the primordial mountain of AN-KI (the universe) which he separated. He was the 'King of the Foreign Lands/Mountains,' where the underworld, to which he was banished and from which he returned, was located.

Because of his importance Enlil was assigned the function of the guardian of the 'Tablet(s) of Destinies.' The Sumerians believed that any act of creation was not finished until the name and the destiny of an element, thing or an individual were pronounced (see above for the beginning of *Enûma Eliš*, p.50). Thus, whoever was in the possession of the Tablet of Destinies had power over the destinies of the universe. Although it was Enlil who had their guardianship, they occasionally ended up in the hands of other deities. One of the most famous stories (Foster 1995) is about the horrifying bird, Anzû (also known as Imdugud), who was given the job as a guardian to Enlil's (Akkadian version) cella, the seat of power as the king of all gods, and then abused his employer's trust by stealing the tablet from him while Enlil was taking a bath. Since none of the deities was brave enough to fight the Anzû bird, Ea (Enki) designed a plan which allowed Ninurta (a warrior god and a son of Enlil) to retrieve the tablet. It seems that at the beginning Ninurta was not eager to return the tablet to its 'legal' owner but eventually he did so and the order was saved again. The others who held the tablets included Enki, Inana and, in the Babylonian *Enûma Eliš*, it was Tiāmat who gave it to Qingu.

The common misconception is that Enlil was hostile toward humankind and that his personality was very destructive (Hooke 1953) rather than creative. Kramer (1959) blames Enlil's bad reputation on an archaeological accident – that is, on the earliest compositions which were published, and which dealt with Enlil – representing him as having 'the unhappy duty of carrying out the destruction and misfortunes decreed by the gods for one reason or another' (p.91). He stressed Enlil's benevolent character and his creation of very useful features of the universe such as the day, plants, trees, the pick-axe, and plow without which agriculture would not be possible. Enlil, as the leader of the Sumerian pantheon, also carried the responsibility to punish all wrong actions in order to assure prosperity, wealth and abundance for all.

The sweet waters of Enki and his gift of wisdom

In contrast to the ambivalent Enlil, Enki (also known as Akkadian Ea and under other names such as Nudimmud or Ninšiku or 'Stag of the *abzu*') has always been considered to be a very positive character especially toward mankind whom he created and whom he saved from the flood. His city was Eridu, his most important temple was *E-engura*, and he controlled the sweet waters as a son of Nammu. In addition he was recognized as the god of wisdom, magic, arts and crafts.

Enki's name and his identity still cause some problems among scholars. While Black and Green (1997) believe that there were two deities with similar or the same name, Enki (Enkig) as the god of the *abzu*, married to Damkina (Damgalnuna) and Enki, 'Lord of Earth,' son of Enlil, married to Ninki, 'Lady of Earth' (p.75), Kramer and Maier (1989) point out to his 'identity crisis' without mentioning two gods of the same name (p.3). Furthermore they suggest that since the name EN-KI with its focus on 'earth,' *ki*, does not really correspond to his association with the freshwater ocean, he might have been called EN-KUR originally, 'Lord Kur' in honor of its conquest. Since the word *kur* has itself a multiple meaning as explained earlier, this might be quite possible.

ENKI'S CLAIM TO FAME AND ORGANIZATION OF THE WORLD

Enki, as the fourth god of the pantheon, was glorified for his contributions to the 'improvement' and 'management' of the earth whose problems he could solve due to his intelligence, wisdom and especially his craftiness. His fame was truly international since he was admired as far as Hittite Anatolia (Kramer and Maier 1989). However, it seems that he was always on a quest to advance his position among other deities either through his benevolent actions or crafty meddling. His claim to authority is particularly obvious in the myth translated by Kramer and Maier (1989) as 'Enki and Inanna: The organization of the earth and its cultural processes.' This poem is not only one of the longest preserved myths of ancient Sumer but is also very interesting and somewhat controversial. It begins with the exaltation of Enki as one of the three most important gods of the pantheon: An(u) (his father), his brother Enlil, ('Great Mountain [Kur]') and himself. It continues with rather a lengthy description of his credentials and accomplishments by the poet and Enki himself. After the recognition of his greatness by the assembly of the Anunna gods (also Anunnakkû gods, very early gods who have never been differentiated by individual names), Enki sets out on a quest to organize the world by pronouncing the fate and functions of various elements starting with the land of Sumer in general, then proceeding to specific cities such as Ur, Meluhha, Dilmun and other lands such as Elam and Marḫaši. After the destinies of these lands and their peoples are pronounced, Enki turns his attention to making the land livable for its people by providing fresh water as poetically described in the following lines: '…once Father Enki had raised it over the Euphrates,/He stood up full of lust like an attacking bull,/Lifted his penis, ejaculates –/he filled the Tigris with flowing water' (Kramer and Maier 1989, p.87).

In her discussion of this poem Leick (1994) focuses on Enki's virility as a bull and the importance of his fluid, semen, represented by the Sumerian sign *A* which has the triple meaning of water, sperm and urine. She points to the sexual overtones of Enki's actions in which his phallus assumes the leading role in the creation process.

After fresh water sources including irrigation canals and rain are established, Enki proceeds with the organization of agriculture (food) and then shelter for humans. Still not tired, he organizes the steppe area with its animals and appoints Dumuzi, the husband of Inana, to attend to it. Once the physical aspects of the world have been taken care of, Enki sets up the 'social structure' and 'division of labor,' prescribing various crafts and functions to different individuals. The poem finishes with Inana (Inanna, also known under Semitic name as Ištar) complaining to Enki that he has not assigned her any function or position. She says: 'Me, the woman, why did you treat in a different way?/I, the holy Inanna: Where are my functions?' (Kramer and Maier 1989, p.55).

Enki's answer is not only lengthy but also somewhat rude in spite of being laudatory. He describes all Inana's powers and accomplishments that she already has without giving in to her demands. Leick (1994) interprets this as the subjugation of the great goddess's powers to the male god, Enki, as the phallus himself. Although this interpretation is possible, it might be better to suggest that Enki's answer indicates his not-so-hidden envy of the many functions she already possessed without his control or involvement. After all it was Inana who outsmarted him by removing *me* from his control as the next story tells.

ENKI – NOT SO CRAFTY GOD: THE TRANSFER OF *ME* TO INANA

While Enki has been praised by many (including himself) for his wisdom and numerous accomplishments so beneficial to his beloved mankind, his mythographers tell a somewhat different story. As Kramer and Maier (1989) noticed, this crafty god has been frequently presented in myths as having a somewhat unstable personality with a strong inclination toward alcohol, women, sex and foolishness.

The story entitled by Kramer and Maier (1989) 'Inanna and Enki: The transfer of the arts of civilization from Eridu to Erech' (pp.57–68) is a favorite example of Enki's fallible character. However, what is even more important is that this story lists ninety-four *me* whose concept was explained above (p.47) and can be referred to in modern terms as 'cultural traits.' It begins with a very fragmentary description of Inana's sexual pleasures with the shepherd Dumuzi after which she decides to go to Eridu to honor Enki, who sometimes was presented as her father (see discussion of Inana, p.82). It is rather unclear what is the reason for her decision but one might try to guess that she was so satisfied with Dumuzi's performance as a lover that she might have wanted to thank Enki who represented both 'water' and 'semen.' This interpretation or rather speculation might be correct considering Leick's (1994) conclusion that, in theory at least, only 'the female erotic experience' in poems with sexual overtones counted (p.129).

Regardless of Inana's reason for her trip she is made very welcome by Enki. His servants give her food and drink, including beer. Although she is described as being the 'young one,' Enki treats her as an equal. Unfortunately for him during the banquet in Inana's honor, they commit a drinking 'no-no' and switch from beer to wine. With his judgement impaired by alcohol, Enki willingly begins to give Inana one *me* after another. Among them he presents her with those which are related to sexuality:

> I will give to holy Inanna,
> to my daughter –
> and it will not be disputed:
> the standard,
> the quiver,
> the 'working' of the penis,
> the kissing of the penis,
> the art of prostitution,
> the art of speeding…

...the art of forthright speech,
the art of slanderous speech,
the art of ornamental speech,
?,
the cult-prostitute,
the holy tavern. (Kramer and Maier 1989, p.61)

These *me* are discussed by Leick (1994) in her attempt to understand sexual and other relations between men and women in ancient Mesopotamia.

Obviously Inana does not hesitate to take all the *me* given to her. One wonders how she was able to outdrink Enki, being just a young woman. But she did. As Kramer and Maier (1989) point out there must have been some obstacles to Inana's departure from Eridu to her city of Erech (Uruk) because Enki has to intervene, issuing a special order for her safe passage. By the time she enters the Boat of An, Enki starts sobering up and realizes that the *me* are missing. Obviously he must have passed out because he needs his *sukkal* (a kind of servant), Isimud, to tell him that he gave them to his daughter. Again the text is fragmentary so we do not know his state of mind upon receiving the news, but then he attempts six times to bring Inana back to Eridu with the *me*. Although her boat is seized, Inana refuses to give them back claiming, rightfully, that they were given to her willingly. She is quite mad at Enki for breaking his word and for what she perceives to be his deception. In spite of Enki's desperate attempt, Inana arrives safely to Uruk where she unloads the *me*. Although the end of the story is too fragmentary for an interpretation, one can conclude that somehow Inana was eventually forced or persuaded to return them. The order has to be restored.

Inana: The unmanageable ultimate goddess

There is probably no other goddess in the history of world religions whose adoration has survived for as long as Inana's. Even today, many mother-goddess religions and/or cults in the United States and elsewhere focus their worship on this very powerful but also very unpredictable divinity of the Sumero-Akkadian tradition.

The original Sumerian form of her name was probably NIN-ANA, 'Lady of Heaven/Sky', which may suggest to some her equal and/or parallel position to the god of heaven, An, who was also sometimes presented as her father or her consort. Her most popular Sumerian name was Inana or Inanna, although in some texts she is referred to as Innin. The Semitic peoples spread her worship under the name Ištar (early Eštar, possibly related to the South Arabian god 'Athtar – Black and Green 1997, p.108) and seemingly as Ashtarte in Syria–Palestine. The name which she 'uses' today in numerous New Age rituals consecrated to the ultimate mother-goddess is still Ishtar.

However, as ironic as it might be, Inana was never the mother-goddess archetype with its focus on nature, nurturing qualities, babies, and so forth. Actually, with the possible exception of Šara, the local god of Umma, who was presented in one of the building inscriptions of Ur III as her son, she never had any children who could have come from her womb (Black and Green 1997). Taking into consideration the fact that her sexual habits were rather on the promiscuous side – Inana's marriage history is non-existent apart from Dumuzi (Semitic Tammuz) whom some scholars regard as her husband, others only as a lover – it is not surprising that she did not have much time to bother with any offspring.

Inana, who over a long period of time gradually incorporated many qualities and attributes of various local goddesses, became "'the goddess" *par excellence'* (Hooke 1953, p.30). As one of the oldest deities whose name, written in the form of the ring-post, appears in the earliest written sources, Inana's powers and greatness were widely recognized not only by mortals but also by her divine 'competitors.' The moon-god Nanna (Nannar)/Sîn (Suen), Enlil, and even Enki 'claimed' to father her, and her mother was Ningal (wife of Nanna and mother of Utu) but it could be even Nammu (if one assumes the original position of Inana to be equal to that of An). Her siblings were the sun-god Utu (Šamaš) who often helped her when she was in trouble, and the queen of the Nether World, Ereškigal, in which relationship one may notice some unhealthy sisterly rivalry.

Inana's main temple, *E-ana*, 'House of Heaven,' was located in the city of Uruk, but she was also worshipped in many other centers such as Kish, Ur, Isin (as Ninisinna), Zabala, Akkad and Nineveh. As the planet Venus, she was believed to be associated with the color red and to represent both the evening and morning stars (possibly as a dual personality: morning for male and evening for female; see Leick 1994). In 'Inana's Descent to the Underworld' she refers to herself as 'the queen of heaven, of the place where the sun rises' or 'I am Inana of the sunrise,' depending upon the translation, which implies her connection with Dilmun, confirmed by yet another text referring to her washing 'her head in the fountain of Dilmun' (Rice 1985, p.103, after Cornwall 1944). Her temple in Ur was known as *E-Dilmun-na* which was restored at least once in the nineteenth century B.C. by Warad-Sin (if a place was important, restoration was necessary because most clay infrastructures in southern Mesopotamia quickly deteriorated) (Rice 1985).

Of the many deities of Mesopotamia, Inana was probably the most unpredictable, whose character and personality often caused trouble to the existing order of Sumero-Akkadian reality as discussed below.

THE 'VIRGIN' GODDESS OF LOVE AND LUST AND KINGSHIP

As explained above, Inana was never regarded as the mother-goddess archetype. Although not a mother in any traditional sense, Inana was invoked in some incantations to help other women in the process of childbirth (Leick 1994). But this was not her claim to fame. The part of Inana's character that fascinated her people the most was her sexuality and sensuality. In spite of her bridal association with Dumuzi, Inana was always classified as the 'ki-sikil,' 'maiden,' before the consummation of marriage, never as an 'old woman' (Leick 1994 p.66). This would make her the ultimate 'virgin,' the Greek *parthenos* to which Leick (1994) refers (p.66); that is, the concept of virginity may have referred to the lack of control by men rather than to physical virginity as we understand it now. In other words, the concept of virginity might have been applied both to women who had multiple sex partners and to those who had none – neither of them 'belonged' to the authority of one man, her husband.

Thanks to the mastery of the ancient Mesopotamian poets Inana was presented as combining both aspects of virginity. The so-called Bridal Songs as designated by Leick (1994) present her as a young girl or woman without any previous sexual experience. According to a composition entitled by Jacobsen (1987) the 'Wiles of Women' (pp.10–12) she has to be taught (at least she is proposed the teachings of) by her suitor, Dumuzi, the art of love and sex. Another text, rather controversial in its translation and interpretation as explained by Leick (1994), refers either to Inana's fantasy or to the reality of possible love-making.

> He made me lie on a honey-smelling bed,
> After my precious, dear one, had lain by my heart,
> One-by-one, making 'tongues,' one-by-one,
> My brother of the fairest face made fifty.
> He became (?) like a silenced man,
> With an 'earthquake' he was put to silence.
> My brother, with a hand put on his waist,
> My precious, sweet one, the time passes!
> (Lover:) Set me free, my sister, set me free!
> Come, my beloved sister, let us go to the palace (*var*, to our house)!
> May you be a little daughter in my father's eye!
> (Alster 1993, lines 27–37)

If the meaning of the above lines is sexual (if, for example 'earthquake' refers to an orgasm) then it indicates Inana's inborn ability to satisfy whomever she chooses to be her lover, even without any previous experience, to the point that he wants to marry her.

Since Leick's (1994) book focuses on the subject of sex and erotica in the Mesopotamian literature, explaining both sexual and sensual symbolism in literary and non-literary texts, there is no need to discuss in any detail all sexual symbolism associated with Inana. However, it must be noted here that the motifs of the garden as both a favorite location for sexual frolicking and a metaphor for the female genitals, as well as the symbolism of apple trees as representing the male genitals, are essential for the analysis of the Genesis paradise story in the creation of humankind (see pp.159–166).

As shy, inexperienced and innocent as Inana might be in the Bridal Songs, she is a different 'virgin' in other stories. The sixth tablet of the Epic of Gilgamesh (Sîn-leqi-unninnī version) presents her not as a sweet girl, but as a woman who knows exactly what she wants: 'To Gilgamesh's beauty great Ishtar lifted her eyes./"Come, Gilgamesh, be my lover!/Give me the taste of your body./Would that you were my husband, and I your wife!"' (Gardner and Maier 1984, p.148).

Then she tells how she would reward him with all possible 'material' goods if he were to become her consort. At first Gilgamesh (the king of Uruk, two-thirds divine, one-third human) tries to brush off her advances by pointing out his low status in comparison with hers, but then he invokes her sexual past:

> Which of your lovers have you loved forever?
> Which of your little shepherds has continued to please you?
> Come, let me name your lovers for you.

For Tammuz [Dumuzi], the lover of your youth.
Year after year you set up a wailing for him.
You loved the mauve-colored shepherd bird:
You seized him and broke his wing.
In the forest he stands crying, 'Kappi! My wing!'
You loved the lion, full of spry power;
You dug for him seven pits and seven pits...
...You loved a shepherd, a herdsman...
...You struck him, turned him into a wolf.
His own boys drove him away,
And his dogs tore his hide to bits. (Gardner and Maier 1984, pp. 149,152)

Gilgamesh continues with a description of Inana's lust for her father's gardener whom she invited to 'take pleasure in your strength. Reach out your hand and touch my vulva' (Gardner and Maier 1984, p.152) and then turned him into a frog. Needless to say the conclusion of his speech was a not-so-polite refusal of the goddess' offer. Insulted, Inana made her father, Anu, create the Bull of Heaven to kill Gilgamesh, under the threat of using her powers if her wish was not met: 'I will smash in the gates of the netherworld;/I will set up the [ruler] of the great below,/And I will make the dead rise, and they will

Figure 6.1 Gilgamesh and his beloved friend Enkidu are slaughtering the monster Humbaba.
  From a clay plaque

devour the living,/And the dead will increase beyond the number of the living'
(Gardner and Maier 1984, p.156).

Since this request was rather out of the ordinary, Anu points out that there is a price
to pay for the creation of the bull: the seven year famine which would kill the people and
the animals unless Inana stored grain and grass for them. She did, and the Bull of Heaven
was sent against Gilgamesh to punish his brutal honesty. But this great king of Uruk was
still able to overcome the divine creation, killing him with the help of his loyal
companion, Enkidu. In order to comply with the divine laws, one of the heroic duo had
to die. Thus, Enkidu was carried off to the Nether World. Inana still got her revenge –
Gilgamesh lost his most beloved friend.

Inana's temper was almost legendary. In the story of 'Inanna and Šu-kale-tuda,'
Šu-kale-tuda, a human gardener, took advantage of her when she was asleep in the
garden, tired after traversing the heavens, earth and different countries (Kramer 1959).
When she woke up and realized what Šu-kale-tuda had done to her, the goddess of lust
became the goddess of fury. After failing to find the mortal who shamelessly dishonored
her, she punished Sumer with a series of plagues.

All the wells of the land she filled with blood,
All the groves and gardens of the land she sated with blood,
The (male) slaves coming to gather firewood, drink nothing but blood,
The (female) slaves coming to fill up with water, fill up with nothing but blood.

(Kramer 1959, p.73).

Nobody gets away with a crime against this goddess.

As stubborn as she was, Inana still listened sometimes to the advice of others,
especially of her twin brother, the sun-god Utu. It was he who convinced her to marry
Dumuzi (Semitic Tammuz, also mentioned in Ezekiel 8:14) in the composition entitled
by Kramer (1959) 'The Wooing of Inanna' (pp.139–142). This is another disputation, a
genre so popular among the Sumerian authors. This time there are two suitors for Inana's
hand in marriage: the shepherd Dumuzi who has Utu's support and the farmer Enkimdu
who has obviously won Inana's first interest. Each of them presents his superior qualities
in comparison to his rival. It seems that Inana is finally convinced by Dumuzi and
marries him. Utu is the one who leads her to the bridal chamber, making sure that all
preparations for her important night are perfect. She is ready as the song describes:'Now
my breasts stand up,/Now hair has grown on my vulva,/Going to the bridegroom's
loins, let us rejoice!/O Baba, let us rejoice over my vulva!/Dance! Dance!/Afterwards
they will please him, will please him' (Jacobsen 1987, p.18).

Inana's marriage with Dumuzi was probably one of the most celebrated events in
Mesopotamia. This shepherd god could have been one of the original heroes of
Sumerian prehistory who, with time, was elevated to the position of a deity. He was
worshipped at Badtibira, a city that he was believed to have ruled before the Flood.
According to the Sumerian King List,

When the kingship was lowered from heaven
The kingship was in Eridu(g)…
…I drop (the topic) Eridu(g);

Its kingship to Bad-tibira(k)
    was carried.
(In) Bad-tibira(k) En-men-lu-Anna(k) reigned 43, 200 years;
En-men-gal-Anna(k) reigned its 28,800 years;
Divine Dumu-zi(d), a shepherd, reigned 36,000 years...

                                        (Jacobsen 1966, pp.71, 73)

However, the same text refers to yet another king with the name Dumuzi, this time after the Flood, who ruled for 100 years in the city of Kuara (Jacobsen 1966), closely associated with Uruk, whose throne must have belonged to him as the husband of Inana. Since there was also a third Dumuzi, a warrior hero of a village near Lagaš (Black and Green 1997), it seems that the Sumerians never tried to clarify which one was the original Dumuzi with whom Inana had a loving but quite stormy relationship.

On the other hand, the Mesopotamians might have never even thought about clarifying the 'Dumuzi mystery' since each and every king whom Inana 'married' in the so-called 'sacred marriage' (Greek *hieros gamos*) was identified with him. The term 'sacred marriage' with regard to Inana's symbolic union with a king is rather misleading. The whole point of the ceremony was a ritual love-making between the goddess and a deified king which would assert the fertility of the land through its connection with Dumuzi – the dying god of vegetation. There are three texts from the Third Dynasty of Ur and the Isin Period which deal with this 'marriage ceremony' in addition to short references in royal hymns (Leick 1994).

Inana's first confirmed sexual union with a deified king is with king Šulgi, the Third Dynasty of Ur, who arrived at Uruk (the main place of Inana's residence on earth) as his first stop during his tour of important temples which he honored with numerous offerings. After reassuring Šulgi of her continuous support, Inana brings up memories of her sexual encounters with him under the name of the shepherd Dumuzi and then they proceed with the ceremony of love-making so well described and discussed by Leick (1994). Leick points out that nowhere in the text is there any reference to Inana being a bride, but rather that she can be perceived as a divine 'hierodule' (especially taking into consideration her make-up!) whom the king must satisfy in order to prove himself. Obviously he did since Inana proclaimed him fit to rule. The second text from the time of Iddin-Dagan of Isin, (also referred to as Amaušumgalanna, another name of Dumuzi) although less clear, refers to a similar event in which Inana's sexual desires must be fulfilled by the adequate performance of the king.

Only the third text from the same period refers to the ritual love-making with Inana as a part of ritualistic ceremonies which took place during the celebration of the New Year festival in Isin. For this occasion the 'sacred bed' was prepared so Inana and Iddin-Dagan could make love. After this act takes place, the king and his queen, Inana, are seated next to each other and she 'is praised as the "*hi-li* (the embodiment of sex-appeal) of the black-headed people"' (Leick 1994, p.101). This particular description might suggest that the actual ceremony was performed between the king and one of the human priestesses or hierodules who represented Inana. Since Inana was sometimes referred in songs as a prostitute operating in her tavern (temple), it should become quite clear that she should have never even been considered as a mother-goddess. Her strength was in her uncontrollable nature which included all aspects of love and lust present among humans. Inana's sexuality and sensuality were essential for the fertility of the land, animals and humans, and those who were responsible for maintaining it, the kings, had to prove themselves to her. This ritual then would emphasize the close emotional bond between the rulers and the divine world, even if they themselves did not make claims to full divine status. Their deification was still possible through their claims to be born of divine mothers, – as for example, Sargon of Akkad or Šulgi of the Third Dynasty of Ur – but there were still mortals like Gilgamesh whose divine status was established through his birth to the Great Goddess but only as two-thirds of his persona. In any event Inana, in each and every aspect of her personality, was essential for the successful maintenance of the kingship, the land and the people.

THE NETHER WORLD AND INANA'S CONTINUOUS QUEST FOR POWER

Inana's sex-appeal was not her only weapon. Her beauty and sensuality were enhanced by her intelligence, wit, compassion and a combination of human characteristics such as vanity, quick temper and unpredictability, which made her more 'accessible' to people than other deities. As has already been discussed above, Inana never stopped trying to increase her authority whether by 'cheating' Enki of *me*, or playing the 'poor little thing' to extort additional powers from him. Thus, it is not a surprise that Inana set her heart upon completing yet another 'impossible' task, to visit the underworld from which, in theory at least, there was no return for deities or for mortals.

It is not quite clear why Inana decided to go to the underworld. In Kramer's (1959) translation of 'Inana's Descent to the Netherworld' she just 'set her mind toward the "great below"' (p.159) while in Dalley's translation (1989) 'the daughter of Sîn was determined to go' (p.155). Both translations might be interpreted as her ambitious intent to extend her domain to the kingdom of the dead. On the other hand, judging from the amount of time Inana must have spent on adoring her body, one wonders whether she just wanted to add to Ereškigal's (her sister, and ruler of the Nether World) misery by showing off her beauty and powers. Of course Inana was fully aware that she might not be very welcome and might pay with death for her arrogance, so she instructed her vizier Ninšubur to intervene, just in case, with Enlil, Nanna and Enki. All plans made, Inana descended to the lapis lazuli temple of her sister where she lied to the gatekeeper, telling him that she had come for the funeral rites of Gugal-ana, the first husband of Ereškigal. Upon hearing this news Ereškigal, quite mad, issued the order to pass Inana through all seven gates but also to strip from her all her clothes and adornments so she would 'be brought naked before me' (Kramer 1959, p.162). In spite of Inana's protests – 'What, pray, is this?' – the order is carried out and she is presented in her full royal nakedness to Ereškigal and the seven judges known as Anunnakû. The welcoming greetings are rather short since '[Ereškigal] fastened her eye upon her, the eye of death,/Spoke the word against her, the word of wrath,/Uttered the cry against her, the cry of guilt,/The sick woman was turned into a corpse,/The corpse was hung from a nail' (Kramer 1959, p.163).

Figure 6.2 Ištar (Sumerian Inana) in her aspect as a war-goddess proudly displaying her assets as a warrior and a woman. From a cylinder seal

The first line of the above passage gives a new meaning to the saying 'if looks could kill.' Inana is dead, and only thanks to her vizier's pleading with Enki (after a rejection from Enlil and Nanna) is she returned to life. But her troubles are not over yet. The law requires that she provides a substitute for her dead body so the order and balance will be preserved. To make sure that she will not weasel her way out of the situation, heartless demons are sent back with her. After making two short stops in Umma and Badtibira, Inana and her not so lovely companions arrive at Kullab (a cult center in Uruk) whose tutelary god is her beloved husband Dumuzi. Unfortunately for him, he does not behave as an upset husband who has just lost his wife. Thus, we are not surprised that the demons carry him off to the Nether World upon the order of Inana. Now is definitely the time for him to cry, which he does, begging his protector and brother of Inana, Utu, to help him escape from these merciless demons. Another poem informs us that he was not very successful in his attempts to avoid his fate in spite of the loyal help of his sister Geštinana (Kramer 1961). Eventually it seems that she agreed to be his substitute in the underworld for six months in a year so Dumuzi can return to the world of the living to spend time with Inana and assure the fertility of the land.

This particular story is not only entertaining and consistent with Inana's 'human' character, but also implies the importance of this great goddess of love and war for the continuation of the prosperous life of earth and on earth. The time when Dumuzi disappears for six months is probably winter, during which time the vegetation dies with him. He returns to Inana at the beginning of the New Year to assure the fertility of the land and the wealth of its people through the love-making ritual with her. This is the same land which Inana as a warrior goddess would protect from its enemy, aiding her kings in each and every battle, depicted sometimes as the 'playground of Ištar' (Black and Green 1997, p.109).

Mesopotamia – summary

Since the Sumerians and their successors in Mesopotamia seem not to be concerned with the establishment of a consistent philosophical system about the origin of the universe, the task of putting together fragmentary and 'accidental' written sources concerning their view is rather difficult and time consuming, but also quite rewarding. The deities discussed above were obviously the most essential for the universe to function and develop according to a once 'encoded' order of nature. An (Anu), Ki, Enlil, Enki (Ea), Sîn (Nanna, Suen), Inana (Inanna/Ištar), and Utu (Šamaš) were the seven deities who had the power to decree the destinies of others but still stay within the limits of the original *prima materia* order, since they too were a part of the creation process. There were also others like Igigi (Igigū), the 'great gods' and Anunnakkû (Anunna) gods who aided them in this process.

In the beginning, the Sumerian universe of deities consisted only of heaven and earth which included the underworld with the Du-ku, 'the holy hill,' situated on the mountain of the universe. This was the place where destinies were proclaimed by deities, where the original Anunna gods lived in immemorial time, and from which all elements of civilization came (Black and Green 1997). Once these above elements were separated, probably to provide space for humans, the universe was perceived by the Babylonians as being divided into three main superimposed spheres: heaven, earth and underworld. Heaven itself – which was possibly believed to be made out of some sort of metal in the Sumerian mythology (Kramer 1959) – or rather its eastern horizon was divided into three zones as the domains of Anu, Enlil and Ea. The 'ways' of these gods were the location for 'the eighteen zodiacal constellations recognized from about 1000 B.C.' (Black and Green 1997, p.37). In yet another tradition the lowest of the heavens was the seat of the stars, the middle, of the Igigi, and the highest belonged to Anu. The idea of numerous heavens survived in the Quranic tradition which refers to seven of them.

The earth was considered to be a flat disc, rectangular in shape, whose four corners were associated with the four cardinal directions and four winds. Beneath the underworld the sweet waters of *abzu* were located. The *Enûma Eliš* tradition preserves this order of heaven, lower heaven as the dominion of Enlil, earth as the price for Marduk killing Tiāmat, and *abzu*, the sweet waters.

However, as little or as much as we know about the creation of the universe in Mesopotamia, the above texts represent what one might call the Great Tradition of the elite
superimposing the so-called Little Traditions (terms proposed by Redfield 1965) which
might have been lost forever. One such tradition, the tradition of the city of Dunnu
known as 'The Harab Myth' (Jacobsen 1984), is quite different from what was presented
above. This short text – whose original can probably be dated to the second part of the
third millennium B.C., although the text itself is of Late Babylonian date – can be used as
an 'illustration' of Freud's reconstruction of the story leading to the establishment of the
Oedipus complex. It presents the story of creation in relation to the city of Dunnu
(within the borders of the Isin kingdom) as a series of killings (parricide) and incest
between deities preceding the ones of the official tradition, such as Enlil and Ninurta. To
provide the reader with an idea of how this myth is narrated, the first fourteen lines are
quoted, after Jacobsen (1984):

> [Harab,] in the first [beginnings, took Earth to wife,]
> [to (found) a f]amily and (exercise) lordship [his heart urged him:]
> 'We will cut furrows in the wasteland of the country!'
> [By] ploughing with their soilbreaking plough they caused Sea to be
> created,
> [the fur]rows by [the]mselves gave birth to Sumuqan.
> His stro[nghold,] Dunnu (the city) of yore they built, the two of them.
> [Har]ab have himself clear title to the lordship in Dunnu, but
> [Earth] lifted (her) face to Sumuqan, his son,
> and said to him: 'Come, let me love thee!'
> Sumu[qan] took Earth, his mother, to wife, and
> Harab, [the father,] he killed and
> in Dunnu, which he loved, he laid [him] to rest;
> also, Sumuqan [t]ook over the lordship of his father, and
> Sea, his older sister, [he to]ok to wife, but... (p.7)

It is quite possible, as Jacobsen suggests, that this myth, although local in its origin,
might have influenced later traditions of Anatolia (Kumarbi's story) and even of Greece
(Hesiod's *Theogony*). Cross (1973) sees similarities between this myth and references to
the Canaanite El's fight against his father, 'Heaven', on behalf of his mother 'Earth.'
After that El marries 'his sisters and emasculates his father' (p.41).

In conclusion one may ask how many other traditions which may have extended our
understanding of the ancient people of Mesopotamia are currently 'lost.' However, at
least one thing is certain: the ancient Mesopotamians were much more tolerant of other
'religious' systems than we are today. They did not feel the need to exterminate and/or
to humiliate deities of other people, but let them exist in many parallel worlds and
traditions.

Egypt

Although some scholars have argued for the monotheistic nature of Egyptian religion
(Budge 1959, 1969; see Hornung 1982 for discussion), there seems to be little doubt
that the ancient Egyptians worshipped multiple deities whose number was estimated by

Budge (1969) to exceed 1200 by the Nineteenth Dynasty. It is reasonable to state that such a high number of deities could not have been worshipped on an everyday basis and, that the pharaoh as a state could not have provided for all of them even with the help of his subjects. It is quite possible that only a very few in ancient Egypt could have named them all. Some of these divine forces are known to modern scholars by their particular characteristics which are sometimes 'encoded' in their names such as Amun, 'the hidden one,' while others are known only by name. Attributes, functions and origins of some or many local deities have never been written down and/or have been forgotten over the millennia. The national deities – that is, those who were continuously associated with the kingdom and its representatives on earth, the pharaohs – are known better but the etymology of their names as well as their origins frequently remains unclear.

In addition to the cosmic and natural forces which were personified as deities by the Egyptians, abstract ideas and concepts such as truth, justice (Ma'at) and localities (the goddess Khefthernebes as the personification of the Theban necropolis) were subjects of a cult too. In spite of extended research on the subject we still do not know what motivated Egyptians in their selection of elements to be personified as the divine beings. Hornung (1982) discussed this subject in detail, pointing out such 'obvious' choices for personification as fire, water, love, fear, and so forth, which were never perceived as deities, although they were associated with some of the deities' aspects. Only a few Egyptian divinities carried animal names, although many were presented in an animal form (Hornung 1982, pp.82–83). Animals such as bulls, ibises, cats and hawks were kept in temples and were worshipped as gods. The concept of their divinity could be similar to the perception of the pharaoh's divinity since they, like the king, were mortal, and required magnificent funeral rituals, including embalming, to be buried with honors. The abundance of divine animal forms in the Egyptian iconography shocked other ancient people such as Greeks and Romans and is still surprising to many. 'Who does not know, Volusius, what monsters are revered by demented Egyptians? One part worships the crocodile, another goes in awe of the ibis that feeds on serpents. Elsewhere there shines the golden effigy of the sacred long-tailed monkey' (Watterson 1985, p.26).

Watterson cited this expression of a horrifying acknowledgment of the strangeness of the Egyptian religion to Graeco-Roman visitors who were also polytheistic. Can this worship of animals be called zoolatry? The answer is well beyond the scope of this book (for a discussion see Hornung 1982), but it must be noted that the trend to anthropomorphisation (attributing human characteristics to those which are not human) of Egyptian religion is already confirmed in the early historical period, although the names of early Egyptian kings (for example, Scorpion, Cobra) still reflect the focus on the perceived superiority of animal-kind. This process never eliminated the existence of animals and animal presentation as deities but actually complicated the matter further, since combinations of both human and animal features in one image started to flourish. For example, one of the mother-goddesses of ancient Egypt, Hathor, was presented in three forms: in her original form as a cow, in her 'intermediary form' as a woman with the ears of a cow or a cow head with a human face, and finally as a fully 'anthropomorphised' woman with a headdress which included a wig, sun disc and horns.

The complexity of the Egyptian gods and goddesses led to the development of many names and images representing different aspects of the same deity. For example, Thoth (Djehuty), god of writing, knowledge and time, was depicted sometimes as an ibis, sometimes as a baboon, sometimes as a combination of either of them with a human body, and/or with a symbolic presentation of the lunar crescent and/or with a scribal palette and leaf or a palm leaf. To make his role and aspects even more confusing some texts referred to him as being the tongue or the heart of the sun-god Re or Ptah.

Each of these names and/or manifestations was important, although not of equal value. The power of names and their 'annexation' was one of the fundamental features of Egyptian religion. Since a 'name' was considered to be one of five, six or eight (depending on the interpretation) elements of any being in existence, including a

Figure 6.3 The syncretic god Re-Horakhte, enthroned, faces another god associated with creation

human, the more names the deity had, the more identities he or she possessed. The name was something to be guarded because the power of being was included in it. Knowledge of the names of others was an easy way to establish the hierarchy of beings as in the order of creation (for instance, Amun, 'the hidden one', his name was unknown to others which made him the first one) and provided the power 'both to repel evil and to coerce other beings' (Hornung 1982, p.89).

The multiplicity of deities, their names, forms, and the expressions associated with them, was already difficult for an average Egyptian to remember and comprehend. Since different deities could have shared the same attributes, characteristics, and/or epithets with regard to their names, the ancient Egyptians developed the idea of 'linking' some of them together, probably in order to simplify religious practices and to make them more cost-effective. This process is known as syncretism and represents another main feature of Egyptian religion. It can be described as the fusion of two or more deities into one being for the purpose of worship. Since Hornung (1982) provided a very eloquent explanation concerning the linkage between various deities which allowed them to 'inhabit' each other but still preserve their separate identity, it is sufficient to mention here only that some of the most powerful deities of Egypt – such as Ptah-Sokar-Osiris and Amun-Re – were subjects of such fusion.

The syncretization of Egyptian deities has led some to believe in the presence of one 'universal' deity whose manifestations and names were plentiful. Of course, the implication is that it would be the monotheistic male god, recognized later on by the Old Testament. This would exclude the presence of female deities who, to my knowledge, were never syncretized with their male counterparts although there were some who could be considered female doublets of the masculine forms such as Amaunet, a doublet of Amun. There are many other problems with this monotheistic interpretation which have been well addressed by scholars. Hornung (1982) summarized this problem as follows:

> It is clear that syncretism does not contain any 'monotheistic tendency,' but rather forms a strong counter-current to monotheism – so long as it is kept within bounds. Syncretism softens henotheism, the concentration of worship on a single god, and stops it from turning into monotheism, for ultimately syncretism means that a single god is not isolated from the others: in Amun one apprehends and worships also Re, or in Harmachis other forms of the sun god. In this way the awareness is sharpened that the divine partner of humanity is not one but many. (p.98)

It must be understood that the polytheistic nature of Egyptian religion and its creativity, lack of clearly defined concepts of divinity within and without, and its syncretism allowed the Egyptians continuously to expand and transform their pantheon. As the old deities were never 'killed' by their worshippers – although they could have been 'transformed' – so the new ones, from foreign traditions of Asia and Nubia, could be assimilated into their pantheon without a major struggle with ideology. While aware of the diversity and disunity within their land, the Egyptians were able to unite all elements of their culture through the religious tolerance and conceptualization of the divine kingship established through the most powerful myth of them all – the creation stories.

The sun-god as the main creator

A large number of Egyptian sun-gods and their combinations indicates quite clearly that the sun was probably the most important deified force in ancient Egypt (for the daily life of sun and other gods of Egypt see Meeks and Favard-Meeks 1996; for a general classification of Egyptian deities see Ions 1983; Silverman 1991; Watterson 1985; for the role of the sun see Allen 1988). As Quirke (1992) stated:

> The sun embodied for the Egyptians more than power in heaven or power over earth; the daily guarantee of sunrise after the sunset of yesterday offered a bright and tangible promise of resurrection, and for this reason the sun-god was considered the central and original power of creation. (p.23)

In general the Sun was believed to be a male deity who was born every morning to sail on his 'day boat' from the east to the west where he would disappear for the night into the Duat, the underworld located in the sky (other expressions used for the underworld included Roseatau and Imhet – for a discussion see Lesko 1991). This was the area which was not visible to the Egyptians, so they imagined that there were many obstacles which the Sun had to overcome in order to be born again. Among demons and other terrifying beings the Sun had to fight was Apep (Greek Apophis), a huge serpent, who was often identified with the negative forces of Seth (for his meaning and the battle see Meeks and Favard-Meeks 1996). The Coffin Text No. 160, for example, makes this connection quite clear: 'Now at the time of evening he [the serpent] turns his eye over against Re, and there occurs a halting among the (solar) crew, a great astonishment (?) within the voyage, so that Seth bends himself against him' (Ritner 1997a, p.32).

Upon leaving the Duat successfully, the Sun directed his boat into the Akhet, 'the place of becoming effective' (Silverman 1997, p.119) before he rose again on the horizon in his visible form. The Egyptians were very creative in searching for images which could be used for the presentation of different stages of the day and night transformation of the Sun. While throughout the Pharaonic Period the most popular images of the Sun were the beetle, the sun-disc and the ram for, respectively, morning, midday and evening, by the Late Period each hour of the day and night was represented by a different creature or being (Lurker 1984).

In addition to numerous images which were associated with the Sun, its different aspects were expressed in the form of various sun deities. Among them the god Re was the most important since he was recognized as the full manifestation of the sun. His name was the term for the heavenly body itself. The sun as a body could also be called as the 'Eye of Re' and was represented by a goddess, usually Hathor. The Sun's name at dawn was Khepri, 'evolving one,' when it was about to be born as a ball. Hence, Khepri was associated with the scarab. Originally he was also a manifestation of yet another sun-god, Atum, and eventually became recognized as Re himself. In Spell No. 83 of the Book of the Dead his sacred history is narrated:

> I have flown up like the primeval ones, I have become Khepri, I have grown as a plant, I have clad myself as a tortoise, I am the essence of every god, I am the seventh of those seven uraei who came into being in the West, Horus who makes brightness with his person, that god who was against Seth, Thoth who was among you in that judgment of

Him who presided over Letopolis together with the Souls of Heliopolis, the flood which was between them. (Faulkner 1997, p.80)

As a morning sun Re was joined with Horus and worshipped as Horakhte, 'Horus of the Horizon.' As a mature sun, his name was Atum, who was not only one of the creator gods but also the sun at sunset. Amun-Re, the most complete manifestation of the combination of powers of the Sun and 'the Hidden One,' emerged as one of the most worshipped gods in Egypt. The powers of Re were so strong that he even merged with Osiris in the Duat where the joining, described as 'the sun at rest in Osiris, Osiris at rest in the sun' (Silverman 1997, p.119), led to the resurrection of both in each other.

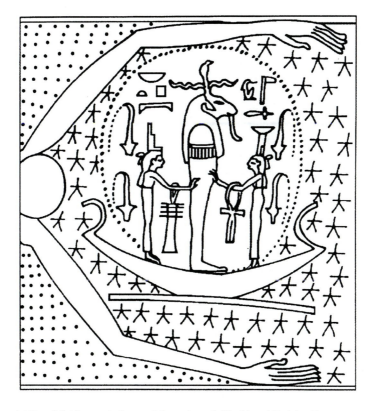

Figure 6.4 Re and Osiris are united as one. The one is touched by Isis and Nephthys. From a papyrus

Finally, the leading god of the Amarna Period (around 1353–1327 B.C.) was also a sun-god known as Aten. He was represented as a sun-disc with rays ending in hands extending toward the earth. Although he was already worshipped in Egypt before his prominence under Amenhotep IV/Akhenaten and his successor Smenkhara, his divinity 'in its own right' is being questioned (Shaw and Nicholson 1995, p.44).

Aten was considered to be a manifestation of Re whose body was supposed to be the sun-disc (Lurker 1984). Owing to the numerous changes which occurred during the reign of Akhenaten many people would like to see Aten as the 'sole' god of the Amarna Period, which would make him the creator *per se* since in any monotheistic religion, by definition, there is no place for other deities to create the world.

> How many are your [Aten's] deeds.
> Though hidden from sight,
> O sole God beside whom there is none!
> You made the earth as you wished, you alone,
> All peoples, herds, flocks;
> All upon the earth that walk on legs,
> All on high that fly on wings,
> The lands of Khor and Kush,
> The land of Egypt.
> You set every man in his place,
> You supply their needs;
> Everyone has his food,
> His lifetime is counted.
> Their tongues differ in speech,
> Their characters likewise;
> Their skins are distinct,
> For you distinguished the peoples. ('The Great Hymn to the Aten' – after Lichtheim 1997a, p.46).

However, in spite of this beautiful hymn referring to Aten as the only god, there is evidence which strongly suggests that other deities were worshipped during the Amarna Period, even on special order from the pharaoh. Thus, monotheism is definitely out of the question. It was rather henotheism or hierarchical polytheism, in which one god is elevated above the position of many others. Since the ideas associated with the leading position of Aten were short-lived and not of the mainstream religion of the Pharaonic Period, the Amarna Period is mostly excluded from the discussion of creation stories of ancient Egypt (for more information see Aldred 1988; KMT 1991; Redford 1987).

The family tree of the Ennead

As explained in the previous section, one of the most important sun-god-creators was Atum. According to the Heliopolitan doctrine of creation he was the beginning of all other elements of nature and universe which were necessary for their existence. His family was accepted by all Egyptians as representations of various forces of the universe. Since Atum was all alone at the beginning of time and existence, 'Atum evolved growing ithyphallic, in Heliopolis. He put his penis in his grasp that might make orgasm with it, and the two siblings were born – Shu and Tefnut' (Allen 1997d, p.7, from the Pyramid Texts, Spell 527).

This act of masturbation was nothing shocking for the Egyptians and should not be for us. Being alone, Atum had a very limited choice in giving birth to others through the sexual act which seems to be the desired mode of creation employed by the priests of Heliopolis. Thus, he was both a mother and a father and sometimes was even referred to as such with the title 'Great He-She' (Ions 1983, p.25). Furthermore, since Atum personified both male and female elements, his hand symbolized his female principle and together they were depicted as the divine couple on coffins of the Herakleopolitan Period (The First Intermediate Period). The importance of his hand was carried on as the title 'god's hand' for Theban priestesses who were believed to be married to Amun (Shaw and Nicholson 1995).

Spell 600 of the Pyramid Texts describes the 'delivery' process of his children as 'you [Atum] sneezed Shu, you spat Tefnut' (Allen 1997c, p.7). They represented the first two elements of the world: Shu, the air, and Tefnut, the moisture. It is not quite clear where this act of birth took place. It seems that some references suggest the primeval

Figure 6.5 Nut, as the sky, arches over her husband, Geb, the earth. From the vignette papyrus of Tameni

mound as the location while others refer to the deep waters where Atum, possibly as the hill himself, remained. In Papyrus Bremner-Rhind, Atum explains that he tended his children with his eye. This eye was obviously separable from him and once it disappeared, Shu and Tefnut brought it back. Although the text is not very clear it appears that Atum replaced the 'lost' eye with a new one which really enraged the first eye upon her return. Thus, 'I [Atum] promoted her [the First Eye] place on my face,/And afterward she began to rule this entire land' (Allen 1997e, 15).

The Eye was probably a metaphor for the sun itself and its rage could have been associated with the scorching powers of the sun's heat in Egypt. This is probably the reason for the description of this eye and other related eyes (Hathor as the Eye of Re) as the destructive goddess whose other aspect was positive, in the form of the goddess Sekhmet saving humankind from certain annihilation. Her dominant place on the face of Atum-Re was probably related to the cobra-goddess Wadjet, whose symbol, *uraeus*, was worn by the pharaoh on his forehead.

The same Papyrus continues with the story of the creation of the world which states that Shu and Tefnut gave birth to Geb and Nut, who in turn became parents of five children: Osiris, Horus (the Elder), Seth, Isis and Nephthys. However, the most common tradition was that Horus was the son of Isis and Osiris, not of Nut and Geb. This generation 'gave birth to their multitude in this world' (Allen 1997e, p.15).

This series of births produced all the necessary forces of life in the universe. While Shu and Tefnut (the etymology of her name, Tefnuty, is still unclear; see Allen 1988) represented dry air and moisture respectively, their children, Geb and Nut, personified the earth and the sky or heaven. However, it must be noted that Shu and Tefnut were already connected with the sun and the moon respectively in the best tradition of the Egyptian duality of concepts. Furthermore Quirke (1992) considers, based on the Coffin Texts from Bersha, that Shu and Tefnut are representation of life and right respectively which he connected with the cyclical perception of time, *neheh* (seasons), and linear sequence of time, *djet* (year by year, generation by generation). Thus, with them time was born, in spite of a lack of agreement between scholars as to proper translations of both terms (Hornung 1992). Allen (1988) sees in them the representation of two parallel principles of existence in Egypt – '*stasis*, the notion of creation as perfect and complete,' as Tefnut, the order, the eternal sameness, and '*change*, the notion of life as dynamic and recurrent,' as Shu, the life, the eternal occurrence (p.25).

It is very interesting that in contrast to many other mythologies, the Egyptians associated a male deity with the concept of earth. But, on the other hand, even the primeval waters were believed to be a male principle, Nun. One might speculate that this association of the original waters of creation with the earth was the result of the Egyptian fascination with dung beetles which were believed to be male, only capable of bringing themselves into being from a mound of dung.

Geb was usually presented as reclining on his side on the ground covered with vegetation. In his aspect as the fertility god he was sometimes presented with his penis erected towards his wife, the sky-goddess, Nut. Geb was also considered to be a protector of the pharaoh since in the story of Horus and Seth, he was the rightful judge who ruled in favor of Horus.

His wife, Nut, the personification of heaven or sky, was often depicted as a woman arched over the earth between two horizons of the east and the west.

(1) Arms   Her right arm is on the northwestern side, the left on the southeastern side.

(2) Head   Her head is the western horizon, her mouth is the west.

(3) Mouth   The western horizon.

(4) Crotch   The eastern horizon. (from the Cenotaph of Seti I; after Allen 1988, p.2)

Since her body symbolized the vault of sky she was also believed to be the mother of celestial bodies to whom she gave birth and whom she swallowed for 'safe keeping,' only to give them birth again. One of the routes of the sun-god Re (also Ihy) was through her body: in the evening he entered her mouth only to re-emerge next morning from her womb.

This idea of swallowing children is not as unusual as one may think. *Tilapia nilotica*, a fish living in the River Nile, is in the habit of taking her young into her mouth at a time of danger and then releasing them again when the danger is gone. The Egyptians were obviously aware of this natural phenomenon and the fish itself was 'the very manifestation of the idea of rebirth' (Manniche 1987, p.40).

Osiris was probably not only one of the most ancient deities of Egypt but also one of the most popular and complex gods. His story, and the story of his siblings, Isis, Seth, Nephthys, and Horus as his brother or son, has survived in many Egyptian texts, although its longest 'edition' is the Greek adaptation of the myth by Plutarch known as *De Isiride et Osiride* in the second century A.D. Although there is a possibility that this version was very much clouded by the Greek tradition, the main theme of the Osirian legend – that is, his death at the hands of Seth – was eloquently preserved.

According to the Heliopolitan account, Osiris, the oldest son born to Nut and Geb, was given the kingship of earth by his father. The Great Hymn to Osiris narrates this event:

> Geb's heir (in) kingship of the Two Lands,
> Seeing his worth he gave (it) to him |Osiris|,
> To lead the lands to good fortune.
> He placed this land into his hand,
> Its water, its wind,
> Its plants, all its cattle.
> All that flies, all that alights.
> Its reptiles and its desert game,
> Were given to the son of Nut,
> And the Two Lands are content with it. (Lichtheim 1997b, p.42)

Osiris married Isis, his sister, whom he had loved while still in the womb of his mother. Isis, one of the most powerful goddesses of Egypt, was a personification or an embodiment of the throne of Egypt, whose image she wore as her headdress. Thus, his marriage to her only strengthened Osiris' claim to the kingship. She was also known as the 'great magic', thanks to which she could have protected her child Horus as well as influenced various events. Isis was worshipped as the mother-goddess because she was perceived as the symbolic mother of the Egyptian pharaoh. Judging from her devotion to Osiris their marriage must have been a very happy one.

However, Seth, Osiris' brother, who married Nephthys (Lady of the Mansion), was jealous of Osiris' good fortune. It seems that he had set his eyes on Isis, whose beauty and sexuality were so enchanting to him that (according to Papyrus Jumihac II, 1–6) he changed himself into a bull and, not being able to catch her, ejaculated. His seed grew in the desert to become plants known as *bedded-kau* (Manniche 1987, p.54). His fascination with her was also referred to during the competition between him and Horus for the throne (Papyrus Chester Beatty I, 6, 3–7, 1 – after Manniche 1987, p.54), but this happened later in the story.

Since Seth was obviously not able to steal Osiris' wife he schemed to steal his kingdom. During the great banquet for deities, Seth offered as a gift a wonderful coffin to whomever would fit in it. Since earlier he had paid the servants to take Osiris' measurements secretly, there was no doubt for whom this coffin was designed. This negative older 'version' of the Cinderella story proceeds with Osiris trying the coffin which fits him like an old shoe. Promptly Seth sealed it and threw it into the waters of the Nile with the king of the earth still inside. Needless to say, since deities were mortal when killed in a violent way, Osiris drowned and with his passing away, the concept of death was born. His drowning in the Nile also became symbolic of the annual flooding of this river.

Isis, the great magician and devoted wife, was looking for his body to resurrect him. Unfortunately, Seth was able to snatch the body again and this time, to prevent Isis' magic, he cut it into many pieces which he then spread all over Egypt. This is why so many cities in Egypt were associated with worship of Osiris because they each claimed to have a part of his body. For example, Busiris was the proud 'owner' of his backbone, the head was 'kept' in Abydos, and the lost penis could have been found at Mendes (Lurker 1984; Shaw and Nicholson 1995). However, the center of Osiris worship was always in Abydos where the first kings of Dynastic Egypt were buried (either as real bodies or as their representations since a second 'set' of tombs for these rulers was found at Saqqara) and where Khentamentiu, the god of Westerners (the dead) who was assimilated by Osiris, was revered in his temple which already existed in the third millennium B.C. (Quirke 1992).

But Isis did not give up. With the help of her sister, Nephthys, she was able to retrieve almost all the parts of her husband's scattered body with the exception of his phallus (possibly a Greek invention since Egyptian texts and images do not refer to this loss – see Quirke 1992). Miraculously, or rather with the help of her great magic, Isis was able to restore Osiris enough to conceive a child, Horus, with him. Although through his death Osiris lost his earthly kingdom, through his resurrection he claimed the kingdom of the Nether World.

In the meantime, Seth tried to enjoy the fruits of his crime – the kingship of Egypt. His happiness was not long-lived since his nephew (or in some versions, another brother), Horus, asserted his right to the throne. Many visual presentations and texts of ancient Egypt refer to a vicious competition between these two for the ultimate award, the throne of earth (for the description and discussion of this struggle for legitimacy see

Figure 6.6 The animated djed-pillar in the center of the presentation represents Osiris with his crook and flail (symbols of power). He is adored by his sisters: Nephthys and Isis, who is also his wife. Above the djed-pillar the sun-god, in the form of a falcon, with a sun-disc formed by the snake, has risen. This event is witnessed by adoring monkeys. From the vignette papyrus termed Spell 16

Meeks and Favard-Meeks 1996; Quirke 1992). Eventually, Horus was proclaimed the ruler and the overwhelming majority of the pharaohs was considered to be his reincarnation. Horus was the rightful ruler of earth since he also was a manifestation of sun and its power over all creations:

> Horus, son of Isis, has become effective since his entrance:
>
> he has become lord of the bark and has inherited the sky;
>
> he has become the representative of the lord to the limit since his entrance into it.
>
> It is this Horus, son of Isis, who officiates over the skies in their totality and the gods in them. (Coffin Texts VI 390d-h; after Allen 1988, p.11)

Seth had to be satisfied with a 'loser's' award, his two new wives, Anat and Ashtarte (Meeks and Favard-Meeks 1996), foreign goddesses worshipped in Syria–Palestine.

The family line of Atum and probably of other deities was not only known widely but also fixed in a particular period of time as indicated by the Turin Canon, a papyrus from the Nineteenth Dynasty which listed various gods as ruling Egypt before humans (Hoffmeier 1997; Meeks and Favard-Meeks 1996). While the number of years associated with reigns of the mortal rulers was within a human life-span, the gods were perceived to rule for thousands of years (Thoth), or for hundreds (Horus) (Meeks and Favard-Meeks 1996).

However, since nothing was fixed forever, according to Egyptian beliefs the world of order, truth, harmony and justice represented by Horus and his reincarnations is continuously threatened by the chaos personified by his uncle Seth. Without rituals, prayers, and the fulfillment of all religious obligations there might come a time when the universe may revert to its non-being state.

Egypt – summary

In contrast to the Mesopotamian tradition of a multiple number of deities whose birth and actions were influenced by the 'encoded' order of creation and whose powers were complementary and 'democratic' in the process of the 'evolution' of the universe, the Egyptians focused mainly on sun-gods as creators, with other deities playing less important role as 'assigned' to them by an all powerful sun-god, be it Atum-Re, Amun-Re, or others. There seems to be no struggle for the title of original creator and/or leader of the pantheon, although competition over the control of various elements is still present in the Egyptian mythology. The emergence of different theologies in Egypt was the result of the power drive of particular religious centers but with the full respect for other creator-gods who were included in a new doctrine not by the description of any battle but through the fusion of names and/or attributes. Furthermore, it should be obvious that in contrast to Mesopotamian deities, whose actions and behavior reflected human emotions and conflicts, the Egyptian divinities were much less comprehensible for a human believer. It is as if the rules of the earthly existence did not apply to them since there was no punishment for actions considered to be unethical or criminal in the human world (such as the conflict between Seth and Osiris and Horus).

Finally, one should pay attention to the very reduced role of female deities in the process of creation as represented by the Egyptian tradition. Neither Tefnut nor Nut, and not even Isis, were assigned any independent actions which would affect the outcome of events. They were 'allowed' to participate in the process but only by association with their male relatives or leaders while goddesses of Mesopotamia such as Nammu, Ki, Inana, or even Tiãmat were not only quite independent in their actions but also equal to their male counterparts.

Anatolia

The sun-goddess of Anatolia – the ultimate goddess of the past

Since the number of texts even alluding to the process of creation or related themes from Anatolia is quite limited, it is impossible to establish the hierarchy of deities which could have resulted from this event (for general discussion of Anatolian religion, see Popko 1995). However, it seems apparent from other texts that it was the sun-goddess of Arinna and her husband, the weather (storm) god of Hatti, who were leading the pantheon in Anatolia. These two deities representing the universal forces of nature were quite a natural choice as the leaders of the pantheon that was a combination of thousands of deities of various ethnic origin.

While the sun-goddess of Arinna makes her first appearance in the annals of Hattusili I, undoubtedly she was originally the Hattian goddess known under the name of Wurusemu. But her relationship with other female sun-goddesses is still a mystery. In all her powers she could have combined principles of other sun deities who were worshipped in Hittite Anatolia. Gurney (1977) points out that there is a strong possibility that the old Hattian sun-goddess, Estan, 'took on the personality of ancient Indo-European god' (p.11), the sun-god of the newcomers, the Hittites. His original name was Sius-summis, 'our god.' The term *sius* meaning 'god' in Hittite is derived from an Indo-European root 'to shine,' and his cognates are *dēius (Proto-Indo-European), Greek Zeus, and Latin *dies, deus* (Gurney 1977) suggesting its original connection with heaven. The further analysis of the old Hittite texts indicate that the 'our god' can be identified with the sun-god, translated as 'our god Siu' which is a parallel name to Zeus as 'god of heavenly light.' While the term 'Sius' became a generic name for god in Hittite, the old Indo-European male sun-god became known as Istanus, an adaptation of the Hattian goddess Estan (Gurney 1977).

The sun-goddess of Arinna eventually became identified with the Hurrian goddess 'Hebat' who leads the procession of female deities represented in Chamber A of Yazilikaya (an open-air sanctuary near Hattussas, capital of the Hittites). This original Hattian goddess, so much embraced by the Hittites and then by the Hurrians, could also have had a connection with the sun-goddess of the underworld to whom sacrifices were made during funeral rituals. Unfortunately, due to the lack of texts her functions and specific characteristics and attributes remain a mystery. They could have been similar to the Ugaritic sun-goddess, Shapsh, who was also connected with the realm of the dead as a sort of messenger between the world of the living and that of the dead (for discussion of her personality see Wiggins 1996). However, the fact remains that the cult of the

Figure 6.7 The central scene of the Hittite open-air sacral place at Yazilikaya. The weather-god (under the Hurrian name Tešub, written with the help of Luwian hieroglyphs) meets his consort, the sun-goddess of Arinna (here under the Hurrian name of Hebat, written in Luwian hieroglyphs), and her son Sharumma. These two deities lead processions of male and female deities respectively

ultimate mother-goddess of Anatolia, the beginning of which can be already seen in the shrines of Çatal Hüyük, survived as the deity of Anatolia under many different names. She was known in Kizzuwatna as Kubaba, and under the name Kybele she was worshipped by the Phrygians of the first millennium B.C., to be eventually identified with the Greek Artemis for whom the famous temple at Ephesus was erected. It seems that her leading position in Anatolia was never endangered and no attempts were made to limit her powers for thousands of years.

The weather god(s) of Anatolia

The weather (storm) god of Anatolia, who was frequently presented as the consort of the sun-goddess of Arinna, was known by many names. His Hattian name was Taru (modified in Hittite as Tarhunna – see Gurney 1977); his Hittite identification was with the God of Nerik (city), the God of Hatti and Hattussas; in Hurrian he was known as Taru Takidu/Darru Dakidu or Tešub; the Neo-Hittites and the Luwians called him Tarhund (Deighton 1982). It seems that in contrast to the mother-goddess of Anatolia, the weather god had to prove himself as the leader of the pantheon. This is clearly illustrated by the native (Hattian) myths of Anatolia about his struggle with the dragon, Illuyanka, which were part of the celebrations of the Purulli Festival, the most important religious event in the Hittite kingdom. This festival was performed at different locations and for various deities. Although it was usually the weather god who was venerated by the Purulli ceremonies, sometimes it could be the underworld goddess Lelwani, often syncretized with the sun-goddess of Arinna (Deighton 1982).

The earlier version (for translated texts of both versions see Hoffner 1990) refers to the storm god of heaven being defeated by the serpent creature who emerged from the hole in the ground. After his defeat he asked his daughter, the goddess Inara, to prepare a feast to take a revenge over the serpent. Inara secured the assistance of a mortal man (the price – a sexual encounter), Hupasiya, to trick the serpent and his offspring whom she invited to her house.

> … The serpent and [his offspring] came up, and they ate and drank. They drank every vessel, so that they became drunk.
> … Now they do not want to go back down into their hole again. Hupasiya came and tied up the serpent with a rope.
> … The storm God came and killed the serpent and the gods were with him. (Hoffner 1990, p.12)

The story proceeds with Inara's dealings with Hupasiya who eventually might have been killed for not following her instructions.

The later version refers to the storm god obviously losing his battle with Illuyanka since the latter ended up in possession of the former's heart and eyes. To get them back again the storm god had to use a trick. When his son of a mortal woman married a daughter of the serpent, he was instructed by his father to request the heart and the eyes as a bride-price (like a dowry) which were delivered to him. Once restored fully to his powers the storm god called for another battle at an unspecified sea in which he killed the serpent and his own son, whose loyalty was obviously to his father-in-law, the serpent.

The texts can barely be called literary compositions. As it should be evident from the above citation, they were rather matter-of-fact stories which needed to be told and possibly re-enacted during the Purulli Festival. Although both texts are being presented as of Hattian origin, one may see in these tales a very prominent motif of the Indo-European battles between two opposite forces, good or order versus evil or chaos, which might have made these stories quite attractive to the Indo-European populations of the second millennium B.C. Anatolia. While chaos and evil forces are represented by the serpent, whose negative qualities have been also stressed by other religions of the Middle East, the 'good' god whose powers had to be restored by this ritual does not seem to be such a positive character himself. His victory is achieved through cunning and with the assistance of his children, whom he simply uses. Whether these features of his character carry any deeper meaning is almost impossible to say, but it is obvious that his powers were limited so he probably was not the creator deity but one of many who appeared in the process.

Another set of typical Hattian stories adopted by the Hittites and others deals with the vanishing gods. The most frequently translated story is the one about the disappearance of the Hattian Telepinu who is often equated with yet another weather (storm) god (Hoffner 1990). The stories usually begin with one of the gods feeling alienated or angry, and deciding to go into hiding. The most common sign of his inevitable departure is his putting the right shoe on his left foot and the left one on the right foot. When he vanishes, all sorts of calamities 'attack' the world of deities and mortals. They are usually listed in detail, as, for example, in the myth of the vanishing Telepinu:

> ... the mountains and the trees dried up, so that the shoots do come (forth). The pastures and the springs dried up, so that famine broke out in the land. Humans and gods are dying out of hunger. The Great Sun God made a feast and invited the Thousand Gods. They ate but couldn't get enough. They drank but couldn't quench their thirst. (Hoffner 1990, p.15)

Of course, depending on which god disappeared, the consequences were somewhat different (Deighton 1982). Then a standardized form of the story proceeds with the massive search for a god. Most commonly it is the eagle and/or the bee who carry out the search, which leads to the return of the god and restoration of the world.

Although Anatolian stories about vanishing gods can be interpreted in the context of a dying god of vegetation (for example Dumuzi of the Mesopotamian tradition), their crisis-related rather than calendar-related character is obvious. This means that the disappearance of the gods was not considered to be a typical seasonal event only but was more tied to the unpredictability of the weather in Anatolia. Again, one must notice the ambiguity of the divine character who just decides to leave without any consideration for the consequences of such behavior, that will inevitably harm all living things. Furthermore, the stress in these stories is on the restoration of the order which cannot happen without each and every divine element in its established place.

The Hurrian competition for the divine kingship

While the central motif of Hattian/Hittite myths seems to be on the restoration of power, the *Kumarbi Cycle* of Hurrian origin focuses on the power struggle between gods for the leadership over the rest. While the sequence of these stories remains uncertain, its main plot is well understood (for complete text see Hoffner 1990). The competition begins with the 'Song of Kumarbi', who invites all deities to listen to his account. The first god listed as the king of heaven is Alalu, who was served by Anu (both of Mesopotamian origin), and ruled for nine years. He was driven out of his position by Anu who took as his servant Kumarbi, a son of Alalu.

> In the ninth year Anu gave battle against Kumarbi. Kumarbi, Alalu's offspring, gave battle against Anu. Anu can no longer withstand Kumarbi's eyes. Anu wriggled loose from his (Kumarbi's) hands and fled. He set out for the sky. (But) Kumarbi rushed after him, seized Anu by the feet/legs, and dragged him down from the sky.... (Kumarbi) bit his (Anu's) loins, and his 'manhood' united with Kumarbi's inside like bronze. (Hoffner 1990, p.40)

The result was rather unexpected for Kumarbi, who became pregnant with many deities including Tešub, Tasmisu and the Tigris River. Although the story is very fragmented and its end is lost, it is apparent that it was Tešub who eventually dethroned Kumarbi, possibly after nine years. However, Kumarbi did not give up and tried to depose Tešub by different means including impregnating 'a great rock' who produced for him his son Ullikummi, his avenger. At the request of Kumarbi, who is addressed as 'father of gods,' the little child was carried by the Irsirra deities to the Dark Earth where he was placed on the right shoulder of Ubelluri (a sort of Anatolian Atlas). Because of his unusual parentage Ullikummi, blind, deaf, and emotionless, grew up very fast and on the fifteenth day his body of basalt stone emerged from the sea. Upon seeing him, Tešub and his allied deities became terrified of his size and perceived powers. Eventually Tešub and his brother Tasmisu went to Ea (this Mesopotamian god frequently appears in Anatolian texts; Kramer and Maier 1989) for advice. Ea approached Ubelluri, asking him

> … Do you not know the Basalt which grew in the water? It is lifted up like a… It has blocked heaven, the holy temples, and Hebat. Is it because you, Ubelluri, are remote from the Dark Earth, that you are unaware of this swiftly rising god?

> … Ubelluri spoke to Ea, 'When they built heaven and earth upon me, I was aware of nothing. And when they came and cut the heaven and earth apart with a copper cutting tool, I was unaware of that. But now something makes my right shoulder hurt, and I don't know who this god is.' (Hoffner 1990, p.59)

Upon hearing these words Ea got an idea of cutting off Ullikummi from Ubelluri's shoulder with the same tool. Although the end of the story is missing it seems that it was Tešub who eventually defeated Ullikummi and, of course, his father.

This Hurrian text is very important because it represents the struggle for power among Anatolian deities. Although both Kumarbi and Tešub are Hurrian deities, it seems that Kumarbi, an underworld god, represented the Hattian/Hittite stratum of well-established deities with their connection with the underground, while Tešub, a celestial deity, was the next (celestial) generation to take over the whole kingdom. If so, the Kumarbi Cycle may be of a similar political importance to the Babylonian *Enûma Eliš*. Furthermore, this story provides the only existing information from Anatolia concerning the creation of heaven and earth, which seems to be the product of the joint efforts of primeval deities whose functions are not known, although some of their names are recorded.

Anatolia – summary

From the above texts, it appears that none of the weather gods was considered to be one of the original creators. Thus it seems reasonable to assume that they achieve their leading position in the Anatolian pantheon through struggle, the same way Zeus did in Hesiod's *Theogony* (the eighth century B.C.) which has been compared to this myth numerous times. Zeus was called the 'Father of Gods' as was Kumarbi, although in both cases it is quite evident that there were many other deities before them. Kramer and Maier (1989) point out that it seems that 'the most significant of the fathers is not the first but the father of the king of the gods – that is, Ea, Kumarbi, Cronus,' (p. 175) who were fathers of Marduk, Tešub, and Zeus.

Although the Hurrian linguistic affiliation is still the subject of scholarly debate, it is possible that the Hurrians represented one of the early groups of Indo-European origins. If so, one might speculate about the Indo-European origin of both stories. This claim can be strengthened by the presence of Ubelluri in whom one can see the beginning of the concept of 'stupid giant' so prevalent in Indo-European mythology.

On the other hand, Hesiod might have 'borrowed' this tradition from Anatolia and adapted details to the Greek reality of his time. Since there is currently no data to support either one of the above suggestions, the interpretation of the role of the weather/storm/sun/sky gods in the process of creation and their place in the original pantheon remain a matter of a personal interpretation. What seems to be the constant feature of the Anatolian religions throughout thousands of years beyond any doubt is the strong and steady position of the mother-goddess whose existence and powers were neither denied nor challenged.

Iran

The fact that the goddess did not play an equal part to that of the male deities of Indo-European tradition is confirmed by the creation stories of Indo-Iranian tradition which are focused on male deities. Not only is Ahura Mazdā or Orhmazd given the title of sole creator, but he does not even need to have a female partner during any part of his life. According to Malandra (1983), it is very characteristic of Indo-Iranian religions that the 'sky-deities' (creators and 'representatives of the highest ethical principles') and 'atmosphere-deities' are usually masculine, while the female deities are more concerned with earth (p. 10). On the other hand, the same tradition also refers to the goddess known as Ardvi Sura Anāhīta, whose origin remains a mystery, but who might have originally represented the female principle of creation and who was eventually – over some period of time – stripped of this honor. Curtis (1993) describes her as 'the goddess of all the waters upon the earth and the source of the cosmic ocean ... as the source of life, purifying the seed of all males and the wombs of all females, and cleansing the milk in the breasts of all mothers' (p. 12). Furthermore, Anāhīta was perceived to personify 'the Heavenly River who feeds, so to speak, all other rivers and streams of the world' (Malandra 1983, p. 117). Thus, in the concept of Anāhīta one might find Homer's idea of original waters known as Oceanus (Ocean) which, in contrast to his name meaning 'ocean', was imagined as the River. If such is the case then Anāhīta could have existed as a cosmic ocean or river even before Ahura Mazdā's creation of the waters of the universe, as the source of life in the 'non-being' state. In this respect she could have represented the older stratum of Iranian religion which might have been patterned on the Sumerian Nammu or Babylonian Tiamat. Her connection with warriors, heroes and anti-heroes who prayed to her for victory could reflect the war aspects of yet another Mesopotamian goddess, Inana (Ištar), and both were connected with the planet Venus. Many authors point to foreign origins of Anāhīta, looking for a similar goddess, in first millennium B.C. Asia Minor (Dresden 1961), or as a combination of at least two foreign goddesses syncretized in the *Avesta* (Malandra 1983). If by the end of the second millennium B.C. Anāhīta was in a way the 'native' goddess of the Middle East (be it of Anatolia, Mesopotamia or Iran), the Indo-Iranians, who were newcomers to the area, might have tried to limit her role by excluding Anāhīta from the official creation ideology but could not have overlooked her already recognized and established powers as a life-giving force. Thus, Ahura Mazdā 'entrusted her with the care of watching over creation' (Dresden 1961, p.353).

While Ahura Mazdā personifies absolute goodness and wisdom, in the best of Indo-European tradition he has his rival, his opposite, Ahriman (Angra Mainyu). According to Zaratuštra, it was in fact Ahura Mazdā who was the father of Angra Mainyu whom he created together with his twin brother Spenta Mainyu (Malandra 1983). The concept of twin brothers is typical of Indo-European mythology which saw twins as the origination of life and death. However, in Iranian tradition, Spenta Mainyu, the 'good god,' is presented as an aspect of Ahura Mazdā in spite of being his son, while Angra Mainyu seems to be an entity by itself (for more discussion see Malandra 1983). It is only between those two male deities that the battle for power over everything occurs, whether in the 9000- or 12,000-year cycle. While Ahura Mazdā – representing the original concept of life and light – is bound to win, he wins his 'war' thanks to his intelligence, not to the involvement of any other being. Angra Mainyu must return to 'the depths' and 'the darkness' in which he fashioned many demons. This motif of the battle for kingship over the rest of existence and non-existence is typical of Indo-European (Iranian) tradition. However, what is not so typical of this tradition is Zaratuštra's sincere belief that Ahura Mazdā will prevail at the end and with the assistance of Saošyants (saviors, sort of prophets) will lead his followers to victory over the dark forces of Angra Mainyu (Malandra 1983). This concept of the savior may have been borrowed by the Judaic tradition and others which developed from it, leading to the creation of a messiah.

But Ahura Mazdā is not the only creator, according to Indo-Iranian tradition. In fact his origins are still a mystery since Ahura Mazdā does not have a counterpart in the Vedic tradition. The closest comparisons can be drawn to the Vedic Varuna, who is also addressed as 'the wise lord,' which is a translation of Ahura Mazdā's name but whose attributes differ considerably (for discussion see Malandra 1983). In contrast to many other deities of the Indo-European tradition, Ahura Mazdā is not exactly a 'flesh-and-blood' god but rather a spiritual, abstract form of deity more common in monotheistic than in polytheistic traditions. The other 'creator' of the combined traditions is Puruṣa (according to the *Rigveda*, the oldest part of the Vedic literature), the flesh-and-blood god who was sacrificed and whose body parts were used in the creation of some elements of the cosmos and the original four castes of the Hindu society (Brandon 1963). These are the same elements to which humans were to return after their death, depending on the original matter from which they came, such as fire, earth or water. This Indo-Iranian (Indo-European) deity could be responsible not only for the methods of disposing of a human body in the Indian tradition but also for similar customs among the Hittites as described later (see p.92).

In addition to the above deities there are other gods such as Mithra, Vayu, Verethragna and Haoma (Indian Soma) who played a very important role in the Iranian pantheon and in the numerous battles which may reflect the human reality at the formative time of their creation. Mithra especially deserves to be mentioned, not only because he is one of the most ancient, confirmed deities of original Indo-European pantheon, but also because Mithraism was a rival religion to Christianity in the Roman Empire. This particular god, the contract-god, was considered to be both a protector and a judge over all living things, especially humans. Since he controlled the cosmic order he could punish those who turned against the truth and rightness. In Roman Mithraism he was also associated with creation through slaughtering the bull representing evil forces in order to create the world by using the purified seeds of this animal. This account was probably based on the Pahlavi books in which Ahriman is represented as killing the primordial bull (Dresden 1961). In the *Avesta* tradition Mithra is presented as being created by Ahura Mazdā himself as his equal, which was probably an attempt to 'pacify' those of non-Zoroastrian circle (for discussion see Malandra 1983). In the *Rigveda*, Mithra was a continuous companion of Varuna. Based on these connections and Mithra's name which can be translated as 'covenant, contract, treaty' and 'friendship' (Malandra 1983, p.56), one can see the focus on the honorable, ethical and just aspects of his divine persona which can reflect the importance of covenant and stability of contracts and structural divisions among the nomadic societies of Eurasia. As such an important concept, Mithra may have been 'transplanted' to the Middle East with the arrival of Indo-European nomadic tribes or groups such as the Hittites and the Persians. This argument about Mithra's 'arrival' might be strengthened by his warrior qualities (a mighty warrior on a chariot killing covenant violators with a mace) and his ability to replenish earthly waters by releasing both rivers and rain. The combination of all the above features may have earned him the title of the Anatolian weather-god whose qualities he obviously represented and it might be for this reason that his memory was carried on by the Hittite pantheon in addition to the *Rigveda* and the *Avesta*.

Finally, it must be mentioned that although the majority of Indo-Iranian deities were somewhat ambivalent in their nature, including both light and dark aspects of their dominion, it was only the original couple, Ahura Mazdā and Angra Mainyu who were presented as the absolute positive and negative respectively (for discussion see Brandon 1963). This allowed for the explanation of the world's ambivalence, the existence of both good and bad, on the simplest possible level without getting into the peculiarities of divine character and the actions of multiple deities of other pantheons.

Pre-Biblical Syria–Palestine

One of the most striking features of the Canaanite religions before the Bible is the territoriality of their deities occasionally compared to the territoriality of Anatolian deities (for example, Baal versus the weather god/Tešub). Deighton (1982) generalized this tendency as follows: 'Elim were nomadic in origin, and the Ba'alim came from the settled agricultural Cana'anites' and both were believed to come from below ground, not from the above (p.95). Each of them was responsible for the maintenance of the part of earth that was their dominion. This territoriality carried on to the Pentateuch with references to the worshipping of the Hebrew god on his own soil (Deighton 1982). However, it must be remembered that Canaanite territoriality did not necessarily refer to the land or physical domain only but also to the functions of different deities. Since they were appointed by El, he is the one whom 'territoriality' issues do not concern – he is a high god.

This territoriality is particularly visible in the Baal cycle which represents a typical struggle for kingship among the gods. However, as Smith (1994) indicates, there is more into this cycle than just divine politics. According to him, this political story should be recognized as integrating three levels – cosmic, human, natural – into one universal unity influenced by Baal.

In order to understand the importance of the Baal cycle one must be introduced to the main players who were the most important deities of the Canaanite pantheon. Their presentation is structured according to their position in the pantheon as it can be reconstructed from the available texts.

The first divine couple: El and Asherah or Yahweh and Asherah?

There is not much doubt that at the head of the pantheon was the god El, whose epithets included titles of 'the King,' 'the Father of Gods' (Coogan 1978, p.12), 'Father of Humanity,' and 'Creator of Creatures' (Smith 1994, p.83; for other epithets see Cross 1973). These titles as well as the title 'Creatress of Gods' given to his wife Ahirat (Smith 1994) or Asherah-Elat (Cross 1973) suggest strongly that El and his consort were responsible for the creation of at least deities and humans, even if they were not an original mover. It must be also mentioned that the root for titles 'creator, creatrix' of the gods is believed to mean to 'acquire/own' so the title of the 'owner' of the gods might be more appropriate in both cases (Handy 1994). This translation is being strengthened by the Hittite myth of Elkunirša – that is, El – where he is addressed as the 'owner of the earth' (Handy 1994, p.76). This does not mean that the title of parents of all gods should be taken away from both El and Asherah since many other texts refer to them as the father and mother of all deities, not necessarily by conception and birth, but rather by status.

Although it is commonly accepted that El's name means 'god' (as *il* – for discussion see Cross 1973) like its cognate 'Allah' in Arabic, its exact etymology is still a subject of discussion focusing on its derivation either from 'strong' or from 'first' (Coogan 1978, p.12). It seems then that El was the first god with creative powers thanks to whom everything was born, even if sometimes there are references to the 'older gods' as in the tradition of Mesopotamia where 'ancient gods' existed almost in parallel to the universe in creation. Furthermore, the creative attributes and the leading role of El in Canaan is confirmed by the Pentateuch itself where Yahweh, the only god, is frequently identified by his name, or by its plural form 'Elohim.' For example, in Exodus 6:2–3 (part of the Priestly tradition) the god addresses Moses: 'I am Yahweh. I revealed myself to Abraham, to Isaac, and to Jacob as El Šadday, but was not known by them by my name Yahweh.' This and many other passages referred to by various scholars (Cross 1973) indicate rather clearly that the only god of the Pentateuch could have been a modified divine form of Canaanite or West Semitic El (Cross 1973). His connection with El is strengthened also by archaeological findings, especially by drawings and inscriptions discovered at Kuntillet Ajrud, Sinai, in the second part of the 1970s (Meshel 1979), and dated to the ninth or the eighth century B.C. The inscriptions contained the names of Yahweh, El, Asherah, Baal and other pagan deities. The most interesting of these inscriptions and drawings were found on two jars (pithoi). Both of them were found in the so-called bench room of a structure which was described as being connected with some sort of religious activity. Since the full description, transliteration, translation, and discussion are included in Meshel's (1979) article, only the most striking features relevant to the subject are presented here. The most controversial drawing found on one of the jars presents 'a seated woman playing the lyre; the god Bes in the center with his genitals (or tail) exposed between his legs; and another unidentified deity on the left

Figure 6.8 The controversial scene from one of the pithoi found at Kuntillet Ajrud (Sinai) which represents the god Bes (central figure) accompanied possibly by Yahweh and Asherah (here as possible consort of Yahweh) playing music in the background. This identification is suggested by the inscription above the headdress of Yahweh

similarly exposed' (Meshel 1979, p.30). Thanks to careful analysis of the inscription associated with this presentation as well as with the support of other material coming from this site, Meshel (and after him others; Dever 1984; Gaber and Dever 1998) was able to identify the 'unidentified deity' as possibly Yahweh and the sitting woman as his wife, Asherah. What a blasphemous notion! Not only that Yahweh is presented not as the 'one and only' god, but also that he 'stole' El's wife! Furthermore, considering the fact that Yahweh was not to be presented in visual arts, seeing him in a rather relaxing environment with Bes and Asherah is a double blasphemy. Finally, if the first figure to the left is really Yahweh, then he is depicted as having his genitals exposed or, at best, as having a tail. Both the drawings and the inscriptions appeared to be anathema to the teachings of the Pentateuch, especially of the Yahwistic tradition which must have been known at the time. Their presence might be explained by the transitional period in the history of Syro-Palestinian religion reflecting possibly the struggle between Hebrew monotheism and deities of pagan traditions as described by the Book of Kings (Meshel 1979). By assuming Asherah as his wife, Yahweh might have been on his way to win the final battle with El, at least in the eyes of the people of Kuntillet Ajrud.

Another association of the Hebrew god with El can be seen in his name, 'Yahweh.' This name, which remains a controversial matter in spite of volumes written about the subject, is considered (by some) to be derived as 'a causative imperfect of the Canaanite-Proto-Hebrew verb *hwy*, "to be"' (Cross 1973, pp.65–66), pointing clearly toward the ancient god of Canaanites, the creator-god.

El's home is a mountain which is also a source of fresh water with two rivers originating at its base (possibly the northern part of the Lebanon Mountains; for discussion of his abode see Naccache 1996). This brings to mind the image of the Mesopotamian cosmic mountain (universe), below which the fresh waters of *abzu* exist (for texts, see Cross 1973; for more precise references see Smith 1994). There he has his tent, not a palace, which may reflect the nomadic tradition of the area before its urbanization. This is quite likely if one takes into consideration the possibility that the Baal cycle could be much older than its first written version (see Smith 1994) and, as with many other oral compositions, had to be adjusted over a period of time with the changing reality of its culture.

In this tent, the tabernacle (shrine) was a central point of El's meetings with his divine council, including Baal, at specially organized banquets during which it seems that El liked to get drunk. The location of both the mountain and El's abode is specified further – 'in the distant north.' However, as Cross (1973) points out, a lot of mountains can be identified with El's abode, including the Biblical description of Eden as 'the garden of God at the Mount of God' and Zion (pp.38–39).

Although El seems to be a somewhat 'withdrawn' or 'retired' leader of the Ugaritic pantheon, with his active position being assumed by Baal, he is also portrayed as an ancient god whose virility is essential for the existence of the world. Some scholars tried to argue that El was replaced by Baal because he was so old that he became impotent while Baal was at the peak of his sexual prowess, but this does not seem to be the case (Handy 1994). After all, it was El who was the father of Dawn and Dusk, who were born after El proved himself sexually to his two wives at the same time (for text see Cross

1973). Furthermore, El is presented as a judge – for example, in the conflict between Baal and Mot – or even as a warrior who protects the legendary ruler Kirta. However, since El was followed by Baal as an active leader of the Canaanite religion, Baal 'inherited' some of El's qualities and associations; for example, Asherah was presented as his wife, not El's (Cross 1973).

Asherah, the wife of El, was considered to be the mother-goddess and creatress in Canaanite mythology. However, her importance in the Canaanite pantheon has been underplayed by many scholars, while others believe that she represented the highest authority together with El. Not only was she represented as El's wife in Ugarit but her consort in Israel was Yahweh himself, and possibly in other cities she joined Baal as a spouse (Handy 1994). Asherah was responsible for assisting El in the selection of individual deities to their designated places and was always the one who could get his cooperation. She was associated with both a lion and a serpent, and addressed with epithets such as 'Lady of the Serpent' and 'Lady of the Lion' (for philological/linguistic discussion of these attributes see Cross 1973).

Baal – the not-so-supreme god

Baal succeeded El as an active ruler in the Canaanite pantheon. Whether there was a Canaanite myth in a tradition of the Kumarbi cycle, Dunnu theogony, or Hesiod's account of the struggle for kingship among generations of divine forces is unknown at this time but quite possible. As mentioned above, El himself was not the first god although he was referred to as such. Even his title as a creator is not very consistent since his father was Heaven and his mother was Earth. But through the victorious battle he has claimed the title of the 'Father of Gods.' But as Kumarbi he was either forced out or resigned to Baal, who was not even his son by birth in most references. Whether this was a 'local' sequence of events such as an agricultural god winning over his pastoral rival (a conflict quite popular in the Middle Eastern and Indo-European traditions) or a tradition borrowed from neighbors in Anatolia still remains a subject of much discussion but little agreement.

However, El was not stripped of his powers: he seems to choose not to get involved in everyday activities which became the domain of Baal. His dominant position is clear in the Baal cycle, when Baal needs permission from El in order to build a palace (temple) for himself. He obviously understands that for some reasons he might not be granted the permit so he tricks Anat into helping him persuade El that he is also a deserving one. Baal's inferior role to El can also be seen in the fact that he, as well as other deities such as Mot and Yamm, was appointed to his office by El, who seems responsible for a properly functioning cosmos (Handy 1994).

Baal was granted the title of a king in Canaanite mythology. However, it is clear that his kingship is limited since the most important decisions are still being made by El with the help of Asherah. On the other hand, he was the most involved deity in everyday affairs of the world. It was his struggle with the god of sterility and death, Mot, the result of which affected the people and the land the most. For this reason Baal is considered to be a typical fertility god by many scholars, although one should argue that his fertility aspects, as related to thunderstorm, rain, and dew, make him more similar to Anatolian weather gods than to a standard dying god of vegetation.

In Ugaritic mythology Baal is presented as the 'Lord of Ugarit,' although he himself boasts that 'I alone will rule over the gods' (Coogan 1978, p.12) implying that his kingdom is limitless. But this seems very unlikely in view of events described by the Baal cycle, where he is often presented as dependent on other deities, not particularly smart (Handy 1994), and always in need of someone to help him win his battles.

His abode is on Mount Zaphon where he probably lives with three women (his daughters; the same number of daughters was ascribed to Allah in pre-Islamic tradition, see Gordon 1961). But before building his own palace he lived with El (Smith 1994). Baal's ambition in life is to be a leader among other deities. Since he is one of the 'younger' deities, like Marduk of *Enûma Eliš*, he must earn his position the hard way, by a victorious battle with his opponents Yamm (the Sea), and Mot (Death).

The Baal cycle begins with Yamm's demand that Baal surrender to him (for line by line analysis of this cycle see Smith 1994). The reason for this demand is not clear, but if any analogy can be drawn between Babylonian Tiāmat and Yamm then the Sea – who might have represented a watery chaos of the beginning – could have perceived a young and overzealous Baal to be a threat to the already established order of creation led by El. If so, there is no surprise that El agrees to this demand, especially in view of the fact that, in contrast to Tiāmat, Yamm does not seem to threaten anyone else and is controlled by El who sometimes calls him 'my son.' It is also El who names Yamm for the battle against Baal, like Kumarbi named his son, Ullikummi, for a battle with Tešub. However, Baal is not willing to submit to the Sea, whom he fights possibly on Mount Sapan (Smith 1994). This battle is very successful, Baal using the weapons prepared by Kothar-and-Khasis (god-artisan): '...strikes the head of Prince [Yamm],/Between the eyes of Judge River./Yamm collapses and falls to the earth,/His joints shake,/And his form sinks./Baal drags and dismembers (?) Yamm,/He destroys Judge River' (Smith 1994, p.323).

The description of the battle and especially the final act of dismembering the enemy echoes older stories from both Mesopotamia and Egypt. However, in contrast to them, nothing new is being created from Yamm's body. Baal emerges as a king but his victory is not as convincing as that of Marduk or of Yahweh in his conflict with Rahab (Job 26:12–13). He could not win if not for magical weapons and the support of the goddess Athtart/Ashtarte. Once again, he is a ruler but with limited powers. It also must be mentioned that Baal's battle with Yamm and his title 'Rider on the Clouds' are very similar to the Pentateuch's description of Yahweh's conflict with the water monster as noted by many authors (Coogan 1978; Smith 1994). Whether they both have their beginning in Mesopotamian tradition or some unknown West Semitic or even Indo-European source remains the subject of ongoing studies (for a comparison of Yahweh's battles and Enûma Eliš see Heidel 1951).

The second main theme begins with the war goddess (Virgin) Anat who is also Baal's sister and wife (for more information about Anat, see Walls 1992). She is battling victoriously enemies of Baal who, in the meantime, proclaims his victory and asks her to cease bloody fighting (in which she might have been on her way to annihilate humankind) and to come to him. Whether it was Baal's conscious attempt to save humans from Anat's rage is unclear, but he uses a trick to get her to visit him. He promises to reveal some sort of a secret to her. Upon making sure that no enemies of Baal are left to be slaughtered, Anat follows her inborn curiosity and with the promise of bringing love and prosperity to earth goes to visit Baal. He welcomes her and instead of telling her the secret, he must have complained to her that he is a god without a house (a temple). It seems that only Anat can convince her father El, the Bull, to give permission for the construction of the abode worthy of this new king. Obviously she is ready to use violence to receive this permission from El. However, Anat's support for Baal's plans was not sufficient since the required permission is obtained only after Baal bribes Asherah, the mother of gods. Then a rather lengthy description of building the temple follows.

The fact that Baal did not have a temple prior to his victorious battle with Yamm indicates that he was not considered to be of any significance until this confrontation. But since there cannot be a king without a palace (Yamm already had his), so the construction of a great abode for a new king was necessary. This reminds us of Marduk who built his temple in Babylon after defeating Tiāmat. The importance of this act is also reflected in the Pentateuch with the description (quite similar to Baal's account) of erecting the temple for Yahweh (see II Samuel, I Kings). Many scholars agree that such an act has its connection with the creation process as either creating cosmos or fructifying it (for discussion see Smith 1994). While it should be obvious that the universe was already created, the building of the temple in Baal's cycle may actually represent the act of repetition as known, for example, from ancient Egypt, where every temple was a recreation of the original act. Then, by building the temple, Baal re-establishes existing principles and preserves the order of existence.

During the process of construction a conflict over the installation of windows arises between Kothar-and-Khasis and Baal. Originally Baal refuses to have a window, possibly because of the belief that Death uses this house opening to claim its victims (Coogan 1978). However, after conquering numerous cities, Baal changes his mind. The window is installed and the setting is ready for a final theme.

Baal challenges Mot (Death) by refusing to pay him tribute. Insulted, Mot reminds him that by conquering the Sea (here referred to by names of Lothan and Serpent) Baal 'caused a cosmic collapse' (Coogan 1978, p.82) or rather the collapse of order. The punishment for such a crime is death. Frightened by the description of Mot's powers, Baal enters the realm of the underworld and dies. He is accompanied on his trip by his children and all elements associated with his life-giving source – rain and thunderstorm. Asherah's attempts to provide successors, her two sons, to Baal's office failed. The world becomes controlled by Death and with him, sterility and drought. Being dead, Baal is completely powerless but his supporters are not. It is again Virgin Anat who combats Mot and kills him. Miraculously, Baal and the world are revived for the next seven years when the challenge is repeated.

The narrative of the above compositions should make it clear that not only was Caananite mythology itself very much influenced by traditions from other parts of the Middle East, but it also constituted the roots of many concepts represented in the Pentateuch and other related sources. As only one god, Yahweh incorporated in his personality characteristics, names, and even actions of two leading deities of the Canaanite pantheon: El and Baal. The result was rather confusing: Yahweh appears to be quite inconsistent and not very merciful, fighting forces which should not have existed in monotheistic religion in the first place.

Conclusions

In contrast to polytheistic traditions of the Middle East, the monotheistic systems, which may have been somewhat patterned on the teachings of the *Avesta* (with Ahura Mazdā as a sort of 'transitional' god between these two ideologies), have had to struggle with the logic of the world organization and its many contradictions expressed by the presence of both good and evil. Although the only god was to be the absolute goodness, he also has to be held responsible for the creation and/or contribution to the existence of negative forces since there is no-one else to blame. The Zoroastrians were among the first ones to see this contradiction and to condemn the Christian god for allowing his creation and his son to suffer (Hinnells 1975).

After the above presentation of numerous gods and goddesses involved in the creation process or in the organization and maintenance of the universe it should be clear that – with an exception of the most ancient sources from Mesopotamia and Egypt – divine forces constitute frequently an amalgam of traditions and attributes selected to advance whatever model of reality was necessary at the time. Since this selection was not done by one author or at one time, many contradictions have found its way into any final version. In polytheistic traditions conflicts in personalities and/or actions of any one divinity were easy to explain by fusing various deities or by 'creating' their negative or any other aspects. Since in these religions deities were perceived as divine 'humans'– that is, often morally and emotionally weak as people are (for example, overindulging in alcohol in Mesopotamia, Egypt, Syria–Palestine) but with inborn power – then knowledge and immortality and all the miseries and injustices of this world could be 'blamed' on them. However, in order for the world to exist, the overall order had to be maintained, so even the deities were the subject of universal justice.

Both henotheism and monotheism were attempts to limit or to eliminate a number of deities in a society, focusing on the ones who were perceived to be the most powerful. This seems to lead to a drastic decrease in the power and involvement of female deities across the Middle East. Their place was assumed by male leaders, causing the emergence of new methods in creation and a new world order. Furthermore, the famous struggles for kingship may reflect a conscious attempt of their creators to solve political, social and/or ideological problems in their area. It is interesting to note that in view of present knowledge of ancient sources, the bloody battles for kingship did not occur until the arrival of nomadic people to the Middle East, be it of Semitic or Indo-European origins. This was the time when changes took place everywhere but in Egypt (because of its isolation): the cunning, unmanageable but 'likable' deities of the Sumerian tradition were replaced by somewhat 'military' characters. The god of political losers would give in to the victorious one. The ancient deities whose meaning became so complicated and confusing would make a place for those who were more comprehensible. The mean gods whose negativity influenced earthly matters would be 'killed' – at least temporarily

– to give the world a chance to revive. However, their past or present existence would be acknowledged, although not necessarily followed by an active worship.

Polytheistic and henotheistic religions could afford to be tolerant. While recognizing the power of their positive divine forces, there was always a place for the negative ones. The Iranian tradition is probably the best example of solving the problems of too many deities by proclaiming Ahura Mazdā to be the only one, good, just, and loving god, responsible for all positive creations, emotions, influence, and so forth. As such incontestable goodness, Ahura Mazdā could not be responsible for human and others' miseries and that is why his evil twin, Ahura Mazdā, was established. Having these two as the main, but not the only, forces of the universe solved all the problems that the monotheistic religions have to deal with.

Whether or not a monotheistic god of Genesis and/or of the Quran is perceived as an ultimate goodness, the fact remains that in spite of his positive attributes and actions, the world is full of suffering and the number of candidates to be blamed for it is rather limited. While the only god often exhibits characteristics of the 'unmanageable' deities of Mesopotamia or Egypt or Canaan, leading to at least questionable decisions (such as the annihilation of the living world with the use of a deluge), his actions still have to be explained in a positive light. Thus, neither the Pentateuch nor the Quran and all other supportive 'holy sources' could try to eliminate the negative elements which could be held responsible. While humans are usually blamed for their own misery caused by crossing the divine law, they do it because they allow negative forces (satans, demons) to invade their thoughts and their actions. Although neither of these forces is recognized as divine, it is still obvious that they carry all godly attributes: power, knowledge and immortality. The only difference is that they are stripped of their divine title.

This leads to the conclusion that monotheistic religions which evolved in the Middle East are in reality henotheistic systems. In order to revere only one god, the others had to be either eliminated or denied a godly recognition. Furthermore, people had to be given so-called 'free will' so the suffering that they occasionally go through could be attributed to their own actions. In this scheme of events there is no place for any heroes who, through their brave actions, can be even admitted physically to the presence of divinity. The new 'monotheistic heroes' are only those who follow the god's commands and to whom the god himself decides to appear. Thus, the followers are not even given a chance to influence the god's will and order in the matters essential for the creation and organization of the universe. The rule is established – divinity is beyond the reach of all mortals so they do not even have to try. In this sense, the polytheistic religions of the Middle East were much more sensitive to human needs, dreams and aspirations. While their role was limited to the divine servants, at least the bravest or most desperate of them could try to change mortal destiny and, at least for a while, join their deities in whichever world they chose to visit. Those were the 'chosen' although not always the 'divine' people.

7

Almost Divine? Chosen People

While the overwhelming majority of people in polytheistic religions of the ancient Middle East could have never reached divine status, there were some individuals whose fate was of special interest to gods and/or goddesses and who reached the status which can be described as semi-divine. In Egypt each and every pharaoh was considered to be divine and some of the legendary wise men (such as Imhotep) were later worshipped as divine beings. In Anatolia a king upon his death was designated as one who 'became God' (Soden 1994, p.69) but this does not mean that he was really perceived to be divine. The situation was probably similar in pre-Biblical Syria–Palestine. In Mesopotamia, kings were perceived as being mortal although some of them, such as Akkadian Naramsin, set a divine determinative before their names. Others, such as Šulgi of Ur, claimed their divinity after performing the ritual of a 'sacred marriage.' However, this type of upgrading one's status did not change the fact that divinity was beyond their reach. Three great heroes of Mesopotamia (Etana, Adapa, Gilgamesh) were able to ascend beyond the human world of the profane, but their conscious or subconscious quest for immortality (which is a part of divine status) was not successful. The fourth one, the survivor of the Flood known under various names in the Mesopotamian literature (including Ziusudra, Atrahasīs and Ūtnapišti), was the only one to whom eternity was granted. In Ugaritic mythology it was a mortal himself, Aqhat, who turned down the chance of immortality. In Genesis and the Quran the first couple carried the honor of being semi-divine, at least at the beginning of their time. Stories of these special people enable us to understand the established rules and regulations which allowed the universe to function after its principles and form were created.

Mesopotamia

The following are stories of three heroes, Etana, Adapa and Gilgamesh, whose memories survived until modern days and who are indirectly or directly associated with the creation and place of humankind in the universe. If these three heroes had succeeded in their endeavors, the world would have been changed forever. The deities provided them with a chance, but as humans, they were not able to use it due to their weaknesses. Thus, the universe and its laws as established at the day of creation remained unchanged.

Etana: The quest for the 'plant of life/birth'

According to the Sumerian King List, Etana, the legendary king of Kish to which the kingship descended after the Flood, was given the name of 'a shepherd, the one who to heaven ascended,/The one who consolidated all lands,/Became king and reigned 1,560 years' (Jacobsen 1966, p.81).

Although the King List does not refer to him as the first ruler of Kish, the legend of Etana gives him the honor of being chosen as the first one to rule over the city that deities themselves just finished building (Foster 1995). The pious king continued the building activities in Kish where he erected a temple for Adad (Sumerian Iškur, the storm god) in whose shade a poplar tree was growing. This tree became home to a snake who resided in its roots and to an eagle who made its nest on the crown. They lived in friendship until one day when the eagle developed an appetite for the snake's offspring, which he consumed. Upon the discovery of this horrible act of betrayal, not even mentioning the loss of children, the snake called on the god Šamaš (Sumerian Utu) to punish the eagle: "'...[The eagle] must not es[cape] from your net,/Th(at) malignant Anzu,/Who harbored evil [against his friend]!'" (Foster 1995, pp.106–107).

Šamaš prepared a rather diabolical plan, according to which the serpent hid inside a dead wild ox's belly and was to wait for the eagle to come for yet another meal. "'When he [the eagle] comes inside, seize him by his wings,/Cut off his wings his pinions and tailfeathers,/Pluck him and cast him into a bottomless (?) pit,/Let him die there of hunger and thirst'" (Foster 1995, p.107). The serpent did as he was told but the eagle did not die. Its pitiful lament was eventually heard by Šamaš who himself could not act as a rescuer so he decided to use Etana as his agent.

In the meantime, the mighty king was very upset because he could not produce an heir. The lack of a male heir appears to be a common source of grief for rulers in the Middle East. The Ugaritic story of Aqhat begins with his father Danel (possibly a prototype of the Biblical Daniel – see Coogan 1978) performing rituals for seven days in order to communicate with his patron deity Baal, to ask for his assistance in bringing a son to his family. While in the Canaanite story Danel was simply granted his wish by El (as was Kirta, yet another hero of Ugaritic tradition) and Aqhat was born, in an older version from Mesopotamia, Etana is only given a chance to produce a son with the help of the plant of birth or life which he must obtain himself. However, he had no means to fly to heaven to secure it. Šamaš advised him to save the eagle and then, in return, the eagle would make his dreams come true. The deal was made and finally Etana was carried to the heavens by the eagle. The description of their trip is one of the most sought-after texts by the advocates of extraterrestrials in the emergence of civilizations on earth, due to the perceived necessity of a plane – if not a spaceship – for such a trip. Upon passing the heavenly gates of various deities, the eagle kept asking Etana about his view of the earth and waters. The higher they flew, the smaller these appeared. Finally, Etana lost his courage because: "'I [Etana] looked, but could not see the land!/Nor were [my eyes] enough to (find) the vast sea!/My friend [the eagle], I won't go up to heaven!/Set me down, let me go off to my city!'" (Foster 1995, p.113).

Since the rest of the text is very fragmented or missing, the end of the story remains unknown. One might speculate that Etana, in spite of divine help, was not able to gather the plant of birth/life, because it would be too much power for mortals to have. This

Figure 7.1 Etana, the legendary king of Kish flying to heaven on the eagle whom he saved. From a cylinder seal

plant of birth may have had the power not only to provide a new birth but also to sustain and/or rejuvenate life (as Gilgamesh's plant), thus to produce 'miracles' which were only the domain of deities. Such an ending would be very consistent with the stories of Gilgamesh and Adapa, two other heroes, who lost their quests for the impossible.

However, in spite of what seems to be an unsuccessful venture to heaven, Etana was given a son by the Mesopotamian tradition, probably by some other means. His son, Balih, appears on the Sumerian King List as the next ruler who reigned in Kish for around 400 years after his father died. Etana, so beloved by deities, was at the end treated as any other mortal and had to descend to the Nether World. The power of creation and eternity was only reserved for the divine.

Adapa: The missed opportunity to become immortal

The story of Adapa must have been one of the most favorite stories in ancient Mesopotamia and probably outside since it survived into modern times in several copies. The oldest existing recording of this story, from the fourteenth century B.C., comes from the Egyptian archives at Tell-el-Amarna, while the others were found in the library of Assurbanipal in Nineveh (Speiser 1955, p.76).

Adapa, the beloved human of the god Ea, was created or begotten by him as a very wise man, a sage (*apkallu*), but was denied immortality at his birth. He resided in Eridu where he attended the temple of Ea in the most admiring way. One day when Adapa was sailing on his boat, the south wind blew so strongly that it drifted. The wisest of men felt so strongly about his right that he cursed the wind and broke 'her' wing. The wind stopped blowing and after seven days had passed, Anu became quite concerned and inquired about the reason. Upon learning of Adapa's improper behavior, Anu demanded to see him. Ea, obviously concerned about the well-being of his son, instructed him how to behave upon his ascension to heaven. He explained to the sage how to amuse the guardians at Anu's gate, Dumuzi and Gizzida, so they 'will say a "good word" to Anu' (Izre'el 1992, p.217). But he also warned Adapa that: "'You will be offered food of death, so do not eat:/You will be offered deadly water, so do not drink'" (Izre'el 1992, p.217).

Adapa trusted Ea and followed his instructions. Unfortunately, trusting Ea also made Adapa unable or unwilling to use his own judgment. He must have amused and/or impressed Anu so much that instead of offering Adapa the 'food and drink of death,' the god of heaven presented the wise mortal with 'the food and water of life.' Both were refused by Adapa. 'Anu looked at him; he has laughed at him./"Come, Adapa, why did you not eat nor drink?/Hence you cannot live! Alas, poor humanity!"' (Izre'el 1992, p.218).

Certainly, poor humanity it was. Adapa, unknowingly, passed up the chance for himself, and probably for others, to share eternal life with deities. Having been tricked by Ea, whose cunningness is praised by Anu (Foster 1995), Adapa was returned to earth after being offered a glimpse into the awesomeness of heaven.

Although the word *adapu* means 'wise,' Kramer and Maier (1989) and others (Jacobsen 1970) suggest that it can also mean 'humankind'. Thus, Adapa, the first antediluvian sage, the 'model of humanity' as he is called by Kramer and Maier (1989, p.116), is being shown his or our place in the universe as servants to the deities without any chance of immortality. Furthermore, the Neo-Assyrian version from the seventh century B.C. indicates that Adapa not only missed the best possible gift from the gods but also brought with him illnesses and diseases for humankind, including even insomnia (Heidel 1951; Kramer and Maier 1989). The only good thing granted to him was his everlasting fame.

Adapa is definitely not Adam of the Yahwistic account, to whom he is sometimes compared, because the death and diseases that he 'brought' upon all humans were not the result of his disobedience. On the contrary, his obedience appears to be his weak point. Since, again, the difference between humans and the deities is in the power, knowledge and immortality of the latter, one might wonder whether humankind is allowed to keep only one of these three characteristics. Adapa was allowed to keep his wisdom, but could not have eternal life because having both attributes would provide him with power reserved only for deities. Adam lost his immortality by eating the fruit from the Tree of the Knowledge of Good and Evil, so he gained the second godly attribute, but had to give back the first. In both cases the original order remained intact.

Gilgamesh: The timeless quest for immortality

Most scholars agree that Gilgamesh, one of the most famous world heroes, was a historical person, a king of Uruk who ruled some time at the beginning of the Early Dynastic Period. However, Black and Green (1997) also point to the existence of the god Gilgamesh who was already worshipped in the latter part of the same period in different cities of Sumer. Tigay (1982) refers to the status of Gilgamesh as a god whose worship could have been established within one or two centuries of his death. According to the Sumerian King List, Gilgamesh was a son of a '*lillû*-demon,' 'a high priest of Kullab' who ruled in the postdiluvian Uruk for 126 years (Jacobsen 1966). As a real person he was probably a contemporary of the historically confirmed rulers of Kish, Enmebaragesi and his son Agga.

In addition to Uruk, Gilgamesh was also associated with the city of Ur where he was especially revered by the kings of the Third Dynasty who referred to him as their "'divine brother" and "friend"' (Black and Green 1997, p.89). One of the Assyrian school exercises is a fictional letter from Gilgamesh which is translated by Foster (1995). In this letter written by Gilgamesh to a foreign king he refers to himself as

> …[Gilgamesh, k]ing of Ur, the Kullabian, created by Anu, [Enlil], and Ea, favorite of Shamash, beloved of Marduk, who rules all lands from the horizon to the zenith like a cord [ ], whose feet daised monarchs kiss, the king who draws in (?) all lands, from sunrise to sunset, like a cord… (Foster 1995, p.368).

Thus, he is presented as the king of both cities, and protected by the most important deities of the Sumero-Semitic pantheon (for more information concerning Gilgamesh's historical background see Tigay 1982).

There are five narratives of Sumerian origin which have survived from the first part of the second millennium B.C. and are known today under the following titles: 'Gilgamesh and Agga,' 'Gilgamesh and the Cedar Forest' (also as 'Gilgamesh and Huwawa'), 'Gilgamesh and the Bull of Heaven,' 'The Death of Gilgamesh' and 'Gilgamesh, Enkidu and the Nether World.' With time these compositions were compiled into one long narrative commonly known as 'The Epic of Gilgamesh' whose most complete version was discovered in the Nineveh library of the Assyrian king, Assurbanipal (668 to around 627 B.C.). The most current reconstruction of this epic, the Standard Babylonian version, in cuneiform and transliteration, is provided by Parpola (1997b). Because of the limited scope of this book, the stories listed above are not summarized here in any detail (for discussion of sources and the stories themselves see Dalley 1989; Tigay 1982), although relevant events and descriptions are referred to elsewhere in this book. The focus of the following discussion is only on Gilgamesh's humanity, his quest for immortality and his relationship with yet another human, Enkidu.

The Epic begins with the description of Gilgamesh, who is praised as the lord whose wisdom carried the knowledge about the antediluvian period (for a translation of the Epic see Gardner and Maier 1984). As the first king of Uruk he is credited with, among other things, the erection of its wall and the founding of the temple of *E-ana*, consecrated to Inana/Ištar. He was two-thirds divine after his mother, the goddess Ninsun ('the great wild cow'), who was married to his father, a deified but still very human king Lugalbanda, from whom Gilgamesh 'inherited' humanity which constituted one-third of his nature. Since he obviously did not have immortality, his divine connection would be limited to both power and knowledge. The Prologue, full of praises, indicates that Gilgamesh must have been quite 'bored' after accomplishing many great things, because he started to terrorize the city, possibly by forcing his citizens to continuous labor and by his sexual appetite directed particularly toward young brides (abusing *ius prima noctis*, 'the right of the first night' with a bride before a groom can enter her chamber). His behavior was definitely considered excessive and abusive, because the deities decided to take some action, instigated by people's lamentations. Aruru, the mother-goddess, was called to create a man, Gilgamesh's double or second image, to stop his actions and to bring peace to Uruk.

> [A]ruru washed her hands, pinched off clay, (and) threw (it) on the
> steppe:
> [...] valiant Enkidu she created, the offspring...of Ninurta.
> His whole body is [cov]ered with hair, the hair of (his) head is like (that
> of) a woman;
> The locks of the hair of his head sprout like grain.
> He knows nothing about people or land, he is clad in a garb like
> Sumuqan.
> With the gazelles he eats grass;
> With the game he presses on to the drinking-place;
> With the animals his heart delights at the water. (Heidel 1946, p.19)

Thus Enkidu, naked and hairy and obviously unaware of his humanity, was brought to life in a fashion similar to Adam. The news about this 'human beast' reached Gilgamesh through trappers and hunters who spotted Enkidu but could not approach him. In order to tame the brute, Gilgamesh sent the courtesan Šamhat to use her charms to separate Enkidu from the wild beasts with whom he liked to roam through the wilderness:

> The lass freed her breasts, bared her bosom,
> And he possessed her ripeness.
> She was not bashful as she welcomed his ardor.
> She laid aside her cloth and he rested upon her.
> She treated him, the savage, to a woman's task,
> As his love was drawn unto her.
> For six days and seven nights Enkidu comes forth,
> Mating with the lass. (Speiser 1973, p.44)

After this time spent with the prostitute, Enkidu was rejected by his previous 'friends,' the animals, and was unable to resume the only life that he had known. Thus, his first passionate encounter with a woman can be explained as Enkidu's realization of his humanity (see Adam and Eve and their 'Fall' in Chapter 10). He started this transition from the 'barbarian' to the 'civilized' state almost as an animal who was not able to control himself upon meeting his own female counterpart, but finished it as a full human. He proved his manhood through six days and seven nights of sexual passion and passed the 'ritual' of initiation into a civilized society.

Since the animals would not associate with him Enkidu followed the holy courtesan to the city of Uruk. There, the confrontation between Gilgamesh and Enkidu took place when the king of Uruk attempted to deflower yet another bride before her husband. The wrestling match between these two powerful humans ended quite unexpectedly. They embraced, and professed their friendship for one another. Their friendship was so strong that Gilgamesh professes his love for Enkidu more than once in the Epic. Leick (1994) interprets their relationship as comparable to the one between the insatiable Inana (here Gilgamesh) and her masculine and very virile lover, Dumuzi (here Enkidu). Like Dumuzi, Enkidu had to die so that Gilgamesh could fulfill his destiny.

Enkidu died after many adventures shared with Gilgamesh. The great king of Uruk became completely overwhelmed by grief and eventually by his own fear of death. In order to avoid the fate of other humans, Gilgamesh made a long and dangerous trip to visit the only mortal, Ūtnapišti (the Flood survivor), who was granted immortality by the deities. Siduri, whom he encountered on his journey, explained the hopelessness of his quest for eternal life in the following words:

> When the gods created mankind,
> Death for mankind they set aside,
> Life in their own hands retaining.
> Thou, Gilgamesh, let full be thy belly,
> Make thou merry by day and by night.
> Of each day make thou a feast of rejoicing,
> Day and night dance thou and play! (Speiser 1973, p.64)

But Gilgamesh wanted more, he wanted the secret of eternal life from Ūtnapišti. Instead he received the wonderful narrative of the Flood story which is the subject of Chapter 11. Upon finishing the story, Ūtnapišti challenged Gilgamesh to defy sleep for six days and seven nights to prove himself worthy of such a great reward as immortality. Needless to say Gilgamesh failed. Obviously feeling sorry for him, the hero of Uruk, Ūtnapišti, urged by his wife, directed him to the place where the plant of eternal youth was growing at the bottom of the sea. Gilgamesh was able to obtain this plant only to lose it to a serpent who carried it off when Gilgamesh was taking a bath in cool water. Gilgamesh returned to Uruk empty-handed, except for the experiences of his journey. Even he had to die.

'The Epic of Gilgamesh' must have been a bestseller in the ancient world since many copies in different languages have been preserved. The lesson to learn from Gilgamesh's hopeless search for immortality is very simple: immortality is reserved for the divine, and no human may change this will of the gods. The only life to enjoy to the fullest is the one on earth since, once it is over, an empty pseudo-existence is all that humans must expect.

Mesopotamia – summary

Of all three heroes depicted above, Gilgamesh seemed to the be the best choice for receiving immortality. Thanks to his mother he had already possessed two of three godly attributes: power and knowledge. However, only one of them, wisdom, seems to be fully divine, since Gilgamesh's powers were limited by his humanity and only impressive to other mortals. When the most important tests were given to him, Gilgamesh failed them as any other human would.

Finally, one must comment on the divine sense of humor. In all three cases immortality and/or different plants of life were 'placed within man's grasp, only to be snatched from him at the last moment' (Armstrong 1969, p.14). This type of 'cruel play' with human emotions is consistent with the imperfect character of the Mesopotamian gods and goddesses, but one is surprised to find it in the Yahwistic story of paradise where the price for obtaining wisdom by Adam and Eve seems to be the loss of immortality (for discussion see Chapter 10). However, the message sent from the above and beyond to humankind remains the same: the quest for immortality is only an exercise in futility. We must resign ourselves to the fate designed for us by the divine: unavoidable death.

Egypt

Duality within the perceived unity of the Egyptian realm

In order to understand the role of a pharaoh in the continuous process of creation or rather preservation of order, truth, harmony, and prosperity one has to realize that the problem with the presentation and interpretation of Egyptian religion is not the lack of sources but rather its wealth – the abundance of ideas and concepts often contradictory to each other and very symbolic in their nature. On the one hand the geographical isolation of Egypt led to the development of a very monolithic and uniform culture – in comparison to other civilizations of the Middle East – with the main principles remaining unchanged throughout the Pharaonic Period (around 3200 B.C. to 332 B.C.). These principles include, but are not limited to, the divinity of each and every ruler, an elaborate and extended belief system in the after-life, the importance of visual images in the perception of the universe, and the consistent use of these images with some stylistic changes throughout thousands of years.

On the other hand, the Egyptians themselves were very much aware of the dualism and disunity of their own land with topographical/geographical and political/religious realms often mixed together. While they referred to themselves as the *remetch en Kemet* (since the ancient Egyptian writing system did not include vowels, modern transliterations often insert an 'e' between consonants to make words pronounceable – see Zauzich 1996), 'the people of the black land,' they also recognized the existence of the *Deshret*, 'the red land,' as a part of their geographical realm (Kees 1977; Shaw and Nicholson 1995). This contrast between the black land and the red land reflected the existing reality of the black, fertile soil of the Nile – whose silt spreading across the land during an annual inundation allowed the Egyptians not only to survive but also to prosper – versus the red soil of the desert which imposed the boundaries on land-adaptation for the living. Since 'the Egyptians experienced duality less as two contrasting elements but rather as two complementary ones' (Lurker 1984, p.48), both lands were necessary to form the unity of their perceived universe. They represented the ever-existing conflict in nature between the fertility of the Nile Valley and the infertility of the desert or, as Lesko (1991) suggests, 'between the consistent, beneficial inundation of the Nile (Osiris) and the unpredictable, generally undesirable storm (Seth)' (p.93). However, it must be noted here that Osiris was not personified as the river Nile or inundation itself although he was the one who commanded it (Silverman 1997), nor was he its cause since an annual flooding of the Nile was believed to be the result of Isis' tears mourning his death (Watterson 1985). In fact, the Nile was never considered to be divine and was always known only as *iteru*, 'the river,' in contrast to the inundation itself which was deified as Hapy, presented as a man with a big belly, pendulous breasts and a beard. This somewhat androgynous look reflected both female and male aspects of fecundity and fertility (Shaw and Nicholson 1995). In addition to the above divinities there were other deities associated with various aspects of the river Nile such as Khnum, Satis, Anuket, and the water creatures such as the deified crocodile, hippopotamus, and frog (Silverman 1997).

However, it was Osiris whose struggle for power with Seth represented symbolically the contrasting nature of the land of Egypt and gave it political meaning without specifying boundaries delineated by cardinal directions. In other words the 'black' versus the 'red' land was a vertical division, with the black, fertile alluvium surrounded by the red deserts to the west and to the east. But there was also a horizontal division reflecting the political disunity or dualism of Egypt, the south (Upper Egypt) versus the north (Lower Egypt), of which ancient Egyptians were perfectly aware. Every time in the history of pharaonic Egypt that the central power was weakened, this land was split into these two entities. When the land was united, its kings were referred to as the rulers of 'the two lands.' This unity was possible, as many scholars would agree, due to 'their common dependence upon the Nile and the accepted dogma that Egypt was ruled not by an Upper Egyptian nor by a Lower Egyptian but by a god, in whom could reside the essential forces of each part of the Two Lands' (Wilson 1968, p.45).

On this horizontal level the battle between Osiris and Seth was still a very important factor but the focus was different. It was no longer Osiris who was an opponent of Seth, but his son by Isis, Horus. Osiris was killed and in his aspect of the dead god he was represented in Egyptian art with his flesh in white, indicating the white bandages of mummy wrappings (Shaw and Nicholson 1995) or in green as a reference to his resurrection ('the great green' – the Pyramid Texts, No. 628; after Lurker 1984, p.55). He still maintained black as his symbol, being also called 'the black one' (Lurker 1984, p.34), with regard to his fertility aspect as well as his leadership over the Nether World. However, it was Horus, his son, who claimed divine power on earth as the rightful heir to his father's throne.

The Egyptian texts are very clear as to the original dominion of Horus being limited to Lower (northern) Egypt. For example, the Memphite Theology established his rulership over the land only 'up to the place in which his father was drowned which is "Division-of-the-Two-Lands"' (Lichtheim 1975, p.52) from where the kingship of Seth over Upper (southern) Egypt extended. However, recognizing the right of Horus to the earthly kingdom of his murdered father, Geb eventually proclaimed him the king of both lands. According to the same text, Horus

> is the uniter of this land, proclaimed in the great name: Ta-tenen, South-of-his-Wall, Lord of Eternity. Then sprouted the two Great Magicians upon his head. He is Horus who arose as king of Upper and Lower Egypt, who united the Two Lands in the Nome of the Wall, the place in which the Two Lands were united. (Lichtheim 1975, p.53)

The division into the two lands and its final unity under the divine leadership of Horus, the first pharaoh, are confirmed by royal titles and crowns as well as by their symbolism. Lower Egypt, the original land 'given' to Horus by Geb, was represented by a red crown (*deshret*). This is quite confusing because the same term, *deshret*, was used in the 'vertical' division of the land for the infertile deserts and was associated with the negative principle of Seth. The possible explanation of this inconsistency might be found in the symbolic properties of red which is usually perceived as an ambiguous color related through its association with blood to both positive and negative aspects of existence (Wasilewska 1991a, 1991b). In Egypt this color symbolized life and victory as well as their opposites – death, destructive fire, and anger (Lurker 1984). Thus *deshret* as the red crown could have symbolized the victory of Horus over his uncle (the most common tradition), and as the desert it could have stood for Seth, the red god, the destroyer, the negative but also necessary force of Egypt.

To complicate matters further, Egyptians associated Lower Egypt with two other symbolic entities related to the color green. One of them was the papyrus plant, the heraldic plant of Lower Egypt, that was believed to flourish on the primeval mound which emerged from the lifeless waters during the process of creation. Its ideogram meant 'green' (Shaw and Nicholson 1995) and Wadjet, the second entity, the protective goddess of this area, was referred to as 'the green' and 'often represented as a snake rearing up above papyrus clumps' (Lurker 1984, p.94).

On the other hand the 'original' land of Seth, Upper Egypt, was represented by a white crown (*hedjet*) sometimes referred to as 'White Nefer' (Shaw and Nicholson 1995, p.74). Again, the positive symbolic aspects of the color white such as purity and sanctity seemed to be in direct contradiction to the perception of the negative god Seth. However, white was also associated with omnipotence and sacrality (Lurker 1984), attributes of each and every 'high' deity of Egypt, even Seth. The heraldic plant of Southern Egypt was the lotus, two kinds of which, white and blue, were known originally in Egypt. This flower was also associated with creation since, according to one tradition, the sun-god emerged from the lotus which was floating on the waters of creation (Clark 1959; Shaw and Nicholson 1995). The protective goddess of this land was known as Nekhbet, the white vulture goddess.

Thus, the inherent disunity of the land was always acknowledged and visible in the official titulature of the Egyptian kings whose classic sequence consisted of five names or titles, fully established by the end of the third millennium B.C. Since it was a pharaoh who was the main force unifying Egypt throughout thousands of years, with his titles and position in ancient Egyptian society he must be addressed as the only divine 'mortal.'

Figure 7.2 The palette of Narmer, verso, showing the pharaoh - wearing the crown of Upper Egypt - in the process of killing his enemy

Pharaoh – the god who was left behind

The term 'pharaoh' which is commonly used today to refer to the ancient Egyptian rulers derives from the Greek form of the Egyptian phrase *per-aa* (*pr*) meaning 'great house.' This expression was employed to differentiate the royal palace associated with the king from 'lesser houses' known as *perw*. Over a period of time this expression came to denote the person of a king 'much as "White House" can denote the president of the United States' (Silverman 1991, p.59). The importance of this connection of the royal palace with the person of the king is also expressed by the oldest recorded royal title, the 'Horus name,' which was added (with three other titles) at the time of a pharoah's official accession to the throne. Beginning with the Early Dynastic Period (the end of the fourth millennium B.C.) the 'Horus name' was placed in a *serekh* ,frame (a hieroglyphic sign representing 'palace-façade,' probably of an early royal palace) on top of which the symbol of Horus, a falcon, was placed. The use of this name symbolized the victory of Horus, or the pharaoh who was his incarnation, over Seth. It is interesting to note that during the

Second Dynasty, one of its kings, Peribsen, changed his 'Horus name' to 'Seth name' and replaced the falcon with the animal presentation of Seth for reasons still enshrouded in mystery. His successor, Khasekhemwy, tried to reconcile both traditions and installed both Horus and Seth on the *serekh*, referring to this title as 'the two powers have appeared.'

Since a living king was a representation of Horus, the falcon, its protective wings often embraced the head of a king as a royal statue (for example, statues of Khafre of the Fourth Dynasty and Pepy I of the Sixth Dynasty). To stress the importance of Horus in the divine kingship over earth the second royal title of a pharaoh also referred to him – this time by an epithet of the divine metal, gold, associated with a shining sun-god – as 'Golden Horus.'

But Horus was not the only god with whom the pharaoh was associated. The last name of the royal titulary sequence was the 'private, proper' name of a pharaoh given to him at birth (a 'birth name' such as Thuthmosis, Rameses and so forth), which was introduced by a title 'Son of Re.' This close relationship with the god Re indicated the importance of the king in the process of creation since Re and other gods such as Atum or Ptah were considered to be creators who had brought order to the universe. Keeping this order or setting it anew was the main function of the pharaoh who was frequently 'shown or described offering *ma'at* [personification of justice, harmony, and truth in the form of a female deity] to the creator gods' (Silverman 1991, p.70; for a discussion of Ma'at see Hornung 1992).

The remaining two titles, 'He of the Two Ladies' and 'He of the Sedge and Bee,' were received by the pharaoh at the time of his accession and coronation, and referred to his role as the unifier of the land. The former is already found during the First Dynasty (Shaw and Nicholson 1995) and refers to the *nebty*, two goddesses, Wadjet and Nekhbet, representing the two lands of Egypt. Wadjet symbolized the royal power as the *uraeus* (a rearing cobra with inflated hood) worn on the royal crown or other headdress. This emblem represented kingship and as such can also be found on the presentation of such deities as Horus and Seth. Both Wadjet and the *uraeus* were sometimes identified with the 'Eye of Re' and in this relationship could have been presented in a leonine form (Shaw and Nicholson 1995). Through Re, the sun-god, the cobra/snake was associated with flames and fire, which explains its appearance as a part of the head decoration of Tefnut in her aspect as the goddess related to fire, Wepes, as well as being the personification of Hathor (Lurker 1984).

While Wadjet represented Lower Egypt where her strongest center of worship was Buto, Nekhbet, the vulture goddess, represented Upper Egypt. Originally she was worshipped in Nekheb (Elkab) from which she derived her name. Nekhbet as a vulture was used as a part of the pharaoh's headdress, although sometimes she was shown also as a snake in connection with Wadjet. These two *uraei* surrounding the solar disc can be seen in the representations of Egyptian queens from the Eighteenth Dynasty onward (Shaw and Nicholson 1995). Both goddesses were sometimes referred to as mythical mothers of the pharaoh.

The title 'He of the Sedge and Bee' (*nsw-bity, nesw-bit, nswt bjtj*) is usually translated as the 'King of Upper [of the Sedge] and Lower [of the Bee] Egypt' for the convenience of the reader and is found from the First Dynasty onward. It is very interesting to note that individuals in ancient Egypt could not address their king by this title unless they used another term, *ʿm*, 'majesty' or 'living embodiment,' to precede it (Silverman 1991). The same term is translated by Morenz (1973) as 'the body' implying the physical, human nature of the pharaoh (p.37). The first part of this name, *nsw*, seems to refer to the divine character of the king or rather kingship itself, while the second part, *bity*, was more oriented toward the individual and his mortal existence (Shaw and Nicholson 1995).

Although the above titles were not the only ones employed in ancient Egypt to address the rulers, they are the most important ones. They reflect very clearly the Egyptian concept of duality which occurred not only with regard to the land (two titles) but also to the person of the pharaoh himself (three titles). While Egyptians were fully aware that each ruler was born as a human and, as a mortal, had to die within the ideal period of time of 110 or 120 years, they also believed that he was a god, and the only visible, living link between the world of the divine and that of the profane. However, this perception of the divinity of the ruler had undergone various changes during the Pharaonic Period (Frankfort 1948; Silverman 1991).

Although there is still much discussion among scholars concerning the divine nature of the Egyptian rulers, it seems quite clear that the institution of kingship itself was divine. According to tradition it was brought to earth in the form of the god-king Re with his daughter Ma'at (Watterson 1985) representing the abstract concepts of truth, justice, harmony and order. This ideal situation was always threatened by negative forces represented by Seth, thus the commitment and the order of existence had to be renewed periodically in the form of festivals associated with the pharaoh, the representative of deities on earth. His claim to the throne was legitimized by his identification with Horus who became the ruler of Egypt after burying his father, Osiris. This means that although the ideal situation was to pass the kingship from father to son, in reality the throne could be claimed by the one who buried the previous pharaoh and completed his mortuary temple and tomb within seventy days, the time allotted for this ceremony (Watterson 1985). Thus, the king's divinity seemed to be obtained through the rituals first associated with the funeral ceremonies of the previous ruler and then through the ones associated with the new ruler's coronation. Only after these ceremonies were other references to his divinity made, including descriptions of his divine birth and/or destiny.

In view of such a perception of divine kingship, the pharaoh was much more than just the head of state. He was an essential element of the cosmos whose order he had to maintain as Horus himself, and, from the Fourth Dynasty onward, as the 'son of Re.' Such a fatherhood was possible as explained by the Westcar Papyrus, which states that the first three kings of the Fifth Dynasty were born as the result of a union between Re and a mortal woman, Reddedet, the wife of a high priest in Heliopolis. Four goddesses of maternity, Isis, Nephthys, Meshkenet and Heket, assisted the birth of these babies on the order of Re. This motif of divine conception and birth of the pharaoh, the royal theogamy, was repeated many times throughout the history of pharaonic Egypt. It was the divine father, Amun-Re, who in the disguise of the pharaoh, had a mystical sexual union with the queen. This concept of divine fathership can be seen much later in association with the conception and birth of Jesus, another being whose divinity is disputed even by some of his followers.

Due to the variety of functions that the king had to fulfill on earth, he was described by different epithets and terms referring to him either directly or indirectly. The three terms – *nswt, 'm, per-aa* – associated with his earthly duties as the administrator of Egypt have already been discussed above. The others dealt with his divine nature. In addition to the official royal titles associated with Horus and Re, from early times on the king was referred to by the term *netjer*, 'god,' which was sometimes written alone and at other times with some other descriptive words (Silverman 1991). The origin of this term and its use have caused a lot of discussion among scholars since both are rather vague (for a summary see Budge 1960; Hornung 1982). However, for the purpose of this book it is sufficient to note, following Meeks and Favard-Meeks (1996), that this particular term had a much more extended meaning and was 'designated [for] any entity which, because it transcended ordinary human reality, received a cult and became the object of a ritual' (p.37). This implies the existence of various degrees of divinity as perceived by the Egyptians since this term was used for all deities, the king and the dead. This is reflected by an example from the Third Dynasty and cited by Hornung (1982) in which the king is addressed with this term as the 'most divine one of the corporation (of gods)' (p.46).

Other epithets which refer to the divinity of the king include *tjt*, the 'image' of the god, and *mj*, being 'like' a god (Silverman 1991, p.59). For example, as a son of Re, the king was perceived as Re's 'living image on earth' (Lurker 1984, p.75). By using such expressions the ancient Egyptians were able to identify their rulers with various deities depending on the need of any particular text. However, since they were fully aware of his human mortality, his divinity as a living ruler was of a different caliber than the inherent divinity of other deities, whether personified in human or animal forms or in a combination of both. In contrast to 'natural' divine forces the pharaoh had to establish his credentials first through rituals of his coronation as well as through his brave actions and decisions (which were possible thanks to his divine favors), then through the rituals of restoration of *ma'at*, performed on a calendrical (for example, the Sed festival or 'royal jubilee' every thirty years) or a crisis basis.

Egypt – summary

As a living ruler the pharaoh was perceived to be a link between 'our' human world and the other one. He was the center of existence as perceived by the Egyptians and in his person all divine powers were united. According to the Pyramid Text No. 1037, his 'head corresponded to the Horus falcon, the face to the "opener of the ways," the nose to Thoth, the thighs to the frog goddess and even the buttocks corresponded to Isis and Nephthys' (after Lurker 1984, p.75). As the 'identification' or 'incarnation' or 'manifestation' of the divine, the pharaoh was a god on earth who had to make certain that the universal order, justice and harmony would be maintained. This included his duties in each and every temple of Egypt which, in reality, he could not perform himself, so others 'chosen' by him, the priestly class, carried them out on an everyday basis.

While the king's divinity on earth remains a controversial subject among scholars, there is no doubt that the deceased pharaoh was an object of worship. Through his death the king was fully incorporated into the divine world and became one with many deities, but especially with Osiris (chthonic aspect) and Re (solar aspect). The Pyramid Texts No. 273–274 known as the 'Cannibal Spell' refer to this incorporation as follows:

> The sky is clouded, the stars disturbed,
> The 'bows' quake, the bones of the earth god tremble.
> But those who move are still when they have seen the king
> With (his) soul manifest, as a god
> Who lives on his fathers and feeds on his mothers.
> (Hornung 1982, p.131)

The universal cycle of death and rebirth was completed. The god who was left behind returned to his divine world. The new god, his successor, was to carry out the duties of divine kingship until his mortal destiny would be fulfilled.

Conclusions: The shortage of divine candidates or too many of them?

While the above examples from Mesopotamia and Egypt indicate the possibility of some special mortals being involved in the process of creation or in its maintenance, the other traditions (which are the subject of this book) did not produce similar texts except for those connected with the emergence of humankind and/or the survivor of divine wrath (flood or freeze) which are discussed in Part 4. In Anatolia there are some stories which involve human/divine interaction but in no way can they change established rules. In Caananite mythology Aqhat was given a chance for immortality by the goddess Anat in exchange for his bow and arrows made for him by Kothar-and-Khasis. Foolishly he turns it down, subduing himself to his human fate and the rage of Anat. Yatpan, her helper, kills Aqhat and leaves his body to be dismembered by vultures. The result is fatal not only for Aqhat but for the whole world since seven years of drought followed his death. Thus Anat, like Ištar, got her revenge on a mortal who refused her offer. However, in contrast to the Mesopotamian story in which Enkidu's death cannot be vindicated, in Ugaritic myth Aqhat's sister possibly kills Yatpan whom she held responsible for her brother's death (for the text see Coogan 1978; Gibson 1978). In yet another myth of Ugaritic origin, the story of a legendary king, Kirta (Keret), preservation of the world was threatened again by the lack of heir and then by the sickness of a king himself which would lead to famine (for the text see Coogan 1978; Gibson 1978; Gray 1964). This was avoided through another divine intervention which did not require too much effort on the part of a human (for parallels with Biblical stories of David see Coogan 1978). Thus, in Canaanite tradition, in contrast to the Mesopotamian one, humans themselves could not threaten the existing order because they never challenge it. They just happen to be a victim of circumstances which are solved by the deities themselves.

In Persia there is no shortage of heroes and anti-heroes who were legendary rulers of Indo-Iranian tradition as described in Šāh-nāma. However, only the first mortals, whether Gayomart or Yima, were given a chance to influence the world and both used it (see Chapter 9). In both the Pentateuch and the Quran such humans cannot exist by definition – there is only one god who is not willing to share his attributes with anybody else. Thus, one must appreciate the religions of Mesopotamia and Egypt which offered hope or chance to their people to become equal, at least in some aspects, to the divine powers. What is even more unusual is the fact that this chance for becoming divine or semi-divine was granted by the religions which either did not focus on the origin and existence of human beings (Egypt) or considered the mortals to be nothing more than the servants created for the divine comfort (Mesopotamia). The others which treated the creation of humankind as the ultimate goal of the god (Genesis and the Quran) have been much less generous.

PART 3

Creation and Destruction
of Humankind

8

Accident or Intention? The Egyptian Lack of Interest in Human Creation

Owing to the character of Egyptian religion the overwhelming majority of both scientific and general writings focuses on the Egyptian 'obsession' with death and rebirth. Only a handful of pages refers to the beginning of humankind, to the reason for their existence. Thus, the subject of mankind's creation is a very difficult one to discuss especially because the Egyptians themselves were not much interested in elaborating on their own 'coming into being.' It almost seems like the existence of humankind was perceived by them so irrelevant in comparison to the cosmic events which brought into being all necessary forces of life that it did not deserve to have a separate text explaining how and why it happened that people populated this earth. On the other hand there is always a possibility that such texts existed but have not yet been found.

There are only two texts – 'The Instructions for King Merikare' composed during the First Intermediate Period (2181–2055 B.C.) and Spell 1130 of the Coffin Texts – which discuss the subject of the human creation in more detail than the occasional references in the sources presented previously and a few additional hymns. Furthermore, in spite of such a shortage of data, the existing information is still contradictory and frequently unclear.

The birth of mankind

Since people are quite a visible part of the universe created by the deities, their existence could not have been ignored and left unexplained by Egyptian theologians. However, this does not mean that people constituted any significant force in bringing order and harmony to existence – that is, the state of being – which had to be addressed in any elaborated way. In fact, sometimes there was not much distinction made between people and animals, as illustrated by Spell No. 80 of the Coffin Texts in which the god Shu is identified, among other things, with the concept of Life itself. Among various accomplishments that are within his power Shu also claims:

> ... I will make firm his [Osiris] flesh every day
> And make fresh his parts every day –
> Falcons living off birds, jackals of prowling,
> Pigs off the highlands, hippopotami off the cultivation,

Men off grain, crocodiles off fish,
Fish off the waters in the Inundation –
As Atum has ordered.

I will lead them and enliven them,
Through my mouth, which is Life in their nostrils.
I will lead my breath into their throats, after I have tied on their head by
the Annunciation that is in my mouth. (Allen 1997i, p.13)

This text not only does not imply that people were of any special significance in the eyes of the god but clearly states that they were looked upon as one of animal forms who were brought to life through breathing the life force into their nostrils. Their association with animals can also be seen in the expression referring to people as the 'cattle of Re.' On the other hand such texts as 'Hymn to Re' and 'Hymn to Amun' (Currid 1997, p.70), which suggest that both humankind and the animal kingdom were created at the same time or thereabouts, clearly considered them to be of different standing. The 'Great Hymn to the Aten', which also lists people together with animals and birds as the god's great creation, is much more specific in its description of people: 'Their [people's] tongues differ in speech,/Their characters likewise;/Their skins are distinct,/For you distinguished the peoples' (Lichtheim 1997a, p.46).

This paragraph is rather unusual because not only does it account for the existence and implied equality of various ethnic and language groups, but also refers to the god as being the one who created them to be this way, including their characters with their both negative and positive aspects. Thus, indirectly at least, in this hymn the god takes responsibility for any disorder that can be caused by humans, while in other texts the people are solemnly responsible for it and must be punished and controlled.

But before the relationship between people and deities is discussed the basic question concerning their origin and the purpose of creation must be answered.

There are two main traditions concerning the origin of people. According to the Coffin Texts Spell No. 1130 people were created from the Creator's tears: '... I made the gods evolve from my sweat,/While people are from tears of my Eye' (Allen 1997j, p.27). Although the name of the Creator is not specified by this text in spite of the common identification with Re (Lesko 1991), Spell No. 80 of the Coffin Texts identifies him as Atum (Allen 1997i) while the 'Great Cairo Hymn of Praise to Amun-Re' gives this honor to Amun in the following words: 'YOU ARE the Sole One, WHO MADE [ALL] THAT EXISTS,/One, alone, who made that which is,/From whose two eyes mankind came forth' (Ritner 1997b, p.39).

Since the practice of the assimilation of divine identities and attributes by other gods has been explained, the assumption of the role of the people's creator by Amun should not be a surprise. However, the reference to two eyes is, since other texts are quite specific (with an exception of a much later text from Edfu) that only one eye was involved. Does it make any difference? Realizing that archaeology is a discipline in which pitfalls abound, one might try to interpret or overinterpret the significance of one or two eyes in mythological terms of ancient Egypt. If this one eye belonged to Re-Atum, then it might have represented the creation of humankind as the action of the goddess Hathor, traditionally associated with this eye. If this is correct, she would have represented not only the destructive aspect of this eye, as in the attempt to annihilate mankind (see Chapter 11), but also her creative force. Thus, as a mother-goddess, also referred to as the 'female soul with two faces' (Lurker 1984, p.59), she might have been a logical choice to destroy her own creation when she felt it was necessary. Furthermore, Hathor was also known as the mother of a king as her name 'House of Horus' indicates, which would make her a wife of Re. This might lead to the conclusion that Hathor, in the form of the eye, represented the female principle of the sun-god and together they gave rise to their human children. A similar concept has already been discussed with regards to Atum who, through masturbation (his hand was his wife), gave birth to the next generation of deities.

However, if the number of eyes involved in creation was irrelevant then one might assume that the act of crying (whether out of joy or sadness) was essential in order to present the creation of humankind as an accident that had to be taken care of and for which a purpose had to be found.

The Papyrus Bremner-Rhind seems to confirm this by referring to this event more as an accident than a deliberate action of the god Atum. After Atum's eye disappeared, his children, Shu and Tefnut, brought her back. And then '... after I [Atum] joined together my parts,/I wept over them:/That is the evolution of people,/From the tears that came from my Eye' (Allen 1997e, p.15).

Most scholars will agree that this version of the creation of mankind actually was a deliberate game of words by the Egyptian theologians because the Egyptian words for people and tears are similar in their consonantal structure, *rmt* and *rmyt* respectively (Allen 1997j; Clark 1959; Hornung 1982; Morenz 1973). Thus the word for 'people' can be etymologically derived from the term for 'tears.' Not denying the Egyptian theologians their sense of humor, I find it quite intriguing that they would have treated their own creation in such a casual way. On the other hand, this creation from tears might be intended to stress the difference between divine forces being created from 'sweat' which emanates a specific fragrance (incense) easily recognized by people (Hornung 1982) in contrast to humans who are made out of 'tears' which lack any smell. Hornung expanded on this idea by referring to one of the Coffin Texts (VI, 344) in which Nun himself is the Creator who states that 'humans belong to the blindness behind me' (1982, p.150; 1992, p.47). In his 1982 work he provided an explanation that 'God overcame the affliction of his eye, but man's origin means that he is destined never to partake in the clear sight of god; affliction blights everything he sees, thinks, and does' (p.150), while in 1992 he believed that the statement 'intimates why humans are so often struck blind' (p.47).

In spite of the eloquent explanations offered by Hornung and others for the creation of mankind from the tears of a creator I have a difficult time accepting this rather sophisticated interpretation of a quite unsophisticated statement concerning this creation from the eye. Since in the Egyptian tradition only a few elements were perceived to be accidental, I tend to believe that the eye of the creator referred to Hathor who, as a mother-goddess, was a significant part of the human creation in other accounts which do not mention any tears, but simple clay as the not-so-original substance from which humans were formed.

The use of clay in the process of originating humankind was the other mode of creation in Egyptian theology. It was usually the god Khnum who was associated with this process since it was he who was depicted in Deir-el Bahari as fashioning a human (Hathshepsut) and her *ka* with the use of a potter's wheel on the orders of Amun-Re. Then the body and *ka* were implanted in her mother so she could bring into this world the daughter of Amun-Re, Hatshepsut. This process was also applied to other children who were to be born of mortal parents (Ions 1983; Lurker 1984).

Khnum's great craftsmanship as a potter is addressed in his description as 'the very great God who has fashioned (*œd*) gods and men, who has molded (*grg*) this country with his hands' (Morenz 1973, p 161). Khnum is also presented doing the same thing on the bas-relief from the temple of Amun-Re in Luxor. However, as Ions (1983) pointed out, this creation was not the full act, since it followed a perceived sexual intercourse between the god Amun and Queen Mutemuia, and was finished with the animation of a pharaoh (Amenhotep III) by Hathor touching the king and his *ka* with the *ankh*, a symbol of life. His creation powers for bringing a pharaoh to life were already recognized in the Old Kingdom since the Pyramid Texts described the pharaoh as 'the son of Khnum' (Ions 1983, p.33).

Figure 8.1 Khnum, the ram-headed god of Elephantine, creates a pharaoh and his ka on a potters wheel. The goddess Hathor contributes to this creation by extending the sign of life, the ankh. From a relief in the temple at Luxor

The choice of material for mankind as 'clay and straw' is also mentioned by other texts (Currid 1997; Ions 1983) and sometimes associated with other gods such as Ptah (Currid 1997). However, the most common association of Khnum with this mode of creation is definitely the most logical, taking into consideration his craftsmanship and virility as the ram-god. His cult centers were located in the islands of Elephantine and Philae where he 'controlled' the flow of the river Nile, allowing for an annual inundation, as recorded on the so-called Famine Stele at Sehel. Since the mud was a part of the regular process associated with flooding he would have logically selected it as the material for molding gods, human, animals, and plants as referred to on the walls of his temple at Esna from the Graeco-Roman Period.

In his other aspect Khnum represented virility and was portrayed either as a ram of a kind which became extinct in Egypt during the Middle Kingdom (Ions 1983; Shaw and Nicholson 1995) or as man with the head of a ram. Since the Egyptian word for ram is *ba* which can be equaled with the spiritual soul, the concept known as *ba*, Shaw and Nicholson (1995) raised the possibility that 'Khnum was regarded as the quintessential ba of the sun-god Ra, who was therefore depicted with a ram's head as he passed through the netherworld in the solar bark' (p.151).

While the creation of humankind out of the creator's eye was a unique event, this act as performed by Khnum can be considered to be a continuous process. Here the ram-god fashions each and every human and his or her *ka* only to place them in the form of a seed in the womb of the mother where life itself is given by Hathor. This motif of continuous creation is repeated by the 'Hymn to Aten' which states:

> [Aten] who makes seed grow in women,
> Who creates people from sperm;
> Who feeds the son in his mother's womb,
> Who soothes him to still his tears.
> Nurse in the womb,
> Giver of breath,
> To nourish all that he made.
> When he comes from the womb to breath, on the day of this birth,
> You open his mouth,
> You supply his needs. (Lichtheim 1997a, pp.45–46)

The same idea of continuous creation as based on the seed being originally made out of clay and then placed in the womb was much later re-introduced by the Quranic tradition.

However, none of the texts that might have reflected the already existing tradition whose texts have not survived, with the exception of the 'Hymn to Aten,' actually provides the purpose of this creation. Even this Hymn just makes the statement that 'You [Aten] bring him [Hapy] when you will,/To nourish the people,/For you made them for yourself' (Lichtheim 1997a, p.46), which may implicate either the god's whim or his need for offerings. One may speculate that since the pharaoh was a guarantor of the divine order, then in order to perform his duties, he needed an army of servants. One of the texts from the Middle Kingdom and the Book of the Dead refers to the king and his role on earth as 'for ever and ever judging humanity and propitiating the gods, and setting order in place of disorder. He gives offerings to the gods and mortuary offerings to the spirits (the blessed dead)' (Baines 1991, p.128).

If this was the purpose for the creation of mankind it would require a very deliberate action by the creator who, in most cases, would have had to create people knowing that the Ennead with Horus would come into being later.

Morenz (1973) suggested that people were created 'in order to carry out his [the Creator's] procreative purpose' using a Graeco-Roman text referring to Khnum as the one 'who made the bulls to make the cows pregnant' (pp.184–185). Unfortunately there is no evidence for this hypothesis either.

Thus, one must conclude that the creation of humankind was either an accident, or its purpose was so well known that it did not need to be referred to in texts. Of course, there is always the possibility that the Egyptians themselves did not have an answer, or that answer was recorded but the text or texts are missing.

A human: What does it mean?

Regardless of whether the creation of mankind was incidental or not, the ancient Egyptians believed it to be not only the act of divine creation but also 'images' of the creator. The most famous text concerning this subject, the 'Instructions for King Merikare,' which was composed during the First Intermediate Period but whose copies date to the New Kingdom, addresses this issue in the following words: 'Well tended is mankind – god's cattle,/He [the Creator – Re] made sky and earth for their sake,/He subdued the water monster,/He made breath for their noses to live./They are his images, who came from his body' (Lichtheim 1997c, p.65).

If this paragraph sounds familiar one should not be surprised because the idea of mankind being created in the image of the god was later employed by the Priestly account of Genesis (see Chapter 9). Unfortunately neither text clearly defines the meaning of the term 'image' or 'likeness.'

Again one can speculate that the word 'image' used by the Egyptian theologians reflected the reality of their religion as projected in visual arts. Since many of the Egyptian deities, including the sun-gods/creators, were portrayed frequently in a human form, this could be believed to be a projected earthly image of a divinity. However, the true, physical manifestation of the greatness that the creator was perceived to be, was to be revealed, comprehended and admired only in the next world (Hornung 1982).

Another interesting idea mentioned by this text is the importance of making breath for the people's nostrils so they could be brought into life. The act of giving breath to humans in the realm of the dead is also addressed by Spell Nos. 54, 55, 56, 57, 58, and 59 of the Book of the Dead (for translations of these texts see Faulkner 1997). However, this divine breath seems to be more than just air which is implied by some other translations of this passage (such as 'he made the air of life so that they might breathe...' Silverman 1997, p.131). Hornung (1992), in his discussion of Ma'at, refers to one of the hymns recited during a daily temple ritual which identifies Ma'at 'with breath for your nose' among other identifications with such elements as 'the robe of your limbs...your bread...your beer...' (p.132). Ma'at is also associated with the nose in one of the Coffin Texts, which instructs Atum to 'kiss your daughter Maat, hold her to your nose' (II.35) (Hornung 1992, p.134). This may suggest that with breath, people received the moral 'code' of life which was necessary to follow in order to keep the universe in its proper order along with harmony and justice, as in the third lament of the Eloquent Peasant who says, 'It is breath for the nose to do *maat*' (Hornung 1992, p.136). Thus Ma'at was created or existed for people as their guiding force.

While the purpose, as it existed, of creation of humankind is very unclear it seems that the Egyptians believed, at least according to some texts, that other divine creations were made for them. The Coffin Texts Spell No. 1130 lists the good deeds which the creator (Re) performed: 'I made the four winds, that every man might breathe in his time./This is one of the deeds./I made the great inundation, that the humble might benefit by it like the great./This is one of the deeds' (Lichtheim 1975, p.130).

The 'Instructions for King Merikare' specifies other creations: 'He [the Creator] shines in the sky for their [people's] sake;/He made for them plants and cattle,/Fowls and fish to feed them' (Lichtheim 1997c, p.65). And even after all necessary elements were made for the benefit of the people, the creator continues to take care of them; as the text states, 'when they weep he hears' (Lichtheim 1997c, p.66).

Conclusions

To maintain clarity, I have treated the Egyptian sources concerning the creation of humankind as a separate chapter because of their distinctive features not present in other cultures of the Middle East; however, there are some motifs that appeared later in Genesis and the Quran. While the creation out of the eye is very particular to Egypt, molding people out of clay is not. The continuous involvement of deities in the creation of separate individuals and their *ka* is a theme that was later repeated by the Quran in somewhat different form. The creation of people in the image of gods is copied also by Genesis but the original source can be found both in Egypt and in Mesopotamia.

Unfortunately, we are still not clear about the purpose of this creation but judging from human obligations toward the deities, the Egyptians could have been brought forth in order to serve them, as in the Mesopotamian tradition. On the other hand, their strong beliefs in the after-world would extend their function beyond their usefulness on Earth. Thus, this problem must remain unsolved until more sources are discovered.

9

Of Mud and / or Divine

While the ancient Egyptians seemed to be barely interested in the topic of the creation of humankind, the ancient people of Mesopotamia discussed it much more frequently although they never focused on it as one of the most important creations. In Mesopotamian mythology, in contrast to many others, including monotheistic religions of the Middle East, humankind is not the ultimate, final act of creation to which all other preceding acts were leading. The Sumerians, whose beliefs provided the foundation on which the Semitic religions of Mesopotamia were built, were not conceited enough to consider themselves and mankind in general to be of any great significance. They understood and accepted the role of humans as servants to the deities, whose wishes and desires must be fulfilled in order for the universe to continue according to its encoded and eternal rules. In contrast to the Bible, which states in Psalm 115:16–17 that 'Heaven belongs to Yahweh, earth he bestows on man,' mankind was in charge of nothing. Its prosperity, wealth and happiness depended on its deities whose actions, sometimes quite temperamental and unjust, could have wiped out all people from the face of the earth without any warning. The best humans could do was to provide for their gods and goddesses to appease them and keep them happy, hoping that their 'godly' power struggles would not interfere with the life of earthlings. Since the deities needed people to work for them on earth, their usefulness was limited only to their lifetime, after which they were sent to the underworld to join all the other, divine and otherwise, creatures in their hopeless and gloomy pseudo-existence. But as long as their servants were alive it was in the best interest of deities to take care of their creation in order to assure the continuance of humans' services to the best of their ability.

Thus, although the worlds of the divine or sacred and of the profane were so interconnected, interdependent and intertwined, the people of the Sumero-Akkadian tradition, like the Egyptians discussed in the previous chapter, did not consider themselves even important enough to place themselves in the center of the creation process. Because their origins are the most ancient, the stories of their tradition are discussed first.

Then, in order to follow a chronological order and to preserve the consistency of available material, the Anatolian approach to the subject of creation or rather the existence of mankind is discussed. It should become clear that people of second millennium B.C. Anatolia shared similar beliefs to the Mesopotamians with regard to their place in the universe. The change in attitude can easily be seen with the birth of the Zaratuštrian/Zoroastrian tradition which centers on the male-kind as the ultimate creation while treating the female-kind as necessary evil. A very similar approach is also represented by the Yahwistic tradition of the paradise which is discussed in the next chapter. Finally, the Priestly account is discussed as a logical continuance of Mesopotamian and Anatolian traditions. However, its inconsistencies with the Yahwistic version are addressed in Chapter 10.

Mesopotamia: 'Workers needed' – creating humankind

Enki and Ninmah: The case of CUI (creating under influence)

The Sumerian story which Kramer and Maier (1989) called 'Enki and Ninmah: The Creation of Humankind,' reconstructed from six different tablets and fragments is one of the oldest and most complete but also most enigmatic stories 'recording' this event. As many other myths referring to the creation of particular creatures and/or objects do, so too this myth begins with establishing the time and the scene. We learn that the event took place after the whole universe was not only created and divided, but years after the destinies were pronounced and all gods and goddesses had already been assigned their functions. It seems that the deities were living normal 'human' lives, multiplying through marriages and working hard to provide for themselves. They had to prepare their own food, some of them carried baskets, others dug canals, and none of them liked this manual labor. Their complaints were loud but not loud enough to awaken Enki who was sleeping soundly in his bed. Finally, Nammu, a personified *prima materia* presented here as the primeval mother, wakes him up to urge her son to take care of the problem by creating servants for the deities. The original translation of the text by Kramer (1959 and 1961) pertaining to the mode of creation – out of clay – 'in the image (?) of the gods' has been somewhat changed. Kramer and Maier's new version (1989, pp.32–33) suggests that Enki 'thought out the project' and then with the help of the team of goddesses (including Ninmah as his helper) carried it out by forming mankind out of special clay above the *abzu*. According to both translations Nammu had already known the name of this new creation before it was brought into the light, thus confirming that she was the original matter in which everything was encoded.

The creation of humankind seemed to be very welcome by the deities since, after a few unclear lines, it becomes clear that they are having a banquet during which they glorify Enki as a great father. Unfortunately Enki and Ninmah have drunk too much beer and she obviously feels that she can do better than being just an assistant to Enki in the creation of people. The agreement is made that whomever she makes out of the *abzu* clay, Enki must decree that creature's fate. Unfortunately, being drunk as Ninmah was, the six beings that she produced were created with different disabilities: 'a man who when reaching could not bend his rigid [?] hands,' 'a man who could see though blind,' 'a man with … paralyzed feet,' 'a man who kept dripping semen,' 'a woman who could not give birth' and 'something without a phallus or a vulva on his body' (Kramer and Maier 1989, p.34). Enki was able to decree a fate or a cure (for example, 'incantation' water for the man who dripped semen) for all of them.

The description of the creation of these six beings and the concept of such a creation are some of the cleverest ideas anybody could come up with as an explanation for the existence of differentable people. Their 'disabilities' or 'differentableness' are explained through this myth as the act of deities who themselves are not perfect, but still their creations are a divine act which makes them equal to the first 'set of humans.' As each and every creature was born out of the divine order so these six beings have their place, an equal place, in relation to the deities. Thus it seems that the Sumerian reality, as well as the Egyptian one, was much more tolerant and appreciative of existing differences between people than many modern societies are today.

The story proceeds with Enki challenging Ninmah to decree the fate of a new creation that he was about to form out of clay. There follows a rather unclear passage relating to the birth in the woman's womb, made possible thanks to semen being poured into it, but the new being, *umul*, is finally born. The meaning of this word remains in dispute. Kramer and Maier (1989) list proposed possibilities as a 'very old man' ('my day is remote'), a 'new-born baby' ('my day [of death] is far [off]'), 'my storm the attacker' (pp.211–212), deciding to leave it untranslated. Leick (1994) refers to this being as Udmul, 'My day is far off' (p.27). This poor being is described in the following words:

> ...its head sick, and sick its...-place
>
> Sick its eyes, sick its neck,
>
> Breath at an end, ribs shaky, lungs sick, heart sick, bowels
> sick.
>
> The hand that supported [?] his head could not put bread in
> its mouth, its splintered [?] spine in pain,
>
> Shoulders drooping, feet shaky, it could not walk [?] to [?]
> the field. (Kramer and Maier 1989, p.35)

Upon seeing Umul, Ninmah protests that there is nothing she can do about this creature who cannot perform basic life functions. Enki responds by listing the destinies he provided for her creatures, challenging her again to decree a fate for Umul. Unfortunately the remaining lines are poorly preserved. It seems that Ninmah gets really mad at Enki, either denigrating him (Kramer and Maier 1989) or lamenting her fate (Leick 1994). We are not sure what happened to Umul but at one point he or she is sitting on Ninmah's lap and there is at least a promise made to build him Enki's house. The story finishes with the statement that Ninmah could not rival Enki.

Since this text is poorly preserved, especially its conclusion, the meaning of the birth of Umul remains unresolved, although Jacobsen's (1987) suggestion that the unclear lines refer to unsuccessful gestation, abortion or premature ejection (discussed by Leick 1994) must be mentioned. In any case, this myth is of great importance because it establishes the main points concerning the existence of humankind. It is clearly stated that people were created by Enki (with some involvement of female deities, especially Nammu and Ninmah) in order to free deities from hard work – they were created as servants. All people, including those who are differentable, are divine creations with a specific purpose in life. Even Umul must have been given a purpose as indicated in some partially preserved lines. People are not holy since they are not related to deities in any way, in spite of the material, the holy mud of *abzu*, from which they were formed. Once created they can reproduce themselves in the 'godly' fashion, through sexual intercourse associated with marriage. It was Enki who provided man with semen, a substance to create life within the womb of a woman. Thus, he is the Father of mankind in spite of the fact that he created it at the request of Nammu, his mother, and with the help of Ninmah, another mother-goddess.

Creation of mankind – ex nihilo?

While the reason for the creation of humankind had remained the same in the Sumero-Semitic traditions of Mesopotamia, the material which was used for this act was sometimes either ignored or 'improved.' For example, the Sumerian story 'Cattle and Grain' discusses the special creation of two deities, the cattle-god Lahar and the grain-goddess Ashnan, in what Kramer (1959) calls the 'creation chamber' (pp.110–113). Their purpose was to provide basic necessities, food and clothes, for the Anunnakû begotten by An. However, their products did not satisfy the great Anunnakû of Duku until mankind was created: 'For the sake of their [Annunaki] pure sheepfolds, the good,/Man was given breath' (Kramer 1959, p.111).

It must be mentioned that this text is not very clear, allowing for the interpretation that humankind was already present before Lahar and Ashnan were created and it was them, not the Anunnakû, who were not able to provide for themselves and for the deities until they were given divine 'breath' (Lyczkowska and Szarzynska 1981). However, it seems that Kramer's translation is more appropriate concerning the Sumerian realm in which each and every creation must have had its clearly described purpose, which in Lyczkowska and Szarzynska's interpretation humans would not have had. This means that although the material of creation as well as the purpose are not so clear in the text, the whole act of human creation happened or was completed by providing these new beings with elements of the divine so they would be capable of carrying out their tasks.

However, according to the story, people were able to become useful, productive and efficient only after Lahar and Ashnan descended from Duku to earth and bestowed their benefits on them. This is indirectly 'confirmed' by yet another Sumerian account found in Nippur which refers to Anu, Enlil, Enki, and Ninhursagga as those who brought forward mankind and only then caused the earth to produce, adding to it animals (Heidel 1951). On the other hand this text may refer to the second creation of humankind, after its destruction (possibly by a flood), which might explain the need for replenishing the barren earth after the catastrophe.

The tablet from Babylon concerning a ritual for the temple restoration contains yet another creation story which refers to people as being created by Ea/Enki to do 'the service of the gods' (Heidel 1951, pp.65–66; see also Kramer 1961). They were brought forth after everything else was created (including Ashnan and Lahar) but the material of which they were made is not clearly stated. Thus, they were either brought into being by just pronouncing their existence or from clay, as the passage at line 26, 'Ea nipped off clay in the Apsû,' refers to all following creations, divine or otherwise, being made out of the holy mud (Heidel 1951, p.65). The latter would suggest that in this magical text there was no difference, at least with regard to material, between deities and humans. Since this notion is rather unacceptable in view of our knowledge of the Sumero-Akkadian religious beliefs, it probably might be better to accept the idea that the 'full' material was simply not essential enough to mention.

There are other Sumerian texts which do not specify the substance of which humankind was made. According to the hymn in honor of the E.engura in Eridu, people came out of the earth like plants during a year of abundance caused by the god An. A similar version is presented in the myth about the creation of the pick-axe, which refers to Enlil placing the seeds of humankind in a crevice from which people later emerged. A much later text narrates the event of people growing out of the earth according to a plan made by the goddess Aruru (Lyczkowska and Szarzynska 1981). This comparison of humans being brought to life in the same way as plants, although it refers to clay, dirt or earth as the original material from which they emerged, does not discuss either the purpose of this creation or the substance of which they were made. This might suggest that neither of these texts actually narrates the story of the creation of humankind but rather refers metaphorically to the process of populating the earth.

By divine and of divine

The Babylonian tradition of the Enûma Eliš follows the Sumerian notion that people were created in order to free gods and goddesses from hard labor: 'They shall bear the gods' burden that those may rest' (Foster 1995, p.38). However, both the mode and the material employed for this purpose differ from earlier accounts.

After Marduk created heaven and earth from the body of Tiāmat and organized the whole universe by creating new elements and establishing various divine domains, there was time to create humankind. Marduk made this decision upon hearing complaints from the imprisoned gods of Tiāmat's 'army' who were turned into his servants and 'punished' by being made to provide the sustenance for the victorious party. Upon consultation with Ea he decided: 'I shall compact blood, I shall cause bones to be,/I shall make stand a human being, let "Man" be its name./I shall create humankind' (Foster 1995, p.38).

It is important to notice that although it was Marduk's idea to create humankind, he had to consult with Ea/Enki whose role as the creator of people with the assistance of the mother-goddess was already firmly established in the Mesopotamian tradition. However, Marduk remains the sole creator of humans because it was he who selected the name for this creation. Again, pronouncing the name and the destiny of a new being or beings was considered to be the final and complete act of creation.

It was Ea's idea that Qingu, the second husband of Tiāmat and the leader of the opposition, should be 'sacrificed' for this purpose as the punishment for his actions. Following the order of Marduk the Igigi gods

> ...bound and held him [Qingu] before Ea,
> They imposed the punishment on him and shed his blood.
> From his blood he made mankind,
> He imposed the burden of the gods and exempted the gods.

> After Ea the wise had made mankind,
> They imposed the burden of the gods on them!
> That deed is beyond comprehension,
> By the artifices of Marduk did Nudimmud |Enki| create!

(Foster 1995, p.39)

While the *Enûma Eliš* preserved the tradition of the active involvement of Enki/Ea in the creation of humankind at Marduk's order, in the Neo-Babylonian text discovered in Sippar it was Aruru, the mother-goddess, who helped Marduk to create people. Although she was the one who 'created the seed of mankind,' it was Marduk who pronounced its name along with names for 'the beasts of Sumuqan |Šakkan, protector of wild animals|, living things of the steppe' and the Tigris and Euphrates (Heidel 1951, p.63). Only after this creation was completed did Marduk create flora and fauna, dry land, and the cities which people were presumably to look after.

The mother-goddess, this time under the name of Mami, and Enki were 'reunited' as creators of mankind in the First Babylonian Dynasty text, possibly a birth incantation, which is badly preserved. The third column calls for the help of Mami, the creator of mankind, to create mankind for thralldom (Heidel 1951; Kramer 1961). It is not clear whether this is the first creation of mankind or the second one because the title of Mami precedes the lines about the task that she was called to perform. Mami, this time presented as Nintu, requests help for this procedure and possibly suggests clay as the substance to be used. Enki seems to volunteer as her assistant by addressing the gods with the proposition to slay a god for this purpose. The blood and the flesh should then be mixed with clay by Mami (here as Ninhursagga) so that 'God and man...[be] united in the clay' (Heidel 1951, p.67).

It is interesting to note that while the Sumerians did not make any claim to even a partial divinity of humans, the Semitic accounts imply it by introducing divine blood into the process. The reason for doing so remains unclear due to the lack of any 'native' explanation, thus making it a subject of speculation by modern interpreters. One of the most common rationalizations for the somewhat divine nature of humans is the lack of moral perfection both in deities and in people. Humankind received its 'evil' nature with the flow of blood of morally imperfect deities such as the rebel Qingu. The untrustworthy nature of human beings, or rather the primitiveness of at least some of them, are also addressed by the Middle Babylonian edition of the text entitled 'Naram-Sin |an Akkadian king| and the Enemy Hordes: The Cuthean Legend' (Goodnick Westenholz 1997). According to this text, Ea, for unknown reasons, created the 'barbarians,' 'mankind |who| scurried into caves' with six kings, and six hundred of their troops. Together with them Ea created 'the terror of lions,/death, plague, fever (?), storm/disease,/|fa|mine, want, and (losses on) the market, which.../...increased, with them, he sent...' Then he spoke to other deities: 'I have created this people. You, its destiny/determine on the condition that they are not to annihilate mankind' (Goodnick Westenholz 1997, p.287).

The story proceeds with the description of the destiny of these nomadic people who eventually attacked the Akkadian empire, approaching its capital, Akkad. The Standard Babylonian Recension of this story depicts Naram-sin's enemy hordes as '|a| people with partridge bodies, a race with raven faces,/the great gods created them./On the land which the gods created was their city/Tiāmat suckled them' (Goodnick Westenholz 1997, p.309).

Although the above passages are concerned only with the enemy of the mighty king Naram-sin and are written from the very subjective perspective of his subjects or followers, one can clearly see that all the wicked things of the world associated with humans were also creations of Ea and other gods. The divinity of the savages cannot be assumed, since there is no reference to any substance of which they were made. On the other hand, it was Tiāmat, the Babylonian *prima materia* mother-goddess who suckled them, which may suggest the origin of their 'evil' nature inherited through the milk of this adversary of Marduk. If such was the case – that is, if the human race in general was perceived as having 'wickedness' attributed to them by deities – then the Mesopotamian beliefs did not include the concept of sin, because people were, by definition, fallible.

The Assyrian story of creation, which was discovered in Assur and is dated to around 800 B.C. (Heidel 1951; Kramer 1961), goes even further than the previous accounts in stressing the divine status of at least the first human beings. The story begins with a typical introduction referring to the creation, separation and pronunciation of destinies for heaven and earth and establishment of the rivers Tigris and Euphrates. Anu, Enlil, Šamaš, Ea and the great Anunnaku gods recount their creations and wonder what else they can do. The Anunnaku suggest to Enlil: 'In Uzumua, the bond of heaven and earth,/Let us slay (two) Lamga gods./With their blood let us create mankind./The service of the gods be their portion' (Heidel 1951, p.69).

The description of all the tasks to be performed by the new beings follows. However, instead of mankind being created *en masse* as in all other Mesopotamian accounts, this text refers only to two humans, Ulligarra and Zalgarra, who were brought forth and whose great destinies were decreed by the mother-goddess Aruru. They were to spring up 'by themselves like grain from the ground' (Heidel 1951, p.71); that is, populate the earth for the service to deities.

This text is rather unusual in light of the existing traditions of Mesopotamia. Not only do we have the first couple here, but their names were preceded with the sign for 'deity' indicating that at least these parents of humankind were considered to be divine (Heidel 1951). One may wonder whether this story influenced the author or authors of the Yahwistic account of the Old Testament, referring to Adam and Eve as the first couple or whether it was vice versa. Although more comparisons between the Genesis accounts of creation and those from Mesopotamia are discussed later, one must point out here that Adam and Eve should be considered at least partially divine, because they were originally immortal, so possessing at least one of the attributes associated with deities, other ones being power and knowledge.

It seems that the above text from Assur was exceptional in the Mesopotamian literature concerned with the creation of mankind. The latest account of this event from 'traditional' Mesopotamia, that of Berossos, remains relatively faithful to well-established principles of Sumero-Akkadian convention. According to him: 'Baal-Marduk/saw that the ground was lonely/that it did not live/he said to one of the gods/"Cut off your head"/rubbed earth in the blood/made people and animals/who can bear his light air' (Doria and Lenowitz 1976, p.240).

As in other accounts of the area people were created *en masse*, as humankind and not as separate individuals, out of mud and divine blood. However, the purpose of creation is somewhat different. Although the service of people to the deities is implied, the main reason seems to be the loneliness of the earth which did not bear any fruit. Furthermore, people are presented on the same level as animals which were created from the same substances and at the same time. And only after them were the stars, the sun, the moon and planets brought into existence.

It might be reasonable to surmise that Berossos had access to various Mesopotamian written and oral accounts of the creation process and could have been familiar with the other traditions (such as that of Genesis) which had been patterned after them. Because of inconsistencies between them he might have tried to combine them into what seemed to him to be a logical sequence of events, but not necessarily the one which was the most popular. On the other hand, Berossos might not have been interested at all in following the order of creation as presented by these traditions, focusing rather on the presentation of specific events in the form which he found suitable for his work, *Babyloniaka*.

Finally, it must be noted that regardless of any possible divinity in humans, the people were perceived as unable to produce by themselves. It was usually Enki/Ea who had to teach them all crafts and sometimes even to create 'work stations' for them. The creation story which Kramer and Maier (1989) call 'The Disputation between the Bird and the Fish' states clearly that Enki, among other things, 'cleaned up the small canals, laid out there irrigation ditches…spread wide the stalls and sheepfolds…set up cities and hamlets, multiplied the Black heads [the Sumerians], supplied them with a king…' (p.87). According to another text, the hymn to Enki's temple, he himself had to set up his own temple so people could tend to it (Kramer and Maier 1989). Berossos also refers to Oan/Ea as the one who 'spent the day with the people/he ate no food/gave them letters learning skill/how to start a city/write laws/mark the land/sowing reaping/everything…' (Doria and Lenowitz 1976, p.238). The conclusion then is quite obvious: without Enki/Ea/Oan's help and advice people would not be able to function and to please the deities with their work.

In reference to Anatolian tradition

It is quite obvious from the above texts that the creation of humankind was mainly associated with the artful work of Enki/Ea even in situations when other gods, such as Marduk, are presented as taking over this process. While this creation seems to come into being as the action of a male god, the contributions of female deities to the formation of humankind were also acknowledged by different texts. Thus, it seems that ancient Mesopotamians did not 'discriminate' – at least in religious texts – against the female gender, treating all creating divinities at the same level. It is also important to note that although there are no texts from ancient Anatolia which describe the event of the creation of humankind, the enigmatic Hittite goddesses known as Gulses and MAH

.MEŠ (Hurrian Hutena-Hutellura) were presented as creators of mankind, goddesses of fate and destiny who presided at birth (Gurney 1977). This presents quite an interesting situation which may reflect, at least to some degree, the perceived status of women in ancient societies. The lack of significant involvement of female deities in the process of creation in the Egyptian tradition may indicate the rather low status of women, while in Mesopotamia, the women's position was much higher, although not quite equal to that of men (possibly with the exception of the Sumerian period). On the other hand the thirteenth century B.C. Anatolia – where the queens had so much power that Puduhepa's 'signature' on official documents accompanied the one of her husband, Hattusili III – gives the honor of bringing humankind to existence to female deities. However, only a few hundred years later, goddesses completely lost not only their role in creation but their right to existence, as denied by the religion of one, single god, Yahweh of Genesis.

Furthermore, one must consider the purpose of the creation of humankind: as servants to the deities. Although there are no texts referring directly to the subject of creation in Anatolian mythology it is quite obvious from various existing texts that the purpose of human existence was the same as in Mesopotamia. The divine forces were the masters who rewarded their servants for good service and punished them for neglect of their duties. In Anatolia it was the king who carried the heaviest burden of this service. If he failed to perform his service properly, then the deities could punish the whole country without even letting the king know the nature of his 'crime.' Once the king discovered the reason for the divine wrath through an oracle or any other means, he was obliged to repay his debt to the deities. The best example of divine-human relations in Anatolia is the collection of so-called 'Plague Prayers of Muršili II' (Beckman 1997a). When he came to the throne, some sort of epidemic was ravaging Muršili II's land. Finally, after 20 years of this plague he realized his own guilt by association with his ancestors and prepared a series of prayers to appease the deities. In the Third Prayer he tried to appeal to the common sense of deities, telling them,

> If you, the gods, my lords, [do not send] the plague [away] from Hatti, the bakers of offering bread and the libation bearers [will die]. And if they die off [the offering bread] and the libation will be cut off for the gods, [my lords]. Then you will come to me, O gods [my lords], and hold this (to be) a sin [on my part] … (Beckman 1997a, p.159)

In the Fourth Prayer he reminded them that

> … since the earliest times you have been concerned with [humans], and you have [not] abandoned humankind. [You have] (rather) very much [safeguarded] humankind. Your divine servants [were] numerous, and they set out for the gods, my lords, offering bread and libation. But now you have turned on humankind, so that it happened that in the time of [my] grandfather (Tudhaliya III) Hatti was oppressed … (Beckman 1997a, p.159)

This remainder was followed by Muršili II's explanation of how he could not admit his guilt since the oracles did not provide any guidance. Now that he knew his guilt he could plead his case.

This understanding of the role of humans on earth, whether in Mesopotamia or in Anatolia, had its consequences in the perception of what was to happen to people after their death; that is, after they were no longer needed (see Chapter 11).

Iran: The male-kind versus the female-kind

The Indo-Iranians introduced to the Middle East the concept of 'the prototype of mankind,' the figure of Gayomart, the sixth creation of Ohrmazd according to the Bundahišn. His name seems to be derived from *Gaya maretan* of the Avesta tradition, who is described as who 'first heard the thought and teachings of Ahura Mazda, (and) from whom he (Ahura-Mazdā) fashioned the family of the Aryan lands, the seed of the Aryan lands' (Dresden 1961, p.342). What is striking, at least for me, is the fact that while Gayomart is portrayed as a single first man (even in the Manichean tradition where he is known as Gēhmurd), actually his Avesta name is a plural. This may indicate the existence of a proto-race of the male-kind – which could be even of divine origin since its substance and how it was created are not specified – which was in alliance with Ahura Mazdā. The female-kind is not even mentioned, although in the later tradition of the Pahlavi book, Zātspram, the demon whore, Jēh, is shown as the queen of her kind, that is of all whoredemons who, as a part of Ahriman's world, causes of the defilement of mankind. Thus even in the Indo-Iranian tradition of the first millennium B.C. we can see a very big, negative change toward women in the Middle East. According to Hinnells (1975) Ohrmazd himself admits that the only reason women were created is the lack of any other vessel to carry the human seed. If so, questions might arise as to why he did not create something else to do the job and why such an important creation was not thought out by him first, but by Ahriman. This negative approach to women and blaming them for the earthly problems is also well reflected in the Yahwistic account of Genesis which is discussed in the next chapter. Since old Mesopotamian accounts of the creation of mankind not only do not specify separate means of creation for men and women, but also do not blame one gender or the other for the fall of humankind, it is interesting to see this new concept appearing both at the east and the west borders of the Middle East within a short period of time (between around 1000 B.C. and 500 B.C.).

Gayomart, as tall and as 'bright as the sun,' but also mortal as indicated by his name 'Mortal Life' (Curtis 1993, p.24), was killed by Angra Mainyu. But his heritage was preserved because upon his death his seed fell into the earth and was purified by the sun. After forty years Mašya and Mašyānag sprang from it in the form of a rhubarb plant with 15 leaves of the 15 years (Bundahišn XV; after Curtis 1993, p.20). These two assumed a human form and 'the breath went spiritually to them.' Ohrmazd addressed them in the following words: 'You are human beings, the father (and) mother of the world. Do your work in accordance with righteous order and a perfect mind. Think, speak and do what is good. Worship no demons' (after Dresden 1961, p.343).

Unfortunately the first couple did not listen to these directions and shortly their minds became corrupted by Angra Mainyu, whom they pronounced to be the creator of water, earth, plants and animals. This switching of alliances was not good for them since it took them 50 years to produce their first offspring, the first set of twins whom they consumed. Then after another long period of childlessness, the second set of twins was born. These twins survived and began the human race.

This story is very interesting because in addition to the introduction of the concept of the 'prototype of mankind' it can also be interpreted as a combination of various traditions. The very Indo-Iranian motif of ethical dualism is quite evident. The first couple was told what was good but they chose the other way. Obviously the choice was theirs as established in the creation of the world according to Zaratuštra: 'Now, these are the two original Spirits, who as Twins, have been perceived (by me?) through a vision. In both thought and speech, (and) in deed, these two are what is good and evil. Between these two, the pious, not the impious, will choose rightly' (Yasna 30.3–6; after Malandra 1983, p.40).

Another element which is quite typical of the Indo-European tradition is the focus on twins from whom the rest of humankind was derived. Gayomart's ancestors included all heroes and anti-heroes of the Iranian tradition as described by Firdausi in his Šāh-nāma where the first ruler is known as Kiyumars (Gayomart). He, the first man, was the one who introduced the elements of the mortal kingdom, the throne and the crown, and ruled for many years over everything. His reign represented the first period in human evolution – pastoralism. It was not until the time of his grandson that agriculture was invented (Curtis 1993, p.31).

The idea of the rhubarb plant with its 15 leaves or branches can be compared to the tree of all races as still represented in traditional nomadic beliefs of the Central Asian steppe, although this tree is supposed to have only 10 branches. If this is the case, the origin of this concept may be very regional (Central Asia, Siberia, Western China) and very ancient, and should be sought in the shamanistic traditions of the early nomads, whether of Indo-European or any other origin.

The early Mesopotamian, or rather early Middle Eastern, tradition in general can be seen in the equality of both genders at the time of creation. Both male and female were created and they are both to blame for choosing a wrong path. Furthermore, they were created obviously as the last element. If the proclamation of Angra Mainyu as the creator of previous elements indicates the order in which they came to being – first water, second earth, third plants, fourth animals – then this order is consistent with the Mesopotamian tradition.

The monotheistic approach

The 'Priestly style'

There is no doubt that the focus of both creation accounts of Genesis is on mankind. The Priestly tradition places this event (1:26–31) as the last creation of the only god who is actually referred in this section as Yahweh Elohim. This title again may recall the role of the Canaanite god El in this event since one of El's epithets is a creator of humankind described as follows: 'Indeed our creator is eternal/Indeed ageless he who formed us' (Cross 1973, p.15).

The plural form of Yahweh's name is very important for the understanding of the formula that the god used as an announcement of his intent. 'Let **us** make man[kind] in **our** own image, in the likeness of ourselves, and let them be masters of the fish of the sea, the birds of heaven' (1:26, emphasis mine). This formula clearly indicates the Mesopotamian and Egyptian origins of this account. Not only does it refer to multiple deities of the Sumero-Akkadian-Babylonian tradition who were involved in the act of human creation but it also points out to the image in which people were to be created. They were to look like deities. One should recall a very similar phrase from the Egyptian literature 'They [humans] are his [god's] images, who came from his body' (Lichtheim 1997c, p.65) and may wonder whether this statement refers to numerous images of deities present in 'pagan' temples of older religions. There is also a possibility that the Priestly redactor(s) wanted to emphasize the difference between animals and humans, being aware that in Egypt many animals were deified (Brandon 1963).

The echo of earlier traditions can also be seen in the word 'man' (Hebrew *adam*) which actually means 'mankind.' This indicates that again we are dealing with creation *en masse*, not of any single person. This is confirmed by the next three lines of the account which state: 'God created man in the image of himself,/in the image of God he created him [mankind],/male and female he created them' (1:27).

Thus, there should be no doubt that men and women were created at the same time, both to be images of the 'one and only' but presented as many (Elohim). However, there is no mention of the material that was used for this creation. Thus, it can be assumed that it was a typical creation *ex nihilo* consistent with preceding lines of this account and also known in the other and older traditions of the Middle East.

The purpose of Yahweh Elohim's creation of humankind is somewhat different than the 'standard procedure' (that is, servants to deities) reason given elsewhere. This time people are to be masters over other creations of the god. However, granting them mastery of earth does not really exclude their role as servants to divine force(s). It might be interpreted that Yahweh Elohim did not want to be involved in the maintenance of earth but still wished for its prosperity so he created people to do 'his' job. He even blessed them for this purpose and ordered them to multiply. Little did he know at the time that soon he would regret this command.

The Quranic style

As explained before, the Quranic tradition of creation seems to be a mixture of the Yahwistic and Priestly ideas with some additional influences. The creation of human-kind is a good example of the 'editing' talents of Muhammad. Although the main theme of this event is the Yahwistic story of the paradise, the elements of other accounts also occupy quite a prominent place.

Again, people were created as the last creation of Allah at the time of 'original' creation. In this act of creation which involved clay, and/or water, and/or soul (breath), there was no difference made between the first man, Adam, and the first woman, his wife (who was nameless): 'He is the One who has created you (all) from a single soul, and made its mate from it, so he may settle down with her [for the purpose of procreation]' (The Heights; X, 7:189 (XXIX)).

In another part of the Quran, Allah explains to the angels his intent of creating mankind: 'I am about to create a human being from ringing clay from moulded slime. When I have finished with him and breathed some of My spirit into him, then drop down on your knees before him' (Stoneland; XIV, 15:16 (II)).

The physical material used for the creation of the humans is clay, while the breath of life so prominent in other mythologies, including the Yahwistic version, is possibly a counterpart of the soul above. However, other parts of the Quran are even more specific in the description of the act of human creation: 'He started out by creating man from clay; then He made his progeny from an extract of discarded liquid; next He completed him and breathed some of His own spirit into him. He has granted you hearing, eyesight and vital organs' (Worship of Adoration; XXI, 32:Intro).

The liquid which is mentioned in this passage is probably the original waters of non-existence since elsewhere in the Quran there are references to everything being made out of water.

However, the masterpiece of the Quranic tradition is a very specific description of Allah's involvement in each and every human being:

> We (first) created you from dust; then from a drop of semen; then from a clot; then from a lump of tissue either shape or else shapeless, so We might explain [things] to you. We cause anything We wish to rest in wombs for a stated period; then We bring you forth as infants; eventually you reach full growth. Some of you will pass away [early in life], while others of you will be sent back to the feeblest age of all, so that he will not know a thing after once having had knowledge. (Pilgrimage; XVII, 22:Intro., emphasis mine)

The above passage is incredibly interesting because its creator so skillfully combined mythological traditions of the creation of humankind with scientific observation of a life cycle of each and every human. Furthermore, it also indicates clearly that in contrast to the god of Genesis, Allah is not a 'one time creator.' He is the one who is actively involved, thus making a relationship between the god and his follower as personable as the ones of the other Middle Eastern traditions preceding the rise of monotheistic religions. Allah's involvement is confirmed by numerous references in the Quran to his personal interest in the affairs of everyday life.

While in the case of the Priestly and Yawhistic accounts references to the plural form of the 'one and only' reflect confusion over a somewhat 'transitional stage' of this newly created religion, references in the Quran to 'we' might be ascribed to the dimension of this god whose name indicates his 'wholeness.' He is not exactly a male god since many of his epithets are also feminine. Allah is rather a representation of the genderless 'divine force' which, in the best tradition of Pharaonic Egypt, incorporates all forces that are unexplainable but believed to exist. This is the reason why the translations of his name should avoid the term 'god' but should stay with the concept itself, 'Allah.'

Thus, Allah created and keeps creating humankind. When he placed the first man, Adam, on the earth, he instructed him and his wife to be overlords on earth. In order to elevate Adam to this position Allah taught him all the names of other creations. This recalls the ancient traditions of naming in both Mesopotamia and in Egypt which allowed Allah of the Quran to raise Adam (or mankind in general) above other spiritual entities also created by him. These entities included angels and the satan (Diabolis) who were created previously by Allah out of smokeless fire (Stoneland; XIV, 15:16 (II)–15:44 (III)). In fact it seems that at the beginning only angels existed and when Adam was created, Diabolis, one of the angels, did not agree with Allah's decision to put a human in charge of the earth. Consequently Diabolis was banished and all of those who followed his way joined his 'extended' family of satanic forces. Once again, Muhammad managed to overcome the inconsistencies of Genesis by explaining that all evil forces were also Allah's creations as originally 'good' spirits but since they were given free will they chose to turn against him. Thus, Allah created everything but he does not command the evil whose existence cannot be denied.

Conclusions

In comparison to other parts of the world, the Middle East is the only region where the development of human thought can be observed for around 5000 years. As incomplete as the written sources of the area are, they still provide a wealth of information concerning the perception of humankind by people themselves. Considering only the accounts discussed above, one must be amazed by how focused, although infrequent, changes appeared during that time. The fact that clay was the most popular material from which humans were created is clearly confirmed by stories from Mesopotamia, Egypt, Genesis and the Quran. It is even suggested by the Ugaritic myth of Kirta in which El uses clay to create a female demon to cure a sick king (Gibson 1978) or in references to the Canaanite El possibly performing creations 'in the image of the potter nipping clay' (Smith 1994, p.83). The choice of this material should not be surprising, not only because of its accessibility, but also due to the fact that the first stories were created in Sumer, the most southern part of modern Iraq which is barren of everything else. It was only natural for the Sumerians to utilize this material to its utmost in art, architecture, writing, everyday life and in religion. For others this choice was also logical due to the clay's qualities: it is easy to gather, to form and to dissipate (like a human life).

Thus, clay has survived all changes in ideological systems of the Middle East. Sometimes it was enhanced with spiritual elements to provide humans with a part of the divine glory, sometimes with divine blood for the same purpose, or it was mixed with the original waters of creation which themselves were the natural choice for a creation material. In the end the clay in the form of dust was 'added' to a male fluid to produce a new being in a 'scientific' way but still through the direct involvement of the supernatural.

Depending on the ruling philosophy, clay was sometimes replaced by the divine blood of the 'not-all-so-good' deity to explain the inherent tendency in every human being to make decisions threatening the established (good) order of existence. At other times there was not even a need to use a material since humans, like everything else, could be created out of nothing, just by a simple thought and pronunciation of the divine wish. But no matter what kind of material was used for the creation of mankind, its limited existence on earth was recognized by all. This limitation also needed an explanation.

It seems that until the birth of so-called monotheistic religions of the Middle East, the ancient people subscribed to the leading idea of humans being created in order to serve deities so the divine lives would be comfortable and full of joy. However, the rise of the 'one and only' god changed this perception a little. This one god, whether Yahweh or Allah, does not need the numerous services that his predecessors did. Thus, having the whole population of earth focusing on the pleasures of one god was quite an illogical concept. So, by default, humans became masters of the earth, freeing the god to attend to his own business, whatever it might be. This seems not to be such a wise decision on the part of the divine force, considering how quickly humans have been destroying his creation. Furthermore, without specific guidance provided on an everyday basis by numerous deities of the polytheistic traditions of the Middle East, there seems to have been too many options open to people to choose a wrong path.

Finally, it should be evident that the status of women has been deteriorating almost simultaneously with the gradual elimination of the number of deities involved in the creation process. The hostile or near-hostile attitude toward women is clearly demonstrated in the accounts of the first millennium B.C., especially if one adds to the above accounts Hesiod's works of the eighth century B.C. in Greece. However, there is one specific story, the story of the paradise of the Yahwistic tradition, which should be held responsible for almost 3000 years of women's misery and their inferior status to the male-kind. This story is presented in the next chapter.

10

Paradise: Divine or Human?

The story of the Biblical paradise is not only probably the single most well-known story of Judaic, Christian and the Quranic traditions, but also the one which has done the most harm to the position of women in each and every society whose ideology includes it. While there is little doubt that the prophet Muhammad's revelation concerning this story was based on his knowledge of the Biblical account, the origin of at least a few themes from this story can be found much earlier in ancient Mesopotamia. Thus, in order to discuss the most important motifs of the paradise myth in the Pentateuch, one must first become acquainted with its Mesopotamian predecessor to see that its final version was an intentional 'manipulation' of the beauty which was turned into the beast. The Quranic narrative is not presented separately but referred to in relevant parts of the discussion.

Enki and the controversial divine paradise

The Mesopotamian story of 'Enki and Ninhursag: A Sumerian Paradise Myth,' as Kramer and Maier (1989) call it, is among the texts referring to the land of Dilmun, the description of which seemS to be at least the inspiration for the author(s) of the Biblical paradise. The myth begins with the description of Dilmun as being a holy, pure, and bright land where the sexual union between Enki and his wife Ninsikila (one of the names of the mother-goddess Ninhursagga or Ninhursag, who is also called Damgalnuna and Nintur in the poem) took place. This is the land not disturbed by birds or wild animals preying on each other, where sickness does not exist and ageing does not occur. Thus, there is probably no death in Dilmun. But this deathless and pure land lacks the sweet water which is necessary for the growth of plants and farming the land. Ninsikila, who was a tutelary goddess of Dilmun, asks Enki to water it, which he does with the help of the sun-god Utu (Akkadian Šamaš). Her city changes into 'the floodgate of the land' (Kramer and Maier 1989, p.24).

It is quite interesting that such a marvelous city as Dilmun could have existed without water. Leick (1994) suggests that the descriptions of its waterless greatness were intended to be funny, implying that Enki was so lost in his love-making with Ninsikila that he simply forgot to create water for the city which he offered her as a bridal gift. Judging him on his encounter with Inana (described in Chapter 6), one may even suspect that he could have been somewhat drunk. However, he is quickly able to correct his mistake, blessing Dilmun not only with water but also with superiority in agriculture and trade.

Once this is done, Enki focuses his attention on his sexual desires. The next few lines of the myth are somewhat confusing and their interpretation depends solely upon which translator's version you use. However, one element is constant: Enki was 'playing' with his phallus in front of his wife, now called Nintu(r), whether as a display of his manhood or as an act of masturbation to fill up the ditches and reeds with his semen. For some reason he needs to assure Nintu that nobody is around to see them. Then Enki turns his attention to Nintu(r) (now called Damgalnuna) and he 'poured that semen into the womb, Enki's semen,/poured that semen into the womb of Ninhursag' (Kramer and Maier 1989, p.25). She becomes pregnant and delivers a baby girl, Ninmu (also translated as Ninnisiga or Nin-sar), within nine days without any pain. We are not told what Enki was doing at the time of her pregnancy so one might assume that he must have left the marshland where he had been frolicking with his wife. In any case, he comes back at a time when his daughter, grown older and beautiful, wanders into the marshland, his territory, where he sees her. It is not quite clear whether Enki was really aware that she was his daughter but the myth tells us that his sexual desire was awakened again. Leick (1994) points out a very metaphorical interpretation of the passage translated by Jacobsen (1987, p.192) as, 'He has put one foot in the boat,/May he not stay the other on dry land.'

Leick sees this as a description of '…vulva [as] a boat, and the "foot" is a likely euphemism for the penis. With one "foot" in the "boat" he will indeed not stay on "dry" land for long!' (1994, p.33).

He did not. Ninmu is pregnant and goes through the same process as her mother did. Ninmu's daughter, Ninkurra (or Ninimma), is born. The story is repeated again, this time with Ninkurra being Enki's choice and Uttu, 'the voluptuous woman' (Kramer and Maier 1989, p. 26), is born.

Although the next passage is very fragmentary it seems that this is the time for Enki's wife Ninhursagga to intervene. It is believed that she instructed Uttu to stay away from the marshes, Enki's sexual dominion, unless he brings her gifts such as cucumbers, apples, and grapes. According to Leick (1994), apples especially were believed to possess aphrodisiac qualities. Enki complies with her wishes but is not very happy about it. 'Enki – his face turned green – grabbed the staff, and headed for Uttu./"You who make demands [?] in her house: Open up! open up"' (Kramer and Maier 1989, p.27).

It is quite amusing that the description of his sexual encounter with Uttu is much longer than that of the sexual experiences Enki had with her mother, grandmother and great-grandmother. She was definitely more demanding and he had to work in order to please her, including possibly offering marriage as suggested by Jacobsen (1987). And then the unexpected happens: Uttu does not seem to be quite happy being filled up with Enki's semen. Her great-grandmother, Ninhursagga, wipes it off. She is also probably the one who plants Enki's seeds, leading to the growth of eight separate plants named in the myth.

Enki is back and ready for more action in the marshland. But instead of a beautiful girl passing by he sees these plants. Since he has never seen them before he knows that he has to decree their fate, but in order to do so he must eat them first, one by one. For reasons which are still the subject of debate (some of them listed by Leick 1994) Ninhursagga is really mad at him for consuming her 'garden' and curses him: 'With life-giving eye until he is dying never will I look upon him' (Jacobsen 1987, p.201). If Leick's (1994) suggestion that the garden has represented a common place for sexual encounters as well as the female genitals themselves is right, one might conclude that the act of eating the plants planted by the mother-earth herself was perceived as a sexual assault on the goddess. On the other hand, since these plants came from Enki's seed, he might have been 'accused' of reversing the order of nature by impregnating himself as has happened in other myths recorded in the Middle East and elsewhere.

As a consequence of eating the eight plants Enki becomes sick in eight parts of his body. Only Ninhursagga can cure him and after some 'negotiation' she decides to do so. For each hurt part of Enki's body she creates a new deity to heal it. The whole process takes place inside of her vulva, possibly implying his return to *prima materia* to have him 'reborn' with full strength and powers. This act of creating a deity at the time of need can be also seen in Canaanite mythology when El creates a goddess to heal Kirta's sickness since nobody else could be found as a replacement (Handy 1994). Among the deities whom Ninhursagga created are Ninti, the 'Lady of Rib,' pronounced in the last part of the myth to be 'the queen of months,' and Enšag, 'Lord of *ag*,' whose function is proclaimed as 'Lord of Dilmun.'

The Yahwistic account and the very controversial human paradise

The Yahwistic story of the creation of the first human couple is preceded by a short description of earlier creative acts (see Chapter 5) which presents the earth as a desert in an image quite similar to that of the original Dilmun. According to this account once the water was provided for earth by Yahweh Elohim he then formed a man (just one – Adam) out of soil and breathed into his nostrils 'the breath of life' (2:7) so he came to life. The god proceeded with the creation of a garden in Eden to be Adam's home. Yahweh Elohim brought to life all kinds of trees, including two important ones, the Tree of Life and the Tree of the Knowledge of Good and Evil, which he 'planted' in the middle of the garden. It was only the latter tree from which Adam was forbidden to eat 'for on the day you eat of it you shall more surely die' (2:17).

Since Yahweh Elohim realized that it was not good for Adam to be alone, he decided to create him a helpmate. Thus, birds and earth animals (but not sea creatures) were created also from soil. But it was Adam who finished this act when he named all of them. Unfortunately 'no helpmate suitable for man was found for him' (2:21). Thus after causing Adam to fall into a deep sleep, the god removed a rib from him and 'enclosed it in flesh' which became a woman whom Adam also named with the general noun 'woman.' This part of the story finishes with the statement that at the time both humans were naked but were not aware of their nudity.

The story proceeds with the serpent which convinces the woman that she and her husband should eat from the Tree of the Knowledge of Good and Evil. He tells her that they will not die as the god told Adam but rather that their 'eyes will be opened and [they] will be like **gods** knowing good and evil' (3:5–6, emphasis mine). Then she ate the fruit and gave some of it to her man. But they did not die as one might expect. The only result was that they noticed their nakedness and run to prepare some clothes from fig leaves.

Upon hearing Yahweh Elohim coming into the garden, the first couple hid among the trees. This was the clue for the god that something was wrong. Upon questioning Adam, the 'one and only' realized that the humans ate from the forbidden tree. The man explained his action as 'It was the woman you put with me; she gave me the fruit and I ate it' while the woman just made a statement that 'The serpent tempted me and I ate' (3:13).

The story continues with Yahweh Elohim pronouncing punishment, first for the snake (crawling on its belly, eating dust and becoming a mutual enemy of women and their respective offsprings), then for the woman (pain in childbearing, 'yearning' [?] for her husband who was to be her lord) and finally for the man (hard work to be able to survive, only to die at the end of it all).

Only after this cursing did Adam name his wife Eve 'because she was the mother of all those who live' (3:20–21). Yahweh Elohim made clothes out of skin for them and then expelled them from the garden (there is no reference to what happened to the animals). This is also the time when the Tree of Life becomes important since the god obviously does not want humans to come even close to it and so he 'posted the cherubs, and the flame of a flashing sword to guard the way to the tree of life' (3:24).

The story proceeds by discussing the next generations brought into life from the union between Adam and Eve.

Common themes of both paradise stories

The paradise: Its location and concept

The land of Dilmun of the Sumerian paradise is mentioned also in other Mesopotamian texts as early as the late Uruk and the Jemdet Nasr periods (between 3500–2800 B.C.) (During Caspers 1986; Nissen 1986). It is recorded as a real place, a location from which ships were bringing loads to Sumer and possibly other lands such as Makkan and Meluhha (Kramer 1986), but also as a sort of a mythical land. In the Sumerian story of the flood, Ziusudra, the Sumerian Noah, is given eternal life by the gods who send him, 'The preserver of the "name" of vegetation and the seed of mankind,/ In the land of crossing, the land of Dilmun, the place where the sun rises' (Kramer 1986, p.193). In view of the story of Enki and Ninhursagga, the choice of Dilmun as a perfect place for eternal life for Ziusudra seems to be logical because of its agricultural wealth and trade contacts. These would guarantee him life without worries in the holy and pure land of Dilmun.

Since there seems to be no doubt that at least the Sumerian paradise was a real place, many scholars have tried to find its location. It is also commonly accepted that there is a strong possibility that both the accounts of the Yahwistic and the Quranic paradise refer to the same location, especially since it is mentioned that the Garden of Eden was located to the east, which must be calculated from Syria–Palestine pointing directly to the Mesopotamian origin of the story. Its Mesopotamian roots can also be seen in two of the four rivers (the Tigris and the Euphrates; the remaining two are the Pishon encircling the land of Havilah with gold and the Gihon encircling Kush) which were flowing from the

Garden of Eden. The Quran does not provide any specific clues as to the geographical location of the paradise. Thus, it appears that if an agreement can be reached with regard to the location of the Sumerian paradise, then the other one would also be discovered by its association with the story (unless you consider this type of research to be an exercise in futility). For this reason the arguments concerning the location of Dilmun, the Sumerian paradise, are presented first and are then followed by a short commentary on the Biblical and Quranic paradise.

According to Kramer (1986), the location of the Sumerian paradise should be sought even farther than to the east of Syria–Palestine, to the east of Mesopotamia, and it should be identified with Gilgamesh's 'Land of the Living', whose whereabouts he placed first on the eastern coast of the Persian Gulf and then farther east to Pakistan and India, where the famous civilizations of the Indus Valley once flourished.

However, most scholars agree that the term 'Dilmun' (also known as Telmun or Tilmun) refers to Bahrain and possibly other islands in the area, although Dilmun's extension in different time periods is still debatable (Al Khalifa and Rice 1986; Mughal 1983; Rice 1984, 1985). For example, even an excavated temple at Barbar (Bahrain) which did not produce any written material can be archaeologically interpreted as dedicated to three important deities of Dilmun from the Sumerian point of view: Ninhursagga, Enki, and Inzag, his son (Andersen 1986; for the discussion of the Dilmunite deities and their origin see Al Nashef 1986). To make the subject of the location of Dilmun even more fascinating, one must mention that the evidence of at least some trade contacts between Bahrain and the Indus civilization have been discovered (Dani 1986; Joshi 1986; Rao 1986), in addition to archaeologically confirmed contacts between both civilizations and Mesopotamia since early times. The trading partners of Dilmun whose names often appear together in Mesopotamian texts are Makkan and Meluḫḫa, which are considered by many scholars to represent the Oman Peninsula and the Indus Valley cultures respectively (Cleuziou 1986; Weisgerber 1986).

Although the majority of scholars do not question the connection between Dilmun and Bahrain, some raise doubts about Dilmun being a Sumerian paradise (Alster 1983; Bibby 1986). They point to the fact that the idea of a paradise where humans lived without any worries for eternity was foreign to Sumerian as well as Mesopotamian philosophy in general. However, the perception of Dilmun as a holy and pure land should not be disregarded, especially in view of the very high number of burial mounds and temples in Bahrain in comparison to settlements (for discussion see Al Khalifa and Rice 1986). As Bibby (1986) suggests it might be that the Dilmunites felt themselves to be blessed people because of the presence of numerous fresh-water springs – some of which emerge from the salt waters – 'given' to them by Enki and they 'convinced' the Sumerians about the holiness of their land. Since this possibility exists one might suggest that the idea of paradise is still of Sumerian origin through the recognition of the Holy Land, which over thousands of years has gone through several 'necessary' transformations to resurface as the Biblical Garden of Eden. Even its Biblical name 'Eden' is of Sumerian origin through the designation *edin* which was used by the Sumerians for their own plain (Gordon 1996; *édinu* as 'plain, steppe or desert' – Brandon 1963, p.125; for more discussion of the extended meaning of this word see Wallace 1985). Certainly, (early explorer) Captain E.L. Durand's description of the islands of Bahrain in the nineteenth century indicates a land of unusual beauty and peace:

> They [the islands] are surrounded by shoal water on every side, which greatly adds to the beauty of the place. Thus, on looking out to sea on the morning of a clear sky and a fresh nor'-wester, it would seem as if Nature, at all times lavish of effect, had here, however, exhausted every tint of living green in her paint box; and then, wearying of the effort, had splashed an angry streak of purple into the foreground. The water itself is so clear that you can see far down into the coral depths, while springs of fresh water bubble up through the brine, both near the entrance of the harbour and at several other places along the coast. (Rice 1984, p.14)

In the Biblical and the Quranic traditions the garden is perceived to be a very special place, with many wonderful trees with great fruit for consumption, in contrast to what was outside of it (wild shrubs and herbs). These contrasting images are in accordance with other Middle Eastern traditions in which the 'greatness' of many places was emphasized by the presence of special trees and/or important sources of water (for discussion see Wallace 1985).

It seems that the Yahwistic editor(s) tried to portray the real geographical or physical location of the paradise by listing the names and attributes of four rivers. Unfortunately, there is no agreement among scholars as to the identification of the Pishon and the Gihon rivers although it is frequently pointed out that the idea of the four streams or rivers flowing from one point is quite common in earlier traditions of Mesopotamia and the area in general (Wallace 1985). Because of the certain location of the Tigris and Euphrates many people believe that two other rivers mentioned by the JE account actually refer to two channels somewhere in the southern part of Iraq, or to the waters of *abzu* which encompass the earth (Brandon 1963). However, there are many other locations (among them the Lebanon, the Amanus Mountains, Assyria and Aden) proposed for the Garden of Eden by different authors (too numerous even to mention) and, as countless discussions on the Internet indicate, general agreement on its identification is not going to be reached any time soon.

Thus, if the idea of the Biblical paradise emerged from the divine paradise of the Mesopotamian tradition, why do we not just accept the same location for the Garden of Eden as for Dilmun? After all, the Yahwistic redactor(s) may have been simply confused as to the geography of the area (as many modern students are today) and were more interested in presenting the idea behind the garden than giving a map of how to reach it.

Finally, it must be mentioned that although there is no concept of the paradise in the Mesopotamian or Biblical sense in the Avestan tradition, the term itself existed as 'the best existence,' probably referring to the high heaven. According to the description offered by Yasna 16.7 it was a place where all the good dwell, including souls of the dead who followed the truth (Dresden 1961). As a 'house of praise' or 'house of rewards' this paradise-heaven could have been located in the Alburz mountains, at the first mountain Hara where Ahura Mazdā and his aspects were believed to live (Dresden 1961). Although, the first glance, the idea of the Iranian paradise has not much to do with the Sumerian tradition, one might see an echo of the earlier account (a place for 'good' souls) and the origin of heaven as a paradise to which people should aspire in monotheistic traditions of the Middle East.

The trees

The final episodes of both paradise stories are associated with special plants or trees and their or their fruits' consumption by those who were not entitled to this act. In both cases the punishment is severe, including the threat of death. Thus the meaning and the importance of these trees must be discussed in the context of available information.

The presence of special trees in many stories of Middle Eastern traditions is nothing unusual. They were used in the description of important places, as marking points of special locations, as locations themselves, or as symbols (Wallace 1985). For example, the Hittite and Canaanite cultic objects or stones known respectively as ḫuwaši and maṣṣēbâ, which were set up 'in temples and rural shrines, were associated with trees' (Gurney 1977, p.37). There is even a possibility that Mesopotamian motifs of the garden as both a favorite location for sexual frolicking and a metaphor

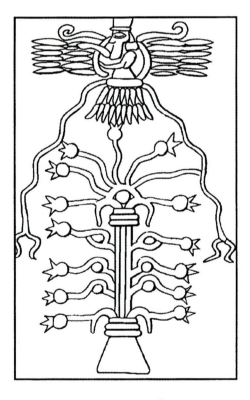

Figure 10.1 The stylized tree (of adoration?) and the sun-god Šamā in his winged disc. From a cylinder seal

for the female genitals, as well as the symbolism of apple-trees as representing the male genitals (on the subject of sex and erotica in the Mesopotamian literature explaining both sexual and sensual symbolism in literary and non-literary texts see Leick 1994), influenced the Yahwistic writer(s) in compiling the story of the paradise.

While the nature of both plants and Enki's crime of eating them remains obscure, the Yawhistic and Quranic narratives are quite specific. According to the JE there were two important trees in the garden: the Tree of the Knowledge of Good and Evil, and the Tree of Life, which were probably located in close proximity to the main source of waters from which the four rivers flow. In the Quran there seems to be confusion, since Allah refers usually to 'the tree,' implying the existence of only one tree which is named the 'Tree of Immortality' in Ta-ha (XVI, 20:116 (VII)) (for the Yahwistic confusion concerning a similar problem see Wallace 1985, pp.101–113). However, this is still the tree from which the forbidden fruit was eaten by the first couple.

The presence of two trees with similar qualities as the ones of the Yahwistic Eden is noted by yet another tradition from the Middle East, the one from Iran. While there is no description of the paradise *per se* in the Iranian (particularly Zoroastrian) tradition, there is a very special place associated with the original creation: the Vourukasha Sea, 'the gathering point of water.' The source of the water and of light was Mount Hara (Curtis 1993). In the middle of this sea there were two trees: the Saena Tree (also known as 'Tree of All Remedies' or 'Tree of All Seeds') – a nest for a legendary bird, Saena (a falcon) – and the 'mighty Gaokerena' plant (White Hom or White Haoma – the source of the immortality drink) with its healing properties and immortality gift for those who were resurrected from the dead (Curtis 1993). The first tree which offers protection for Saena, who can cause all seeds to grow with her winds, is protected by various beings from contact with any harmful forces.

Although the existence of two trees in the Biblical paradise have bothered some interpreters (for discussion see Brandon 1963), in view of the story itself and the Iranian tradition as an additional source it should be quite clear that both trees were needed because they represented very specific qualities: one gave knowledge and the other gave life.

The Tree of the Knowledge of Good and Evil does not seem to have any direct 'ancestors' (for discussion see Wallace 1985), and it is the tree around which the whole story of the Fall evolves. This is also the tree whose fruit, from the beginning, is specifically forbidden for human consumption by the god himself under punishment of death. Thus, the first information provided about this tree (except for its location) is that whatever knowledge can be obtained by eating from it, this knowledge will be fatal for Adam (Eve has not been created yet). The second information is that this tree was occupied by the snake who could speak, and who ended up being successful in tempting the woman to take the fruit. The similarity can be seen here with the *huluppu* tree of Mesopotamian tradition. According to the story it was Inana who, shortly after the creation, found this tree (torn off by the South Wind, the same wind which caused trouble for Adapa; see the story in Chapter 7, pp.121–3) on the banks of the Euphrates, carried it to Uruk and replanted it in her sacred garden with the purpose of making a throne or bed out of it for herself.

> The tree grew large, but she could not cut off its bark.
> At its base the snake who knows no charm had set up for itself a nest,
>
> In its crown the Zu-bird had placed his young,
> In its midst Lilith had built for herself a house. (Armstrong 1969, pp.15–16)

Inana cried for help and Gilgamesh cut the tree which was then used for her throne or bed, and of its base Gilgamesh made *pukku* and of its crown he made *mikku* (probably musical instruments). Two of the three inhabitants of the *huluppu* tree, the snake and Lilith, were incorporated into monotheistic religions of the Middle East.

The third quality of the Tree of the Knowledge of Good and Evil becomes obvious after the act of disobedience is committed by the first couple. Exactly as the snake informed them, their eyes became open and they discover their nakedness. The Quranic tradition is even more specific because it refers directly to this quality of the tree by saying:

> So Satan whispered to them to show them both private parts which had gone unnoticed by either of them. He said: 'Your Lord only forbids you this tree so that you will not become two angels, or lest you both become immortal... Once they had tasted the tree[s fruit], their private parts became apparent to both of them, and they started to patch together leaves from the Garden for themselves. (The Heights; VIII: Intro. (II)7:25 (II))

Thus the fatal knowledge that came with the tree's fruit was not death but the realization of their sexual differences; in other words, the sexual awareness which would inevitably lead to procreation. However, at the time, the only action that they took immediately was to cover their bodies with clothes. Samuel Kramer liked to refer to an obscure Sumerian text which mentions 'the tree which establishes the use of clothes.' Was it the same tree as the Tree of the Knowledge of Good and Evil? Was this tree a fig-tree (the first clothes were made of its leaves) or an apple-tree (representing male genitals in Mesopotamian tradition) which awakens sexuality in the first couple?

The long-term results of this discovery were realized by Yahweh Elohim. With their act of disobedience the humans received the power of creation through mating. While some authors suggest that the god's concern about the 'fatal' knowledge obtained by Adam and Eve was caused by his fear of the future overpopulation of earth (Brandon 1963), I rather believe that his main concern was more selfish. Since humans were created in the image of divine force(s) (see Priestly account, Chapter 9, p.154), carried his breath, and were immortal (there was no command against eating from the Tree of Life), by eating from the Tree of the Knowledge they obtained one more divine attribute and thus became deities themselves. In this sense they could have become like the younger gods of the *Enûma Eliš* tradition who, after realizing their 'equality,' decided to strive for more power! This had to be prevented. Yahweh Elohim realized this and uttered the following words: 'See, the man[kind] has become like one of **us**, with his knowledge of good and evil. He must not be allowed to stretch his hand out next and pick from the tree of life also, and eat some and live for ever' (3:22–23, emphasis mine). In order to keep them away from the garden, the 'one and only' banished the first couple and, just in case they were ever to find their way back, posted the guards (for discussion see Wallace 1985) of the Tree of Life.

Thus, the presence of the second tree in the Garden of Eden was very logical, not, as some suggested, a result of two confusing traditions (for discussion see Wallace 1985). Once Yahweh Elohim had cursed people with death, 'for dust you are and to dust you shall return' (3:19), the Tree of Life had to be off limits to humans. Since the Quranic edition seems to use only one tree, the punishment imposed by Allah was the same, death, but there is no mention of guarding the Tree of Immortality because its fruits of knowledge were already consumed. Thus, it can be interpreted that humans received both knowledge and immortality from one tree in the sense that their memories would be carried through generations of their descendants thanks to the ability to procreate. Furthermore, Allah's curse gives some hope to humans: 'You will live on it [earth] and you will die on it, and from it will you be brought forth [again]' (The Heights; VIII: Intro. (II)–7:25 (II)).

The 'prototype' of the Tree or Plant of Life can be found in earlier stories of the Middle East (Wallace 1985). Since Gilgamesh's adventures in search of immortality were addressed in Chapter 7, only the other tree of the Sumero-Akkadian-Babylonian tradition remains to be mentioned. This tree, known as the *kiskanu* tree, required special care from the king and was presented frequently on seals;

> In Eridu there is a black *kiskanu*-tree growing in a pure place,
> its appearance is lapis-lazuli, erected on the Apsū.
> Enki, when walking there, filleth Eridu with abundance.
> In the foundation thereof is the place of the underworld, in the
>   resting-place is the chamber of Nammu.
> In its holy temple there is a grove, casting its shadow, therein no man
>   goeth to enter.
> In the midst are the Sun-god and the Sovereign of heaven, in between
>   the river with the two mouths.
> (Armstrong 1969, p.10 after Widengren 1951, pp.5–6)

Also in the Egyptian tradition there were references to the 'prototype' of the Tree of Life. The tree goddess was the one who provided the deceased with both food and drink to sustain him or her and the *ba*. Although in most cases she remains anonymous, in some others she is Hathor as the mistress of the west or Nut, the mistress of heaven in the realm of the dead (Hornung 1992). In some presentations she emerges from a tree trunk holding water and food for the dead, in others she is a tree herself, with only hands and breasts revealing her identity. Thus, in a way, she is the tree of life which allows for its continuation after the physical death.

It seems then that the Yahwistic writer or writers were very much aware of the existence of trees with special powers in numerous traditions of the Middle East. While the trees of life of the earlier traditions were to provide either eternity after death (Egyptian and Iranian accounts) or 'eternal' youth (Gilgamesh), the Yahwistic tree was the last divine attribute which had to be kept away from any other beings than the 'one and only' god himself.

Adam and Eve or Adam before Eve

While the mode of creation of the first man in the Yahwistic account is very consistent with other stories from the Middle East (see Chapter 9), his original loneliness in the Garden of Eden is rather unexpected. He was brought to life in order to take care of the garden which was full of trees and water but lacked all other living beings. Thus Yahweh Elohim created birds and 'earthly' animals in the 'hope' of finding company suitable for Adam. This action raises two questions: why the god did not know who would be the most suitable partner for the man, and what does 'suitable' really mean? Obviously the Quranic tradition must have recognized the problem with answering both questions and eliminated this part from its narrative completely.

The first point which needs to be made is the fact that animals seem to be created in the same fashion as the man with the help of soil and possibly with animation which is not mentioned in the text. If this is the case then Adam was considered by Yahweh Elohim to be not much more than the leader of the animal kingdom (he was created first and he was the one who named all the animals). However, it must be assumed that there was something more special in the first man since only he was given prohibition to eat from the Tree of the Knowledge of Good and Evil, implying that he was the only one who could even get such an idea.

The animals were supposed to be his original helpmates but it is apparent that he was not satisfied with them. Since the Yahwistic story of paradise is full of sexual innuendoes, many interpreters suggest that this lack of suitability refers to sexual mating. In fact we should not be too surprised by the implication that Adam was copulating with animals created for him by the god. In addition to the story of Enkidu of Gilgamesh fame (see Chapter 7), there are other texts from Mesopotamia which strongly suggest physical love between man and his flocks (Šakkan and his flocks – Cooper 1996). The practice of sexual contact between men and animals among the nomadic societies, both of the past and of the present, is not as unusual as we would like to think. The ancient laws of the Hittites even addressed this subject by permitting some sexual pairing between a man and 'selected' animals (mule, horse) while forbidding bestiality with others (for these laws see Roth 1997).

His failure to satisfy Adam with the companionship of animals only is the reason given for the creation of the woman by Yahweh Elohim. Thus, the god put Adam into a 'deep sleep,' obviously very different from an ordinary sleep (although it is not clear why he needed it in a land where pain did not exist), in order to perform the cosmic surgery. The choice of material for the creation of the woman – the man's rib – has no precedence in Middle Eastern literature and no followers in the Quranic tradition (the 'rib' story is only mentioned by the Hadith). It seems to be an original thought from the Yahwistic writer(s). In spite of many attempts by scholars to explain this mode of creation, there is simply no satisfying answer. On the other hand one must remember that the Yahwistic editor(s) must have been familiar with the story of the Sumerian paradise which also includes reference to the rib. This was the sick rib of Enki which was eventually cured by the goddess created especially for this purpose by Ninhursagga. Her name was Ninti, 'The Lady of Rib.' Owing to the nature of Sumerian writing, the ideogram which was used to express the word 'rib, side' (ti) was the same as the one for 'life' (til). If this connection is accepted then the Lady of Rib can also be read as the Lady of Life (Kramer 1961), which brings us close to the interpretation of Eve's name, ḥawwâ, 'because she was the mother of all living' (Wallace 1985, p.143). Many scholars reject this connection because 'no instance of Sumerian interest in this homonymity has yet come to light' (Brandon 1963, p.127). However, I believe that this is still the best explanation for such an unusual choice of material to create the woman. And it does not matter whether the Yahwistic editor or editors were aware of the Sumerian homonymity. It was enough that her name was associated with both terms, and since the 'life' could be logically incorporated into the text of the Yahwistic paradise in connection with ḥawwâ, so the rib must have been 'fitted' somewhere because the linguistic connection did not make sense in the Hebrew language. However, the reader must be aware that there are many other explanations, some of which are quite outrageous – for example, the creation of Eve from a dog's tail, since the dog ate the rib and ran away from the god who was only able to catch its tail.

Although there is no agreement among scholars as to the 'origin' of the rib, not many people can deny that this choice of material only contributed to the establishment of the woman as the 'inferior' or 'secondary' creation in comparison to the man. The purpose of her creation was to find a suitable helpmate for the man and no amount of sophisticated semantics (see discussions in Meyers 1988) is going to change this common perception. Sometimes the straightforward statements should be accepted in their simplest form.

While there is general agreement on the meaning of the name Adam as being related to the clay, dust, soil of the ground, there is not much agreement as to the significance of the name of Eve, ḥawwâ. The existing interpretations as discussed by Wallace (1985) focus on linguistic and other associations of this noun with sexuality, fertility and the snake. There are also some interpreters who explain her name as being the 'long forgotten or ignored' creatress since her name, as the name of Yahweh, can supposedly be derived from the Hebrew verb 'to be.'

However, the name of Eve is not as important as the role she played in the Fall and the punishment imposed on her. According to the Yahwistic narrative she was the one who was tempted by the snake and then shared her fruit with her husband. In his response to the god, Adam blamed her for his disobedience, or rather blamed Yahweh for creating her as his helpmate, implying that without the woman he would have never eaten from the tree. One might then argue that not only were women perceived as the origin of evil (see Chapter 9 for comparison, pp.152, 157) by the Yahwistic redactor(s), but were also somewhat threatening to men because of their inherent curiosity and a special pact with snakes (up till this moment). (See the punishment for eating from the tree, p.161) While the serpent was punished first, the woman was the second one on the list. She was cursed with the increase of pain in childbearing and with the yearning (see below) for her husband to whose rule she was to submit. This punishment raises some problems. If the god were to increase her pain in childbirth this would mean that she had already given birth to a child either with minimal pain or none. Since there are no records of such an event, one might speculate that the Yahwistic writer(s) had in mind some sort of a story in which women were bearing children without pain. Why not then the Sumerian story of the divine paradise in which goddesses were doing just that in nine days?

The second punishment remains somewhat mysterious because there is no agreement as to the exact meaning of the term 'yearning.' Again, one may speculate that in view of other, older traditions, divine females were in charge of their own sexuality and the successful sexual encounter was the one in which a goddess was satisfied (see Chapter 6). Thus, the curse of this account was intended to reverse this situation. Only male satisfaction was to be counted and he was pronounced to be the only one to initiate sex. Her husband was to be the lord over her.

The 'Quranic women' escaped both the blame and the punishment as directed only toward them, because this narrative considers the action of eating the tree's fruit to be the fault of both the man and the woman at the same time. Thus, both of them were punished 'only' with death, without any sexual overtones directed toward one or the other.

The difference in the two accounts might be used as an explanation of human attitudes toward marital sex as presented by the religions based strictly on the Yahwistic account or on the Quranic one. In general, the Islamic tradition encourages married couples to enjoy sex with each other on the initiation of either of the partners. The Judaic and Christian traditions are much more strict, by regarding sex as necessary for procreation and probably initiated by man for whom woman is to 'yearn.' Thus, one may wonder whether the folk tradition of the Middle East was not 'right on the money' in the attempts to combine two contradictory (the P and the JE) accounts of human creation from Genesis into one logical whole with the use of sex. According to these folk stories, the first man and the first woman were created at the same time and in exactly the same manner as narrated by the Priestly version. His name was Adam, but his wife was not Eve, but another woman known as Lilith (the demoness in Mesopotamian tradition). Their sexual life was not much to the liking of Lilith who wanted to have more variations in frolicking with her husband than just the missionary position. Obviously dissatisfied with his performance and continuous fighting, Lilith left Adam and moved to the area of the Red Sea. Since the man could not be alone, Eve was created with the goal of making her very obedient. As we know by now, this failed too. However, since Lilith was not in the garden at the time of the Fall, she remains immortal and enjoys herself wherever she feels like it (for more information about Lilith and her stories see Hurwitz 1992).

This story is obviously of much later origin but it reinforces interpretations of the Yahwistic account which focus on the sexual aspects of the story. Furthermore, even the late folk tradition illustrates clearly the popularity of ancient stories of various origins, from which themes can be skillfully connected, expanded and 'manipulated.'

The serpent

There is no doubt that one of the important points to be made by the Yahwistic version of the creation process was to put to an end the special relationship enjoyed between women and serpents. This relationship is indicated not only by the action of the serpent addressing the woman (not the man) but also by possible linguistic associations between the name of Eve and the terms for 'snake' and 'life' in Semitic languages (see Wallace 1985). This connection between all three is definitely of much older origin as indicated by both archaeological and literary (including linguistic) evidence from Mesopotamia, Egypt and Canaan.

In the Yawhistic account the snake is presented as a special being, 'the most subtle of all the wild beasts' and with the power of speech (possibly human). He also has a great knowledge, probably comparable to the divine, because he knows what is to happen to the first couple if they eat from the tree. There is nothing about his creation in the story of paradise of the Yahwistic origin, but the Quranic tradition describes the snake or satan as created from smokeless fire like the rest of the angels in the service of Allah. Obviously, he is a malevolent character in the J version and exists almost in parallel to the god but still can be punished by him.

Figure 10.2 Ningizzida (with horned snakes) leads Gudea, the prince of Lagaš, towards Enki, god of sweet waters and of wisdom. From a cylinder seal

No specific origin needs to be assigned to the idea of the snake living among the trees since it is a normal occurrence in nature but one should mention the Sumerian association between trees and snakes in the person of a god. In Mesopotamia both trees and serpents were connected through one god known as Ningizzida, 'the lord who makes the tree be right,' who was married to his female counterpart properly called Ninazimua, 'the lady who makes the branches grow rightly' (Jacobsen 1987, p.58). He was particularly associated with the roots of trees, the growth of which was essential for their vitality. According to Jacobsen (1987), it was assumed in Mesopotamia that roots and snakes are identical, so somewhat by default Ningizzida became the king of serpents. In visual arts when he was to be portrayed as a human, there were two serpent heads in addition to his human head growing from his shoulders while he was riding a dragon (Jacobsen 1970).

Snakes were both feared and admired in ancient cultures of the Middle East. They were associated with longevity (the snake snatched the plant of eternal youth from Gilgamesh; see Chapter 7) and sometimes even with immortality, due to their ability of rejuvenating their bodies. So they would be at least partially divine and could die only by violent death (Wallace 1985). They were believed to have healing abilities and occasionally were objects of cult (Brandon 1963). They were not only crafty as the snake of the paradise story, but also possessed wisdom which they could share with the chosen members of human society. Finally, they were connected with fertility because of their shape. The evidence for this is mostly in the visual arts, where serpents are placed in close associations with naked women. In Caanan this aspect of the reptile's powers was possibly connected with Ashtarte as the mother-goddess (Brandon 1963; Wallace 1985). Furthermore, it was suggested that since Tiāmat of the *Enûma Eliš* was described as the mother of monster-serpents she herself could be considered to be a powerful snake. But as Heidel (1951) correctly noticed, Tiāmat also gave birth to many benevolent deities and nowhere in the text is she referred to as a serpent. On the other hand, in a poorly preserved text entitled by Foster (1993) 'The Serpent' and dated to the second part of the second millennium B.C., the serpent is presented as being born out of the ocean and it is the mother-goddess who must provide her most violent offspring, Nergal, to fight the snake. This may indicate that the serpent was considered to be an independent being capable of emerging by itself from the waters with destruction on its mind. This emergence from the waters of its own accord might be an explanation of why the Yahwistic account did not mention the creation of water-creatures. Were they considered to be fathered or mothered by the snake as an independent being? Was the snake not a creation of Yahweh? Was the snake his main adversary in the same fashion as Angra Mainyu was to Ahura Mazdā in the Iranian tradition? If so, women would be the snake's natural allies, even if created by Yahweh.

Thus, we should not be surprised that it was in the god's best interest to sever the relationship between the snake and the woman in the paradise story. The serpent must have been somewhat divine and obviously in search of an ally to oppose the will of one god. If there was even a slight possibility that someone could have considered the first woman to be a divine figure thanks to her curiosity, name and 'ancient connections,' then the alliance of both forces could have threatened the creation as ordered by Yahweh. In this sense, the serpent represents possible chaos which has to be fought, and was known in the Egyptian tradition. His return, although unavoidable, was feared by the Egyptians. Was it also feared by Yahweh or by Allah? If so, then the Biblical and the Quranic serpent would be the Egyptian non-being which encircles the world and which renews itself continuously in the body of a snake (Hornung 1992).

Conclusions

While at first glance the story of the Yahwistic and Quranic paradise may seem very different from its predecessor, the Sumerian divine paradise, there are enough similarities between them and other additional sources to see much more ancient origins of this account. Both stories are about sex and its consequences. In the case of the Biblical and Quranic paradise the act of eating from the tree led to the discovery of procreation, the result of mating between a man and a woman. In the case of the Sumerian counterpart, one might suggest that Enki, after eating the plants which sprang out of his seed planted by the mother-goddess, also received the ability to procreate but this time without any female involved. This type of procreation was considered to be an abomination in ancient Mesopotamia where deities were 'patterned' on people and often created in pairs to continue the act of creation as encoded in Nammu. Since Enki could not be sentenced to death for the crime which he committed unwittingly, he had to be punished some other way, so he could not use his newly acquired powers (a conception of child of his own seed) of which he seemed not to be aware. The pain and sickness of the eight parts of his body probably prevented the unwelcome birth and kept the universe in order as it was intended.

However, in the case of the first couple, their punishment had to be death since they knowingly committed the act of disobedience against the god. This act demonstrated clearly human irresponsibility and other inherent weaknesses which had to be controlled. Thus, the death sentence also allowed the god to regulate their life-span, slowing down the inevitable overpopulation of earth.

Finally, the concept of 'sin' which did not exist in earlier religions was also introduced by the Yahwistic account. When in the past people committed wrongful actions it was simply because from day one they were created as 'faulty' beings. Thus, as correctly noted by Heidel (1951), man could not fall from the state of moral perfection, since such a state did not really exist. Furthermore, only individuals who committed wrongful actions were punished, although sometimes the divine wrath could have been carried on to the next generations or overdone in the state of rage (for example, the Deluge, Inana's plagues). But never before Genesis were humans considered 'guilty of sin' at the day of their birth. In some ways, wrongful choices in pre-Genesis traditions were the result of human 'stupidity,' not of their conscious choice of committing an act of disobedience against the divine force for personal gain. Striving for moral perfection is always a goal of any religious tradition but believing that it was once achieved and then lost is the product of the Yahwistic writer(s).

11

Were Gods Mad?
The Destruction of Humankind

It seems that the subject of annihilation or near-annihilation of humankind is one of the leading themes in creation stories around the world. Thus, one should not be surprised to find stories relating to this event in the Middle East. While an attempted destruction of mankind took different forms in the region, the underlying reason for its occurrence seems to be the same: divine realization that the earth is overpopulated. The different types of calamities which were sent by deities to exercise their right of extermination of their own creation appear to depend on geographical conditions of the areas as well as on the traditions from which these stories developed. In contrast to Egypt, where the river Nile is considered to be a life-giving force and its flooding is much awaited and predictable, the floods of southern Mesopotamia are very violent and sudden. Many such floods can be seen in archaeological material, (for example, at Ur or Shuruppak), although none of them was as extensive (that is, flooding more than one city at the time) as the most popular story of the Middle East indicates. There are many hypotheses as well as speculations concerning the historical basis of the Deluge but their discussion is well beyond the scope of this book. However, there is no reason to doubt that the violent floods of Mesopotamia led to the idea that if there had ever been a divine attempt to destroy humankind, this would be the means chosen by deities.

This idea became very popular in other areas of the Middle East, such as Anatolia and Syria–Palestine, where violent floods are very rare but the story itself was very appealing or entertaining. Since the beginning of everything was perceived to be in the waters of non-existence (whether representing order or chaos), its end could as well be seen there. This is probably the reason why these areas 'adopted' the Deluge as their own means for an attempted annihilation of humankind.

The same theme can be seen in Iranian tradition. However, here the flood was replaced by a big freeze which made more sense in view of the possible origin of nomadic traditions of the region which can be traced back to the area of Central Asia, southern Siberia, and western China.

In Egypt and Canaan, drought was perceived to be the most feared force of nature, capable of eliminating thousands of people. However, it was not dramatic enough – it was a slow process which would not guarantee annihilation of the whole population.

Thus, the wrath of deities in the form of slaying humankind in a short period of time, for whatever reason, became a means of choice of divine destruction.

The following is a presentation of catastrophic stories from the Middle East which are connected with the theme of creation. Since the people were the creation of divine order or forces, their ultimate well-being and existence in general depended on the gods. Destruction was yet another means to maintain the order of the universe and, as demonstrated in previous chapters, this task was the ultimate responsibility of all divine forces in the Middle East.

Mesopotamia: In search of solutions to control an overpopulation of the earth

In view of existing data there is no doubt that the earliest story of the Flood was written down by the Sumerians. As mentioned previously, the Sumerians even divided their past into two time periods: before the Flood and after the Flood (the Sumerian King List). This division and the existence of the Flood as a reference point of the past was accepted throughout Semitic Mesopotamia and from there spread to Anatolia (the Hittite capital, Hattussas), Syria–Palestine (ancient Ugarit, modern Ras Shamra) where it became an essential part of Genesis, as well as to other parts of the ancient world such as ancient Greece.

This story was so popular that numerous texts referring to or describing this event have been discovered in Mesopotamia, dated to different periods. The best-known edition has been found in the library of Assurbanipal at Nineveh as a part of the 'Epic of Gilgamesh' into which it had already been incorporated by the second millennium B.C. The oldest story relating the events of the Flood has been found in Nippur and although the tablet itself is of the Old Babylonian Period, the text is undoubtedly older, representing the Sumerian tradition. This is also the poorest preserved tablet concerning this narrative.

According to the Sumerian tradition the mortal who survived the Flood with his family was Ziusudra (or Ziusura; 'he saw life?' – Heidel 1946, p.227) who was eventually granted everlasting life in the land of Dilmun (see Chapter 10). In Akkadian/Babylonian tradition he is known as Atrahasīs ('the very wise' or 'exceedingly wise one') while the Gilgamesh Epic refers to him as Ūtnapišti (possibly 'he found life'). The hero of the Berossos narrative is Xisouthros, his name being a Greek version of the Sumerian original.

Since all the stories are in a different state of preservation and are very similar to each other with regard to the main motifs, the following discussion is based on all of them, focusing on the subject directly referring to the creation or destruction theme.

The Mesopotamian tradition identifies Shuruppak (modern Tell Fara) as the city where the flood began. Ūtnapišti specifically refers to this city which he describes as 'situated [on the bank of] the river Euphrates/That city was (already) old, and the gods were in its midst' (Heidel 1946, p.80).

The Sumerian King List presents this city as the last one before 'the Flood swept thereover' during the reign of Ubar-Tutu(k) (Jacobsen 1966, pp.75–77) and this is confirmed by the Sumerian account (Kramer 1973). Ūtnapišti is presented as the son of

Ubaratutu. Ziusudra himself was a king of Shuruppak, although in the account of Berossos this city is not mentioned while Sippar (yet another antediluvian city) is described as the city where the ancient writings were stored. His father is called Ardates, possibly the Greek interpretation of the Sumerian Ubar-Tutu. According to 'The Instructions of Shuruppak' (dated to the early third millennium B.C.), who was the king of the city by the same name, it was Ziusudrawas, his son, who received the advice. Thus there should be no doubt that the traditional Flood was associated with the city of Shuruppak as the place of its origin. Furthermore, the deposits of a considerable flood were discovered in this city and can be dated 'towards the end of the Jemdet Nasr period, c. 3000 BC.' (Rice 1985, p.260; see also Kramer 1986).

The reasons for the Deluge survived thanks only to the Atrahasīs Epic (for the standard translation see Lambert and Millard 1969; Dalley 1989; Foster 1993). The Sumerian account listed them but unfortunately this part is missing. The Ūtnapišti version relates the story from his point of view so he cannot list the reasons because he did not 'attend' the meeting of deities during which this horrible decision was made. However, the Atrahasīs story, whose best copy dates to around 1635 B.C. (Cohn 1996), explains this godly decision very clearly:

> The land became great, the peop[le mu]ltiplied;
> The land became stated (?) like cattle.
> The god became disturbed [by] their gatherings.
> [The go]d heard their noise
> (And) said to the great gods:
> 'Great has become the noise of mankind;
> With their tumult they make sleep impossible. (Heidel 1946, p.107)

In spite of slightly different translations (for example by Foster 1993) it seems obvious that when deities created humans as their servants to free the lesser gods and goddesses from labor, they did not take under consideration the fact that mankind would multiply to the point that its presence would bother them. It took only 1200 years for the noise to start to bother Enlil and other deities. The first solution for the problem was the plague. It reduced the population and the noise was gone, but only for another 1200 years. This time withholding rain and causing drought helped somewhat for another 1200 years. The irritated deities decided on what was to be possibly a final solution and for six years they did not provide any water to their people, causing starvation and cannibalism, sometimes even of children by their parents. But the people still survived, enough in number to repopulate the earth in a relatively short period of time. Their survival was possible thanks to their protector, Enki/Ea, who always listened to the prayers of the pious king, Atrahasīs, whose reign lasted for around 4800 years (Cohn 1996). Since Enki was able so many times to outsmart the plans of Enlil and other deities, Enlil decided, as a final solution, to wipe out all of humankind with one catastrophe – a flood. When even this left some people alive, Enlil and other deities had to become more inventive. Instead of destroying humankind in one act, Enki/Ea decided to lower the number of births by making some women barren, forbidding others to marry, and using a demon, the Extinguisher, to snatch some babies away from their parents (Kilmer 1972; Lichty 1971).

As we have already seen in *Enûma Eliš*, noise must have been a popular and quite justified reason for annihilating its makers. While the Babylonian Epic of Creation did not directly connect it with the overpopulation of the divine domain of Tiāmat and Apsû, the Epic of Atrahasīs is very specific in making this association. Such a severe reaction of deities to their noisy 'children' should not surprise anyone because the divine forces of the Mesopotamian pantheon were never perceived to be perfect and calm. Thus, the Mesopotamians presented us not only with the location of the Flood but also with the logical reason for sending it.

But Enki obviously could not handle the thought of losing his beloved mankind. Although sworn to secrecy about this divine plan, he indirectly informed his favorite Ziusudra/Atrahasīs/Ūtnapišti about the disaster which was to happen. He transmitted the message through the wall of the reed hut. The story proceeds with the hero's preparation for the avoidance of the Flood. A boat is built according to specific instructions. There is even an element of humor in the story of Atrahasīs when he complains to Enki that he has never built a boat and asks for its plan to be drawn on the ground.

When the hero was ready and the boat was filled with his family, animals and the seed of all life, the Flood came. So terrible was its force that the deities themselves were horrified, cowering like dogs, especially Inana who was one of the very few who protested against the original idea (the story of Ziusudra; Parrot 1955). Only then they realized that with humankind gone, so was their food and drink. Since the description of the Flood is irrelevant for the topic of this book, it is only necessary to mention that it is quite similar to the Biblical narrative (Cohn 1996; Heidel 1946; Kramer and Maier 1989; Parrot 1955) although it lasts only for seven days and seven nights (the Sumerian version) or six days and six nights (the Gilgamesh Epic).

When the waters finally receded, sacrifices were made by the survivors of the Flood. But Enlil still remained angry at his orders not being completely carried out. Finally Enki opened his mouth in the story of Gilgamesh and puts Enlil, the warrior god, in 'his place':

> Punish the one who commits the crime; punish the evildoer alone.
> Give him play so he is not cut free; pull him in, lest he be lost.
> Instead of your bringing on the Flood, let lions rise up and diminish the people.
> ...[repetition E.W.] Let the wolf rise up and cut the people low.
> ...[rep. E.W.] Let famine be set up to throw down the land.
> ...[rep. E.W.] Let plague rise up and strike down the people.
>
> (Gardner and Maier 1984, p.240)

It seems that Enlil listened to the ingenious plan of Enki/Ea for the creation of what Kramer and Maier (1989) call 'a kind of ecological balance' (p.133). As mentioned above, population growth was eventually decided by the assembly of gods to be controlled by the birth of new creations. Ziusudra/Atrahasīs/Ūtnapišti was rewarded with immortality, one of only two humans granted such an honor (the other was his wife). In order to speed up the process of providing offerings to the deities (in the Atrahasīs version), the mother goddess, Mami, and Ea created 14 new humans with the help of 14 women (goddesses or survivors of the flood?). The manner in which they were created was somewhat different from the other creation stories. The 14 women were gathered together and the clay was placed in front of Mami. Ea recited incantations which were followed by Mami's magical words over the piece of clay from which she pinched off 14 pieces, seven to the right and seven to the left with the brick in between. With the help of the 14 wombs, seven boys and seven girls were born. The world was ready to continue.

Egypt: Too many servants and a too fragile universe

As beneficent as Egyptian deities were toward humans, their altruistic nature could not have been taken for granted. At any time they could have turned against the people if they did not follow the *ma'at*, or simply because they were not in a good mood, so the people were given magic to protect themselves from divine hostilities (Morenz 1973). Since the deities themselves could be imperfect, their creation too had a big 'flaw' – free will.

> I made every man like his fellow; and I did not command that they do wrong. It is their hearts that disobey what I have said. This is one of the deeds. I made that their hearts are not disposed to forget the West, in order that sacred offerings be made to the gods of the nomes. This is one of the deeds. (Spell No. 1130, Lichtheim 1975, p.132)

This text clearly indicates that the consequence of this freedom of choice given to the people is the beginning of 'the primary source of unrest in the world' (Silverman 1997, p.130). Nobody else but the people are responsible for their actions since deities never commanded evil into their hearts (for divine commandments and guidance see Morenz 1973). The Papyrus Beatty IV, 6, 5–7, warns: 'Beware lest thou say: "Every man is according to his [own] character; ignorant and learned are all alike; Fate and upbringing are graven on the character in the writing of God himself"' (Morenz 1973, p.137).

It seems that the created universe was rather fragile: it almost disappeared right at the beginning of its existence. The famous Spell No. 175 of the Book of the Dead, which probably originated in the First Intermediate Period, refers to this event as:

> O, Thoth what is that happened through the children of Nut? They have made war. They have raised disturbance. When they committed evil, then they created rebellion. When they committed slaughter, they created imprisonment. Indeed, they converted what was great into what is small in all that I have done. (Ritner 1997c, p.28)

Since the universe was so frail, even the people could cause the return to chaos. In order to prevent this, deities had to react to any rebellious human actions. The text known as 'The Destruction of Mankind' refers to such a situation in which humankind plotted against its creator, the god Re, and the same event is mentioned by the 'Instructions for King Merikare.' When the creator learned about this plotting he called for a secret 'assembly' of his Eye, Shu, Tefnut, Geb, Nut and Nun, as well as other primordial deities who were with him in the waters of Nun, to decide what to do with people. The verdict was unanimous: 'Cause your Eye to go that it may catch for you who scheme evilly. The Eye is not foremost in it in order to smite them for you. Let it go down as Hathor' (Lesko 1991, p.110).

Thus Hathor, who could have been one of the original creators of mankind (see Chapter 8), destroyed some of Re's (and possibly her own) children with pleasure. 'Then the majesty of Re said: "I shall prevail over them as a king in diminishing them." That is how Sekhmet came into being, the [beer] mash of the night, the wade in their blood beginning from Herakleopolis' (Lesko 1991, p.110).

It is interesting to note that annihilation of all humankind was not on Re's mind. He just wanted to decrease their number, which raises the issue of an overpopulated land, a theme so popular in the Mesopotamian tradition. In order to prevent the total destruction of humankind, the creator ordered the production of beer (yet another creation) mixed with hematite (or red ochre) to look like human blood. 7000 jars of this beer were carried to the location where humans were to be attacked by the goddess.

> Then the fields were filled with liquid for three palms [depth]... When this goddess went at dawn she found this place full of water, her face was beautiful therein. She drank, and it was good in her heart; and she returned drunk, without having perceived humankind. (Lesko 1991, p.111)

Humankind survived but with it also survived the potential for chaos, injustice, disorder and unrest.

Iran: Too cold

Although the beginning of humankind in Iranian tradition is associated with Gayomart, there is yet another mortal, Yima, who is referred by Ahura Mazdā as the first mortal who was worthy of listening to his teachings (Brandon 1963). According to the Avesta, Yima was not the first mortal, but the first king who ruled in the golden age during which there was no death in his land. While people reproduced and obviously aged, nobody 'seems to have advanced beyond the ideal age of fifteen years' (Malandra 1983, p.175). But even his great kingdom did not last forever. After a long time, sometimes described as 900 years, something evil occurred which made Yima choose a wrong path. According to somewhat obscure passages from the Gāthās, Yima was among the ones who were accused of depriving humanity of happy life and of immortality. His offense was specified as giving 'people flesh of the ox to eat' (Brandon 1963, p.199). Thus it seems that killing oxen was forbidden at that time. This act might be connected with some sort of primordial animal sacrifice which was to ensure either prosperity in life or warding off death. (For discussion and identification of Mithra as a twin brother of Yima see Brandon 1963.)

There is yet another story associated with Yima which is of a later edition and appears in Vendīdad 2. According to this account, Yima was such a good ruler that under his care the world expanded enormously after the first 300 years of his power given to him by Ahura Mazdā: 'Then the earth became for him (too) full of livestock and draft animals and men and dogs and birds and blazing red fires. They did not find space (enough) – livestock and draft animals and men' (Malandra 1983, p.179).

Realizing the problem, Yima expanded the earth to 'one-third larger than before' with the help of a golden whip and a golden goad given to him by Ahura Mazdā at the time of his rejection to becoming Ahura Mazdā's first prophet; instead he became a king. This solution worked for only another 600 years, and then the same problem occurred. This time Yima expanded it 'to two-thirds larger than before.' After another 900 years of rule, the problem returned. The earth was enlarged 'to three-thirds larger than before.'

It seems that this continuous expansion caused by the overpopulation of earth by both people and animals made Ahura Mazdā call an assembly of spiritual deities, to which Yima was invited. There Ahura Mazdā informed Yima about the great winters which would come and freeze the area. He instructed Yima to build *wara* (its meaning is not clear) in which he was to store 'the seed of all men and women who are the largest and the best and the most beautiful of this earth,' as well as the seed of all animals, plants, and foods, all as couples 'so that their seed will be inexhaustible' (Malandra 1983, p.181). The exact instructions for the construction of the *wara* followed. It seems that Yima was able to survive the great freeze and after 40 years (or possibly days) the seed started to produce in the structure made by Yima.

While at first glance the above story is a variation of the ever-popular story of the Deluge, it also carries memories of the Proto-Indo-European tradition to which Malandra (1983) refers in his discussion of Yima. As with many authors before and after him he points to Yima as being the first mortal man and the king of the dead in the same way as Yama of the Rigvedic tradition. In the Vedic tradition it is Yama who '[t]o please the gods he chose death, to please his offspring he did not choose immortality' (after Hinnells 1975, p.39). The reconstructed version of the Proto-Indo-European myth refers to the first twins, Yama (a twin from *yemo) and his brother *Manu (asterisks indicate reconstructed PIE words) who were interpreted as the first king and the first priest. Then, the priest sacrificed the king in order to create cosmos out of his dismembered body.

Since Yima and Yama are of the same origin, Malandra (1983) suggests that the Iranian version of the flood story is actually a later corruption of a very old myth of Indo-European, nomadic roots. He emphasizes the role of Yima as a pastoralist who in the original version of the story was probably told by a 'high god' or gods simply to build a shelter for himself and his people and animals in order to survive long winters of the steppe or mountainous area. However, over the period of time this story was transformed under the influence of Mesopotamia. While I support his idea of the nomadic origin of the variation on the subject of flood, the fact remains that in Iranian religion this story was accepted without much argument about its origin; its prototype referring just to the 'creation' of a shelter for long winters of the steppe was forgotten or abandoned in favor of a more dramatic story of an intended annihilation of mankind.

As with the other 'destruction' stories from the Middle East, this one implies the reason for the freeze to be an overpopulation of the earth. Since a flood does not appear to be a logical solution in the Iranian reality, the snow and freeze of the nomadic homeland were used as the threat to the world. Finally, the time period used in this myth also indicates its Mesopotamian connection. If multiplication of the reigning years of Yima was a sequence of 300s by one, two, three, and four, then the freeze was to occur after 1200 more years of Yima's rule. Since the number 12 is a sacral number in many cultures this would not be very unusual but its continuous appearance in the flood stories of the Middle East is definitely worth mentioning and seems to be relevant.

Yima, the hero of the flood and the first king, became the symbol of a great ruler in Iran. To celebrate the event of his coronation the holy festival Nauruz, the Persian New Year Festival, was introduced. Even today this festival is celebrated on the 21st of March in some countries (Curtis 1993).

Genesis: The Deluge

The tradition of the Mesopotamian Flood in connection with the Epic of Gilgamesh made its way to many other locations in the Middle East. As one of the bestsellers at the time, texts narrating this story were found in Anatolia (Hattussas) and Syria–Palestine (Megiddo, around 1400 B.C., and Ugarit). Sarna (1996) suggests that the Hurrians, whom he calls transmitters of this tradition, were responsible for changing the place of the landing of the ark from the tradition of Mount Nisir (east of the Tigris) to Mount Ararat of the Bible; that is, the area that was under Hurrian control.

The story of the Deluge as it appears in Genesis 6–8 (or 6–9 including god's blessing and an establishment of the covenant) is a combination of both the Yahwistic and the Priestly accounts. Modern scholars are able to 'dissect' this one general story (for separate texts of these accounts see Habel 1988; Parrot 1955) and to demonstrate contradictions appearing in this one text as being the result of two different authorships (for comparative studies of both accounts see Habel 1988). The most obvious contradiction is the duration of the Flood which, according to the Yahwistic version, lasted for 40 days, and according to the Priestly account for 150 (Heidel 1946; Parrot 1955), although there are also other numbers suggested (Cohn 1996). Neither of these accounts mentions the place where the Flood was to originate. In fact the Mesopotamian accounts are the only ones in the Middle East which identify the physical location where the calamity had its beginning.

The similarity of the Biblical Deluge (and the Quranic one) to the Mesopotamian tradition is unquestionable. The main events are the same: a decision to send the Flood by one or many gods; the saving of a 'chosen' human (and his family); the 'ordering' of the construction of a boat; the boat to be filled with animals (and seed of life in the cuneiform tradition); the Flood comes and all people with the exception of the chosen man (and his family) die; the hero learns about the subsidence of the waters by sending birds; offerings are made by him to his divine protector(s); Yahweh/the gods smell a 'nice' smell; there is a reconciliation with god(s) (P) and blessing of the hero (J) (after Parrot 1955, p.43).

The main difference between the Mesopotamian and Biblical account is the reason given for destroying the people. The obvious reason in the latter account is stated by both the Yahwistic and Priestly authors as the evil behavior of humans.

> Yahweh saw that the wickedness of man was great on the earth, and that the thoughts in his heart fashioned nothing but wickedness all day long. Yahweh regretted having made man on the earth, and his heart grieved. 'I will rid the earth's face of man, my own

creation,' Yahweh said, 'and of animals also, reptiles too, and the birds of heaven; for I regret having made them.' But Noah had found favor with Yahweh. (6:5–8)

The above passage of the Yahwistic version (the P account talks about corruption of earth as seen by Elohim; 6:9–13) clearly indicates that the fall from the state of moral perfection continued with the first couple who were expelled from the paradise for disobedience. This is not surprising, given the weakness of human character. However, what is almost shocking is the very angry reaction of the god who was supposed to be all mercy and all goodness. Not only that he decides to eliminate all humankind, who arguably deserved this punishment, but also all animals and birds! (The sea creatures are obviously not his concern – see Chapter 10.) What did they do to be punished for the sins of mankind? Such an unjust decision would be quite consistent with actions of temperamental deities of polytheistic religions of the Middle East, but absolutely inappropriate for the creator and protector of the universe. But for the writers of Genesis this decision was valid in order to make the point: obedience is to be rewarded, wickedness is to be punished severely. This means that they consciously removed the original reason for the Flood, an overpopulation of the earth, from the narrative.

However, since the editors of Genesis were rather 'sloppy' in their work, the original reason, somewhat veiled, is still visible in the passage preceding the one cited above.

When men had begun to be plentiful on the earth, and daughters had been born to them, the sons of God, looking at the daughters of men, saw they were pleasing, so they married as many as they chose. Yahweh said, 'My spirit must not for ever be disgraced in man, for he is but flesh; his life shall last no more than a hundred and twenty years.' (6:1–4)

The above lines indicate that Yahweh was very much concerned about humans populating the earth rather rapidly. Once the 'fatal' knowledge was gained by the first couple they, and their children, were able to produce plentiful offspring. Their daughters were in special demand by the sons of **god**. Who were these sons? How could the 'one and only' have sons if their mother is not mentioned, since, by definition of monotheistic religions, she was not to exist in the first place? If god had sons, were they divine or semi-divine? In any case, their marriages with earthly females must have 'improved' the human genetic, spiritual and physical make-up; something that Yahweh was obviously not pleased with. This 'improved image' could have included a very long life-span which the god decided to shorten to 120 years. The only reason to do so would be again the fear of the overpopulated earth as in all other similar accounts from the Middle East. This obviously did not work because the infusion of divine blood could have also caused more success in reproduction. Thus, a flood was a 'logical' final solution.

However, as in the case of the Mesopotamian deities, Yahweh of Genesis regretted his action after seeing such horrible destruction. After smelling the 'appeasing fragrance' offered to him by Noah, Yahweh said to himself, 'Never again I will curse the earth because of man, because his heart contrives evil from his infancy. Never again will I strike down every living thing as I have done' (8:21).

Although highly speculative, this interpretation of the Genesis Deluge seems to connect the traditional accounts of the Flood with the new, religious and moral reasoning for an extermination of humankind. The 'regret' is still of the 'old date' (the same as in ancient Mesopotamia) but the divine commands after the Flood (see below) are a new addition. While the Mesopotamian deities selected less terrifying means of population control, predicting the same problem in the future, Yahweh seems to 'forget' about his original concerns, be it the wickedness of mankind or its speedy increase in number. He blesses Noah and his sons and tell them to '[b]e fruitful, multiply and fill the earth' (9:1–2).

The influence of the earlier traditions can also be seen in the number of years as the limitation for a human life, 120. This echoes the Egyptian tradition (see Chapter 12) and the sacrality of the number 12 as in the cycle of 1200 years when attempts to control population are made by other deities.

The proposed interpretation is not as creative as it may seem to the reader. Many authors realized that the reason for the Biblical Flood was still the overpopulation of the earth, although their reasoning was not exactly along the lines discussed above (Brandon 1963).

Of the two versions of the Flood in Genesis, the Priestly account is much more precise than the Yahwistic. The Priestly writer(s) provided such information as the construction of the boat (ark), its dimension (including the number of stories and of the rooms), the date for landing (8:4 – 'in the seventh month, on the seventeenth day of the month') and its location (Mount Ararat).

The Quranic account of the Flood refers to Noah more than 30 times but its main outline is very similar to the Biblical tradition and for this reason it does not have to be discussed in detail. Since the main focus of this chapter is the importance of the destruction stories for the understanding of the process of creation, a lot of fascinating and important issues of the Flood story itself must be omitted from the discussion. For more specific information the reader should explore such sources as Cohn 1996; Dalley 1989; Dundes 1988; Heidel 1946; Kramer and Maier 1989.

Conclusions

From the discussion above it should be quite clear that attempts to annihilate humankind were made by divine forces in order to prevent the overpopulation of earth. However, while in Mesopotamia and Egypt it was a decision of the whole assembly of angry deities, in other countries it seems to be the action of a single deity. In Iranian tradition it was Ahura Mazdā who sent the freeze in order to decrease the population so the survivors would have a more comfortable life. Since Ahura Mazdā represented the whole goodness, his motives for destruction are never presented as a decision of a mad god, but rather as a logical outcome of a situation that was out of control. In contrast, the Canaanite and Biblical traditions tried to present such an attempt as the result of the divinity's really bad mood. In Ugaritic tradition it was Anat who in Baal's cycle seems to be slaughtering people without any particular reason. In Genesis Yahweh Elohim seems to have had enough of bad human behavior so he decides to annihilate almost all living creatures. However, the underlying reason is still god's concern about the overpopulation of the earth.

It is so interesting that the ancient people were very much aware of the limited resources that their land could provide to sustain human life. This realization allowed them to compose stories which would explain the need for the destructive behavior of nature as commanded by divine forces who were responsible for maintaining the stability of their own creation. Since there was no concept of sin in its Biblical meaning before the Yahwistic account came into being, the reasons for the deities to send any calamity were sought in the very human behavior of divinities who ruled over them. Their deities then were not mad. In the Iranian tradition, the freeze was sent by the 'one and only' representing all goodness only after all other attempts to provide humans with a comfortable life failed. Thus, in some ways it was the act of mercy and sacrifice – some people had to die so that future generations could enjoy the earth. However, the Flood of the later tradition which was produced on the principle of the existence of only one god was commanded by this god as the punishment for people's numerous sins. If Yahweh's command to people after the Deluge to 'Be fruitful, multiply and fill the earth' (9:1–2) can be interpreted as god's 'joke' on humankind, one can say today that the destruction stories came the full circle: from physical and environmental reasons for all calamities, through the moral fall of mankind, to physical and environmental abuse of the earth by people of the twentieth century who may not need the 'help' of divine forces to destroy themselves. Thus, following the god's command, we are doing a pretty good job of destroying ourselves.

PART 4

The End

12

Where Do We All Go?

If there is the beginning, the end will usually follow. Sometimes the perception of the final act is associated with the perception of its beginning, sometimes it is just an unrelated event. In the case of ancient Mesopotamia and Anatolia the creation of humankind and its end were closely related to the purpose for which people were brought into this world – the service to deities. Once death claims the servant, his or her usefulness comes to an end so they have to be disposed of properly without being any bother to the deities. In other cultures the reasoning is not that transparent but can still be deduced from various texts. However, in each of these cultures the concept of the underworld existed in a form appropriate to, although not always consistent with, ruling ideology.

Mesopotamia: Workers no longer needed

The Mesopotamian perception of the underworld could constitute the origin of the later concept of 'hell' if such origins were to be sought and possible to prove. It was the place without any hope to which Enkidu referred as:

> ...the house of darkness, house of Irkalla,
> the house where one who goes in never comes out again,
> the road that, if one takes, one never comes back,
> the house that, if one lives there, one never sees light,
> the place where they live on dust, their food is mud;
> their clothes are like bird's clothes, a garment of wings,
> and they see no light, living in blackness:
> on the door and door-bolt, deeply settled dust...
> (Gardner and Maier 1984, p.178)

The Assyro-Babylonian tradition added to this description an excessive number of monsters and demons who made the life of the dead even more unpleasant than it already was. The most common name for this place was the Sumerian *kur* (Akkadian *erṣetu*), but it was also known as '*arali, irkalla, kukku, ekur, kigal, ganzir*' (Black and Green 1997, p.180). The Nether World was believed to be located either under the fresh-waters of *abzu* and/or in the inaccessible land of desert or mountain, possibly to the west, but the eastern location somewhere in the Zagros mountains is also possible.

This was the final destination for all mortals notwithstanding their good or bad deeds and/or status on earth. The only exception to the rule was the survivor of the Deluge (Sumerian Ziusudra, Babylonian Atrahasis, Assyrian Ūtnapišti, Biblical and Quranic Noah) who was rewarded with everlasting life. The spirit of the dead known in Sumerian as the *gidim* never had a chance to leave this gloomy place once the name of the deceased was written down by the scribe of the underworld, the goddess Geštinana or Akkadian Bēlet-ṣēri. The deceased's underworld life could have been slightly improved if survivors on earth remembered to provide him or her with regular offerings of food and drink. By no means do these offerings attest to the presence of ancestor worship. On the contrary, they were a sort of protection for the living that the dead will not be rootless and unhappy enough to haunt them since at death, the dead person is 'endowed...with demonic power to take revenge for his neglect' (Brandon 1962, p.76). The fear of the dead was so strong that Inana used it upon her descent to the Nether World whose gates were closed to her. She threatened to smash the gates so the dead would descend on the earth and eat the living 'so that there may be more dead than living' (Brandon 1962, p.80). This threat obviously worked since Inana passed through the gates as described previously.

But people were not the only inhabitants of the Nether World. They shared its space with some dead deities who ended up there as the result of their actions, horrifying demons to make their life miserable, and the deities whose professional duties were associated with the *kur*. The most important of them was Ereškigal (Semitic Allatu), the 'Queen of the Great Below,' an elder sister of Inana, whose first husband, the god Gugal-ana, died. As the queen of the land of no-return she herself could not leave its seven gates. Thus, according to the story 'Nergal and Ereškigal,' when the deities prepared a banquet, she had to send her vizier, Namtar, in her place. He received a wonderful welcome from all the gods but one who 'did not rise before' him, thus insulting Ereškigal, was summoned in front of her. But Nergal, the disrespectful god, was obviously not intimidated by her. Once the gates were open:

> ... Inside the house he seized Ereškigal,
> By her hair he pulled her
> From the throne to the ground in order to cut her head.
> 'Do not kill me, my brother. Let me say a word to you.'
> Nergal heard her, his hands loosened.
> She wept, she was depressed.
> 'You should be my man, and I should be your wife.
> Let me make you hold kingship in the wide land,
> Let me put a tablet of wisdom in your hand.
> You should be master, I should be mistress.'
> Nergal heard this speech of her,
> He held her, kissed her, wiped off her tear(s).
> 'Whatever you ask me from those months...' (Izre'el 1992, pp.224–225; for another translation and discussion see Dalley 1989)

Obviously Ereškigal must have been quite lonely to give in to Nergal (also identified with Erra, Meslamta-ea or Lugar-irra), the violent god as represented by other texts. But she was not lonely enough to look forward to Inana's visit as described in Chapter 6.

In summary, the above description of the Mesopotamian underworld indicates clearly that it was not a place to which anyone wanted to go. However, this was the place where all servants of deities ended up eventually, since their purpose in life was fulfilled with their death. Their bodies had to be sent to somewhere where they would not interfere with the world of the living. Thus, their state of existence on earth, which was so connected with the prosperity and wealth of their gods and goddesses, was to enjoy, because there was nothing for them to look forward to after they died. However, one must mention a possible exception to such a perception of death as represented by written sources discussed above. There is archaeological evidence (for example, from Ur and Kish), dated to the early period of the Sumerian culture, which indicates lavish preparations for the after-life which even included human sacrifices. Since they are somewhat in conflict with the literary evidence as to existence after death, there is no satisfactory explanation which can connect both 'traditions.' One might speculate that the Royal Tombs of Ur represent the original hope that life continues in its glory after death, but with time this belief was either abandoned or strongly modified. Thus, it should be accepted that the ruling belief on death and the after-life was the end of human existence in any pleasant form after physical death had occurred. This belief is consistent with the overall philosophy of the Mesopotamian religion(s). This perception of the non-being state after death could have indirectly promoted the hedonistic approach to life in Mesopotamia, making people realize that since they have only one life to live, they'd better make proper use out of it and enjoy it.

Egypt: Workers still needed

This was definitely not the case in ancient Egypt. Here, people were almost obsessed with planning their after-life existence which was to be the same or better (depending on their preparations) than the one on earth. This fascination with the after-life in the case of the pharaohs, who, as gods, were to be reunited with the rest of their divine family, is quite understandable. However, ordinary peoples could not hope for such a reunion since they were only mortal and their purpose was to maintain the order, justice, truth and existence of the only world they were familiar with. One might surmise that belief in the after-life was promoted for the benefit of the dead kings who would be helpless in the divine world without their devoted earthly followers. If such was the case, then the Egyptians needed to develop the means which would make the trip to the Other World also possible for all of those who were interested in serving their pharaoh and other deities in the after-life. To make this transition possible or comprehensible, the Egyptians believed that every human being consists of various spiritual elements who could live after the physical body lost its primary use.

In addition to the physical body and the breath of life (*ma'at* – see Chapter 8), humans were believed to consist of other non-physical elements which needed to be taken care of, as demonstrated by the Late Period text of the Book of the Dead:

> O you who fetch ba-spirits, O you who fell shades,
> O all deities within, at the head of the living,
> Come, bring the ba-spirit of (the deceased);
> May his heart be sweet, may it join his body,
> His ba-spirit to his body, to his heart;
> May his ba-spirit embrace his body and his heart;
> May they fetch him, the gods in the shrine of the primeval stone
> In Iunu beside Shu son of Atum,
> His heart like that of Ra, his heart like that of Khepri;
> Twice purification to his ka-spirit, to his ba-spirit, to his
> Corpse, to his shade, to his mummy;
> He shall never perish before the lord of the sacred land (the necropolis).
> ('Incantations for going out in the necropolis by day'; after Quirke 1992, p.105)

Because of the intricacies involved in the meaning of the concepts *ba* and *ka*, these spiritual components of the human being can be translated into English by different terms (for a discussion of these and other components see Hornung 1992; Quirke 1992). Usually the *ba* is referred to as a 'soul' or a 'spirit' but its meaning is much deeper because it relates to personality, psyche, psychic force, and can be extended to the power and manifestations of some gods. Since without the *ba* the deceased could not survive in the after-life, many spells from the Book of the Dead recommended ways to keep the *ba* united with the body. The *ba*, usually depicted in the form of a bird with a human head, was to rejoin the *ka* in order for the dead to be transformed into the *akh*, the form in which the deceased was to live in the underworld, unchanged for eternity.

The *ka*, usually presented as a pair of arms or another human being, has been translated as the double, the sustenance, and the second-self. It was born with a human being (see Chapter 8) and when the individual died it tended to wander, so offerings of food and drink had to be given in order to keep it with the body and nourish this life-preserving force.

Finally, one has to mention both the shadow and the name which were the remaining essential elements (there may be others but our understanding of these is very limited) of the human being. Since the importance of the name has been discussed elsewhere, here only the explanation of the 'shadow' is provided. This force was necessary as it was believed it protected a human from any possible harm. Of course, the power of this force was associated with the solar shadow which protected those on whom it fell during his or her passing through the underworld.

In order for the person to survive the trip to the underworld and life there, all these non-physical elements and the physical body itself had to be preserved (hence, the custom of mummification) and kept linked through various offerings and other necessary nourishment.

However, the life itself of people, deities and other creatures was limited in its length. According to Hornung (1992) the most desired life span for humans on earth was 110 years, although this ideal time was sometimes extended to 120. Even for deities the immortality was limited to 'millions of years' after which they too had to die and go to the kingdom of Osiris (Hornung 1982, 1992; Morenz 1973).

The limited immortality of the Egyptian deities meant that the universe had to end eventually and revert into the state of non-being. In the eyes of the Egyptians it was not the question of if it happens, but when. According to the text cited by Meeks and Favard-Meeks (1996),

> The Pelican will prophesy, the Shining One will come forth, the Great One will rise up and the Ennead will begin to cry out; the plain will be walled round, the two extremities will be reunited, the two riverbanks will be rejoined, the roads will become impassable for travellers, and the hillsides will be destroyed for those who would flee. (p.17)

Atum himself depicts this event in Spell 175 of the Book of the Dead:

> 'What is the span of my life' – so says Osiris.
> 'You shall be for millions of millions (of years),
> A lifetime of millions. Then I shall destroy all
> That I have made. This land will return into the
> Abyss, into the flood as in its former state. It is I
> Who shall remain together with Osiris, having
> Made my transformations into other snakes
> Which mankind will not know, nor gods see.' (Ritner 1997c, p.28)

Only the creator will survive as the serpent, the chaos, from which he emerged and to which he will return. This is the snake, the non-being, which at the time of the existence of the universe encircles it, only to assimilate it within itself at the end. This is the ultimate symbol of eternity, the Greek 'Ouroboros' who bites its tail. He is the beginning and the end which, with time, transforms itself into one of these two.

In summary, although the purpose of the creation of mankind was not spelled out in the Egyptian texts, one may deduce that people were on earth to tend to the needs of their god-pharaoh and all other deities who ruled the universe. But their usefulness did not end with their mortal death as in Mesopotamia. It might be inferred that the reason for regular people's extension of life after death was the god-pharaoh himself who needed his servants after his mortal existence came to an end. The pharaoh was the one who was changing his place of residence and who was entering the world of deities in which 'division of labor' was already fully established. Since no divine forces would serve him, he had to use the ones from his previous life: the people. Their reward was 'immortality' as limited as the pharaoh's, since he too would eventually cease to exist.

At this time the *neheh* and *djet*, two Egyptian concepts of time which together describe more or less our concept of eternity, will be reunited as one, in the unity of Atum and Osiris, while everything else will cease to exist. 'I [Atum] and Osiris will be the remainder...then I will come to sit with him in one place' (Spell 1130 of the Coffin Texts; after Silverman 1997, p.131).

This reunification at the end of time, time as perceived by humans, will bring closure to the familiar reality, but still offers hope for a new reality to be born as the eternal motion of creation must continue: 'Everything, including the divine, has an end, insofar as it dies, but is also endless, insofar as it is reborn' (Alfred Wiedemann, after Hornung 1982, p.152).

Anatolia: In, out and forever

While in Mesopotamia the concept of the underworld was associated with the end of life and in Egypt with the beginning of a better life, in Anatolia it was possibly the beginning and the end of everything. As Deighton (1982) argues in her book, the Hittite deities of Anatolia were frequently of the chthonic origin due to specific features of the Anatolian landscape. As she points out, 'In Anatolia, however, the gods in general descend into holes and underground whenever they are either afraid or in a fit of pique. It is not a place of dread, but a place of refuge, indeed it is home' (Deighton 1982, p.49). The vanishing gods of Anatolia frequently disappeared into a hole – as, for example, the God of Nerik did – to have a rest from any problems that they encountered.

In this sense the Hittite underworld was quite an ambiguous concept. On the one hand, it was the place that could be visited by deities seeking withdrawal from the earthly matters. On the other hand, it was also the place of the final disappearance judging, for example, from its description in the text entitled by Beckman (1997b) 'The Wrath of Telepinu': 'Below, in the Dark Earth, there stand bronze kettles. Their lids are of lead. Their latches are of iron. Whatever goes into (them) does not come up again, but perishes therein' (p.153). Thus, one may speculate that the Hittite underworld was divided into two parts at least: one which allowed for a return to earth and one which meant the end of existence for whoever or whatever was thrown into it and locked in.

It was the domain of the primordial or ancient deities as clearly indicated by such texts as the incantation entitled 'Purifying a House: A ritual for the infernal deities,' translated by Collins (1997). According to this incantation, the ancient gods (also addressed as Mesopotamian Anunnakû) were asked to come out of the underworld to take the uncleanness of the house back to the underworld where it was supposed to be locked forever.

However, we cannot be sure to which part of the Hittite underworld mortals, including the king, were sent after their death. The best preserved text of the 14-day-long funeral ritual entitled 'If in Hattussas a great calamity happens, (namely) either the king or the queen becomes a god' (fully discussed by Gurney 1977), indicates the possibility of 'no-return' for a king as well as for the people. On the thirteenth day of the ritual, a rope smeared with oil was thrown into a hearth accompanied by the words 'When you go to the meadow, do not pull the rope!' (Gurney 1977, p.62). This passage suggests to me that without a rope, kings and others could not pull themselves out of the hole which was the passage to the underworld.

Although the Hittite kings were probably not to return, their bones (after cremation) were rested in a 'Stone House' (E-NA), a huge establishment consisting of lands, villages, people to serve, who were forbidden to leave the place forever (Gurney 1977). While such a house has not yet been identified, the niches in Yazilikaya and the underground chamber in Gâvur Kalesi are often cited as possible candidates (Emre 1991, p.7). It is also interesting to note that a similar house, the 'house of clay,' is mentioned in the Indo-Aryan Rigveda (7.89). This house seems to be associated with the Other World of Indo-European traditions and possibly signifies a special enclosure for the dead. A similar enclosure is mentioned in the Hittite texts as a 'ḫesti-house' in connection with ceremonies consecrated to the underworld (Gurney 1977) which were conducted in open-air sanctuaries. However, according to Gurney this house was 'originally a cult-centre for Hattian Underworld deities' (1977, p.41) which, if correct, would exclude any Indo-European connection.

The name 'house of clay' in Proto-Indo-European tradition could have been reserved for tombs artificially constructed out of clay or earth such as kurgans (Lincoln 1991), and the term 'house of stone' could have been used for natural rock formations and those 'reinforced' with stone burial structures.

The practice of cremation in Anatolia and in Central Asian sites of the second millennium B.C. (such as Tamgaly), as well as their association with specific 'houses of dead' (which could have been reserved for the most important people in the society), may indicate a common origin in Proto-Indo-European tradition which I believe is also a nomadic tradition.

It should be noted that the Hittite 14-day funerary rites which were performed after the death of the king are somewhat similar to Indo-European tradition. Based on Gurney's (1977) interpretation of this ritual the following elements of the so-called Indo-European traditions can be observed in Anatolia: death of a ruler perceived as a violation of the divine order; cremation of the body; sending the soul through a slaughtered ox; sacrifices to the sun deity (the sun-goddess of the underworld); presence of the 'stone house'; sacrifices of oxen, sheep, horses and mules, which need to be provided with a 'piece of meadow' (emphasis on grazing, not on agriculture); and presence of chariots.

Based on this limited documentation, it seems that the Hittites believed in the tradition of the underworld as being a kind of combination of the Mesopotamian and Egyptian beliefs. Since there is no mention of life after death for people – in spite of kings and queens being divinized after their death – one can assume that, as in Mesopotamia, their role was fulfilled with their death so they had to be disposed of properly. It is interesting to note that the practice of cremation and inhumation as existing side by side among the Hittites (for a brief description of these customs see Macqueen 1996) can be explained by the instructions provided by the Indo-Aryan prescriptions, including the Rigveda, for the disposition of the dead – return the body to the element of the cosmos which is right such as sky and wind (through fire?) and earth (inhumation?). Furthermore, the presence of animal sacrifices among the burials associated with the Hittites in Anatolia might indicate the continuation of very early rituals which survived in Indo-Aryan tradition as related to the continuous replenishment of the cosmos through sacrifice (Lincoln 1991). Human sacrifices are also present in the Hittite sources in connection with the king as the sun. This is consistent with the underlying Proto-Indo-European ideology of the king who 'embodies the totality of the social order and is willing to sacrifice himself [and his people] for his people' (Lincoln 1991, p.8). If this is the case then one might want to look for the origin of the Anatolian mythology concerning creation not only in Anatolia itself but also in the Indo-Aryan tradition carried by both the Sanskrit and Vedic texts, especially since some of the Hittite texts mention the names of Indo-Aryan deities such as Mithra, Varuna, and Indra.

However, as in Egypt, kings and queens at least were given not only quite an elaborate burial, but they had the whole establishment – land, farmers, servants, and so on – associated with them. But since there is no indication that they were given ever-lasting life, one may assume that these establishments were set up to show the reverence for the dead and possibly to prevent any spiritual elements of a dead human being from haunting the living. Unfortunately, at the present time, this is not more than a plausible hypothesis.

Iran: Double jeopardy

While it was definitely Ahura Mazdā who was to prevail at the end of the 9000- or 12,000-year cycle, only the people who were following his good example were to enter the future life in which they would obtain inconceivable rewards. Since humankind was created by Ahura Mazdā, the ultimate goodness, their death was not meant to be the final end. This would mean that Angra Mainyu would win the battle, since death was his main weapon. However, in order to achieve immortality the deceased had to go through the Bridge of Judgment where decisions concerning his or her good deeds would be made (for description see Hinnells 1975). Those who did not 'make it' would be thrown into the darkness, into 'a long life of darkness, bad food, (and) lamentation' (Yasna 31.20, after Malandra 1983, p.23). Thus, the origin of the concept of the day of judgment and the idea of 'hell' could also be sought in the Iranian tradition which may have adopted the visual appearance of the Nether World from ancient Mesopotamia.

The beginning of this trip to immortality was believed to be in the Alburz mountains, the original creation spot. Here, after passing the judgment, the good souls would proceed to the paradise-heaven (see Chapter 10), the bad ones would be thrown to hell, the entrance of which was believed to be marked by the Arezur ridge (Hinnells 1975). However, the Zoroastrians recognized also the third group, 'so-so sinners,' those whose good deeds equaled their bad ones. The 'undecided' were to wait for the final judgment in Hamestagan (Hinnells 1975), an intermediary place which can be compared to Catholic purgatory.

The Avesta refers to the term *frašo.kereti*, the exact translation of which is unknown, but which indicates some sort of wonderful transformation described by Yašt 19.11 as 'ageless, immortal, undecaying, not-rotting, ever-living, ever-prospering, self-sufficient' (Dresden 1961, p.360). Based on the later Pahlavi books, this transformation is the final judgment which is also the end of the limited struggle between the forces of good and evil, with Ahura Mazdā emerging as the victor. At this event all bodies will be resurrected and reunited with their souls to go through the final trial: an ordeal by molten lead. Those who were damned already (during an individual judgment) would be damned again, and the others will be given the immortality drink, the white Haoma, by the Saošyants (the three posthumous sons of Zoroaster) so 'the material world will become immortal for ever and ever' (after Dresden 1961, p.360).

When was this judgment to occur? The answer can be found in the writings of Zoroastrian tradition, according to which the material world was to exist for 12,000 years:

the first 3000 years were the creation period; the second were the world according to the will of Ohrmazd; the third were the co-existence of good and evil; and the fourth were the final defeat of Ahriman (see Hinnells 1975). According to the Zurvanism, the first 9000 years represent the mixing of good and evil, while the last three thousand it was the final defeat of evil. Thus, from the ideal state of creation the universe had to go through the cycle of 12,000 years to be revived in the ideal state again but this time spiritual, not material, in its nature.

It is rather unclear what was to happen to Ahriman, whether he was to be killed or just immobilized in his hole, the entrance to which would be sealed by Ahura Mazdā (Hinnells 1975; p.68). With the absence of evil, the rest of existence would be a very pleasant event since the universe would continue, but in a different form. It will never cease to exist because its end would mean the victory of evil.

Pre-Biblical Syria–Palestine: The jaws of death

The Ugaritic literature makes it perfectly clear that both people and their rulers were mortals, although the latter were recognized among deities after their death (Dietrich 1996). For example, in the story of Aqhat, he is offered immortality by Anat but he refuses this gift saying, 'A mortal – what does he get in the end?/What does a mortal finally get?/Plaster poured on his head/lime on top of his skull./As every man dies, I will die;/Yes, I too will surely die' (Coogan 1978, p.37). The reference to plaster and lime probably reflects an old custom of plastering skulls in Syria–Palestine, evidence of which was found during the Neolithic Period in such places like Jericho.

As in the Mesopotamian tradition, the Nether World was not a desirable place to be. It was associated with the desert, the domain of the god Mot, Death, who himself resided in a dark, damp and watery place called 'the Swamp,' 'Muck,' 'Phlegm' and 'sanatorium' (Coogan 1978, p.15). The entrance to Mot's house was blocked by two mountains. There, Mot awaited his victims whom he devoured on their arrival. His appetite seems to be insatiable, as described in Baal's cycle: 'My throat is the throat of the lion in the wasteland, and the gullet of the 'snorter' in the sea;/And it craves the pool (as do) the wild bulls, (craves) springs as (do) the herds of deer;/And, indeed, indeed, my throat consumes heaps (of things), yes indeed, I eat by double handfuls' (Pardee 1997, pp.264–265).

Thus, it seems logical to assume that Ugaritic mythology, similarly to Mesopotamian tradition, was not much concerned with life after death. While resurrection was possible for deities (for example, Baal), death was final for all others who were considered to be merely food for Mot. Even the kings, who could have been addressed as a 'son of El,' as Kirta was, had to die. They might have been semi-divine through special interest, protection or their relationship to the gods, but they were also mortals who should not be saved from the jaws of Death; however, they should be buried properly (especially kings) and should receive commemorative offerings (for discussion of funeral and mortuary liturgy so rare among Ugaritic texts see Pardee 1996).

While some scholars argue that Mot might not have been even a deity since no offerings were presented to him, and that his domain was not as unpleasant as it seems to be (Handy 1994), I rather believe that the existence of Mot was simply a natural and logical outcome of the functioning of the Canaanite pantheon. Mot obviously held a very high position among deities since he is one of a very few with the title of 'king.' Furthermore, he was presented as the beloved of El who 'was assured of receiving all things in the end' (Handy 1994, p.106). Accordingly, El may have been perceived as a beginning of everything while Mot was its end.

Conclusions: Genesis and the Quran as 'closing chapters'

The limit of 120 years of life for people was established by the only god of Genesis in his attempts to control the population just before he decided on a final solution, the Deluge. Only chosen people such as Moses were able to reach this ideal age, whose origin can probably be found in Egypt (Hornung 1992) or even in Mesopotamia with its focus on the number 12 (with additional zeroes whenever needed). But what was to happen to them after their death? The author(s) of Genesis faced the problem which was very difficult to resolve in order to be consistent with the ideology to which he or they ascribed.

It should be obvious by now that a lot of motifs, themes, and events of Genesis were freely borrowed from earlier traditions of the Middle East, especially from Mesopotamia. But one idea, so popular in the area, that the purpose of the human creation was as an army of servants to the divine forces, was consciously avoided by the Biblical writers. This means that problems must have arisen regarding how humans should be disposed of after their life on earth came to an end. The Yahwistic idea of paradise and mortal sin committed by the first humans was possibly intended not only to explain the obvious – the existence of death – but also to dispose of humans in a more or less 'Mesopotamian' manner. As Brandon (1963) states, 'the Yahwists accordingly denied that the dead had any effective *post-mortem* life, and that what remained of a person after the dissolution of death departed to a miserable and hopeless existence in Sheol, which was very much the counterpart of the grim kur-nu-gi-a, the "land of no-return" of Mesopotamian eschatology' (1963, p.122; for more detailed discussion see Brandon 1962).

However, as Heidel already noted in 1946, 'Nowhere in the Old Testament is death regarded as a part of man's God-given constitution, or as the natural end of life. Nor is it indicated anywhere that death already existed before sin but became a punishment through sin' (p.143). Thus, this dilemma was solved both in Genesis (35:18) and other books of the Pentateuch (I Kings 17:21; Jonah 4:3; Eccles. 12:7) as well as in the Quran by providing humans with a soul which was to depart at the time of their death while the body was to return to dust (for discussion of the Pentateuch beliefs on death and the after-life see Heidel 1946). However, the Pentateuch is not clear as to whether all spirits would go to Sheol or only the ones of the wicked people, while those of the good would ascend to heaven (Enoch and Elijah ascended to heaven alive). Since Sheol can also be interpreted as a grave (Heidel 1946) it might be that this was perceived as the residence of all bodies but only of some of the souls. This way Sheol can be interpreted as a 'temporary residence' in a manner similar to the Iranian tradition: either as a 'temporary hell' for 'wicked souls' or a sort of 'waiting room' where all souls would wait for the final day of judgment. Only after this day comes would the souls of all humans be assigned by god their proper place, either to remain with god in his celestial kingdom or to be forever banished to Sheol. The same idea is repeated by the Quran. (For more detailed discussion of various traditions which emerged as the result of the development of Judaism, Christianity and Islam see Brandon 1962.)

In view of the above discussion it seems that the Pentateuch writers struggle with the development of consistent beliefs concerning death and the after-life. While the earlier traditions of the Middle East accepted the fact that people were created mortal, the Yahwistic account and the Quran deny this idea by introducing death as the punishment for the disobedience of the first couple. While in earlier traditions people were to be treated either with equality after death to enter the state of pseudo-existence (Mesopotamia, Anatolia, Canaan) or given an equal chance to enter the stage of their prolonged life (Egypt), the Iranian, Pentateuchal and Quranic traditions use the concept of an initial and then of a final judgment to provide a proper residence for various people depending on their moral deeds – that is, dependent on human actions on earth. Furthermore, in Mesopotamia, Anatolia and Canaan, people were to be punished or rewarded for their behavior when they were still on earth, during their mortal existence. In Egypt this approach was slightly modified. Since, technically speaking, people were not really to be reborn in the other world but to continue their lives in the same manner as on earth but without its problems, the rewards and punishments were distributed among them also on earth. While the concept of judgment also existed in the Egyptian ideology, it occurred after a long trip that was taken by those people who were interested (everyone had a chance to undertake this trip), to the kingdom of Osiris, and an entry into the after-life was not necessarily based on moral standards. It must be remembered that among those who were denied the entrance to the kingdom of the West were also those whose bodies and/or names were destroyed either on purpose or accidentally. It is quite obvious then that such a destruction was not necessarily the result of their wicked behavior on earth.

Morality and good deeds became the basis for human distribution after death only with the birth of religions based on conceptual duality of the world existence: the struggle of good with evil. In such religions both rewards and punishments were promised to be 'just,' not on earth (the suffering of innocents on earth is not a 'just' punishment) but in the non-specified future after death.

This development could be the result of many different factors of which the character of deities and the increasing inequality in access to material resources played a very significant role. Since deities of polytheistic religions were perceived to be ambiguous in their behavior – both good and bad, depending on their mood – many human mishaps and calamities could be explained as consequences of unpredictable divine behavior. In religions where the ruling god or the 'one and only' was expected to represent all possible 'goodness,' another explanation for the misfortunes had to be introduced. Their existence is either blamed on people as the 'payment' for their wickedness or, since bad things happen to good people, on the higher purpose of the god who, for unknown reasons, tries man's loyalty to him.

The second factor may have been the realization that there is not enough material wealth to be distributed in a satisfactory manner among all members of a society. The gradual limitation of access to the goods produced by many people and of possibilities in climbing the social and economic ladder might have caused the gradual development of the perception that hard work and moral life on earth, if not rewarded by divine forces in this life, would be compensated appropriately after death. This understanding of life on earth has led to the development of the concept of religion as a set of actions pertinent to *Homo religiosus*. Thus, religion in the modern sense of the word was born.

This type of 'religion' seems to be the concept most commonly defined by modern scholars such as Stark and Bainbridge who in 1987 proposed a set of rules which govern all societies as a theory of human action. It is a general 'optimality' model which stresses that '[h]umans seek what they perceive to be rewards and avoid what they perceive to be costs' (Stark and Bainbridge 1987, p.27). Their line of inquiry, reported in the form of axioms, propositions, and definitions, led them to the statements that some of the desired rewards are limited in supply, some might not exist, and their distribution is unequal among persons and groups in any society. Owing to this inequality in distribution, some individuals or groups may acquire greater resources than others, and with them more power, defined by Stark and Bainbridge as 'the degree of control over one's exchange ratio' (1987, p.33). Since this power is usually used to confer still more power, eventually some of the most desired rewards become relatively unavailable to others. In addition, some rewards are so rare that they seem not to exist. Thus, 'in the absence of a desired reward, explanations often will be accepted which posit attainment of the reward in the distant future or in some other non-verifiable context' (Stark and Bainbridge 1987, p.35).

In other words, compensators – substitutes for desired rewards – must be offered as rewards for human efforts, and must be taken on faith. This concept 'is the key to the theory of religion' (1987, p.36). These substitutes seem not to be offered until the introduction of the 'one and only' god representing only goodness of being and non-being states of existence, independently of the number of other divine, ambiguous or evil, forces involved. This concept of 'religion' was possibly born in the Middle East with the development of religions based on Genesis, the Avesta, and the Quran in which the concept of the final judgment after a waiting period is so prominent.

In view of modern knowledge, only in the Middle East can we observe the transformation and/or 'evolution' of concepts and ideas which have led to the development of the current understanding of the term 'religion.' As demonstrated throughout the course of this book the ancient civilizations of the region did not even have a word for this concept in their vocabulary. The reality that they perceived was also the reality that they lived. In the polytheistic world of many deities there was no need for competition between ideological systems. Any ideological conflicts which arose as the result of new migrations, conquests, and interactions between different ethnic and cultural groups were resolved through the 'manipulation' of existing data, leading to the compilation of various sources, incorporation of new deities and/or concepts, and the gradual elimination of less 'effective' forces from the more suitable pantheon. Thus, until the first millennium B.C. there were no 'wars' between ruling ideologies, although the battles between various individual deities reflect the 'birth' or 'introduction' of new notions.

At the beginning of human thought as represented by the written sources of the Middle East, the understanding of existence focused on the recognition of two states: that of 'non-being' and that of 'being.' Whether the state of 'non-being' was considered to be orderly or chaotic in its nature, the fact remains that only thanks to its existence could the elements of 'being' emerge according to the logic dictated by the reality lived and observed. These elements included all necessary components of the cosmos represented as divine forces, often anthropomorphized, and the people. In order for this world to continue in its recognizable form, each and every element of creation was given his/her or its place in the continuum of time. All that existed was interconnected and equal with respect to its designed role in the state of 'being.' In this sense the universe itself was to be used, not abused, because of the fear that it could disappear, dissolve, or revert back to the 'non-being state.' Its probable 'collapse' did not depend on one individual action but on the inability of those involved to repair the damage caused by crossing once-established boundaries of existence. Thus, the rewards and punishments were prescribed in order to be carried within the perceived life-span of both divine and human elements since they were the only ones who could have threatened the established order.

However, this well-balanced universe to which all creatures were to contribute equally according to their original destinies seems to disappear from later ideologies. The old order in which there was no separation between reality and spirituality or religiosity was replaced by the new one in which the distinction between these two has become the cornerstone in redefining the place of an individual not only in the universe but in any given political, economic and social situation. The old order did not call for the identification of an individual as a follower of any particular religion, not only because this concept did not exist but also because such an identification was simply illogical and unnecessary as long as there was a place for yet another deity or his or her selected attributes to fit into the perceived reality of polytheistic systems.

Since nothing ever seems to be created in a vacuum, one should not be surprised that our Western tradition carries on memories of many earlier traditions of the Middle Eastern 'religious' stories, concepts and ideas. After all, 'The process of cultural acquisition inevitably operates a selection in the available cultural input. The outcome of this selection is that certain features are recurrent because they are more likely to be entertained, acquired, and transmitted by human minds' (Boyer 1994, p.IX).

Unfortunately, as can be seen from this presentation of creation stories from the Middle East, in this process of cultural acquisition, the tolerance and relative equality of the older traditions gradually became concepts of the past. In contrast to the world of the Sumerians and others before the first millennium B.C., the new reality, the one with which we are familiar today, claimed 'victory' for one male god, inequality of genders, and an attitude that says, 'the universe is for us, not we for the universe.' No longer do we focus on the existence of only two states, the one of 'non-being' and the one of 'being.' Currently the focus is on ourselves, mankind alone, who has became the center of creation stories of the leading religions. However, this too might change in the future, since the need to adapt to ever-changing reality is a natural component of human nature and of the universe, whether it was created by many deities, by one god or by itself. As long as there are questions that cannot be answered by modern science, so there will be creation stories, whether old, transformed or new, which will fill the gap, making sense of what seems to be incomprehensible.

References

Al Khalifa, S.H.A. and Rice, M. (eds) (1986) *Bahrain through the Ages: The Archaeology.* London and New York: KPI.

Al Nashef, K. (1986) 'The deities of Dilmun.' In S.H.A. Al Khalifa and M. Rice (eds) *Bahrain through the Ages: The Archaeology.* London and New York: KPI.

Aldred, C. (1963) *The Egyptians.* New York: Frederick A. Praeger.

Aldred, C. (1988) *Akhenaten, King of Egypt.* New York: Thames and Hudson

Allen, J.P. (1988) *Genesis in Egypt: The Philosophy of Ancient Creation Accounts.* Yale Egyptological Studies 2, edited: K. Simpson. New Haven, CT: Yale Egyptological Seminar, Department of Near Eastern Languages and Civilizations, The Graduate School, Yale University.

Allen, J.P. (1997a) 'From the "Memphite Theology" (1.15).' In W.W. Hallo (ed) *The Context of Scripture. Volume I: Canonical Compositions from the Biblical World.* Leiden, New York and Cologne: Brill.

Allen, J.P. (1997b) 'From Coffin Texts Spell 76 (1.6).' In W.W. Hallo (ed) *The Context of Scripture. Volume I: Canonical Compositions from the Biblical World.* Leiden, New York and Cologne: Brill.

Allen, J.P. (1997c) 'From Pyramid Texts Spell 600 (1.4).' In W.W. Hallo (ed) *The Context of Scripture. Volume I: Canonical Compositions from the Biblical World.* Leiden, New York and Cologne: Brill.

Allen, J.P. (1997d) 'From Pyramid Texts Spell 527 (1.3).' In W.W. Hallo (ed) *The Context of Scripture. Volume I: Canonical Compositions from the Biblical World.* Leiden, New York and Cologne: Brill.

Allen, J.P. (1997e) 'From Papyrus Bremner-Rhind (1.9).' In W.W. Hallo (ed) *The Context of Scripture. Volume I: Canonical Compositions from the Biblical World.* Leiden, New York and Cologne: Brill.

Allen, J.P. (1997f) 'Coffin Text Spell 261 (1.11).' In W.W. Hallo (ed) *The Context of Scripture. Volume I: Canonical Compositions from the Biblical World.* Leiden, New York and Cologne: Brill.

Allen, J.P. (1997g) 'From the Berlin "Hymn to Ptah" (1.14).' In W.W. Hallo (ed) *The Context of Scripture. Volume I: Canonical Compositions from the Biblical World.* Leiden, New York and Cologne: Brill.

Allen, J.P. (1997h) 'From Papyrus Leiden I 350 (1.16). In W.W. Hallo (ed) *The Context of Scripture. Volume I: Canonical Compositions from the Biblical World.* Leiden, New York and Cologne: Brill.

Allen, J.P. (1997i) 'From Coffin Texts Spell 80 (1.8).' In W.W. Hallo (ed) *The Context of Scripture. Volume I: Canonical Compositions from the Biblical World.* Leiden, New York and Cologne: Brill.

Allen, J.P. (1997j) 'From Coffin Texts Spell 1130 (1.17).' In W.W. Hallo (ed) *The Context of Scripture. Volume I: Canonical Compositions from the Biblical World.* Leiden, New York and Cologne: Brill.

Alster, B. (1983) 'Dilmun, Bahrain, and the alleged paradise in Sumerian myth and literature.' In D.T. Potts (ed) *Dilmun: New Studies in the Archaeology and Early History of Bahrain.* Berlin: D. Reimer Verlag.

Alster, B. (1992) 'Interaction of oral and written poetry in early Mesopotamian literatures.' In M.E. Vogelzang and H.L.J. Vanstiphout (eds) *Mesopotamian Epic Literature: Oral or Aural?* Lewiston/Queenston/Lampeter: The Edwin Mellen Press.

Alster, B. (1993) 'Two Sumerian short tales and a love song reconsidered.' *Zeitschrift für Assyriologie 82*, 186–201.

Andersen, H.H. (1986) 'The Barbar temple: Stratigraphy, architecture and interpretation.' In S.H.A. Al Khalifa and M. Rice (eds) *Bahrain through the Ages: The Archaeology.* London and New York: KPI.

Angela, P. and Angela, A. (1993) *The Extraordinary Story of Human Origins.* Buffalo, NY: Prometheus Books.

Armstrong, J. (1969) *The Paradise Myth.* London and New York: Oxford University Press.

Baines, J. (1991) 'Society, morality, and religious practice.' In B.E. Shafer (ed) *Religion in Ancient Egypt: Gods, Myths, and Personal Practice.* Ithaca, NY, and London: Cornell University Press.

Beckman, G. (1997a) 'Plague prayers of Muršili II.' In W.W. Hallo (ed) *The Context of Scripture. Volume I: Canonical Compositions from the Biblical World.* Leiden, New York and Cologne: Brill.

Beckman, G. (1997b) 'The wrath of Telepinu (1.57).' In W.W. Hallo (ed) *The Context of Scripture. Volume I: Canonical Compositions from the Biblical World.* Leiden, New York and Cologne: Brill.

Bibby, G. (1986) 'The land of Dilmun is holy.' In S.H.A. Al Khalifa and M. Rice (eds) *Bahrain through the Ages: The Archaeology.* London and New York: KPI.

Bielinski, P. (1985) *Starozytny Bliski Wschod: Od Poczatkow Gospodarki Rolniczej do Wprowadzenia Pisma. (The Ancient Near East: From the Beginning of Agriculture to the Introduction (Invention) of Writing.)* Warsaw: Panstwowe Wydawnictwo Naukowe.

Biggs, R. D. (1974) *Incscriptions from Tell Abu Salabikho.* Chicago, IL: University of Chicago Press.

Black, J. and Green, A. (1997) *Gods, Demons and Symbols of Ancient Mesopotamia: An Illustrated Dictionary.* Austin, TX: University of Texas Press.

Bower, B. (1995) 'Indo-European pursuits.' *Science News 147*, 120–125.

Boyer, P. (1994) *The Naturalness of Religious Ideas: A Cognitive Theory of Religion.* Berkeley, CA, Los Angeles, CA, and London: University of California Press.

Brandau, B. (1998) 'Can archaeology discover Homer's Troy?' *Archaeology Odyssey 1*, 1, 14–25.

Brandon, S.G.F. (1962) *Man and His Destiny in the Great Religions.* Toronto: University of Toronto Press.

Brandon, S.G.F. (1963) *Creation Legends of the Ancient Near East.* London: Hodder and Stoughton.

Bryce, T. (1998) *The Kingdom of Hittites.* Oxford: Clarendon Press.

Budge, E.A.W. (1959) *Egyptian Religion.* New York: Bell.

Budge, E.A.W. (1960) *The Book of the Dead.* New York: Bell.

Budge, E.A.W. (1969) *The Gods of the Egyptians or Studies in Egyptian Mythology: Volume 1.* New York: Dover Publications.

Charlesworth, J.H. and Evans, C.A. (eds) (1993) *The Pseudoepigrapha and Early Biblical Interpretation.* (Journal for the Study of the Pseudoepigrapha Supplement Series 14. Studies in Scripture in Early Judaism and Christianity 2.) Sheffield: Sheffield Academic Press.

Clark, R.T.R. (1959) *Myth and Symbol in Ancient Egypt.* London: Thames and Hudson.

Cleuziou, S. (1986) 'Dilmun and Makkan during the third and early second millennia B.C.' In S.H.A. Al Khalifa and M. Rice (eds) *Bahrain through the Ages: The Archaeology.* London and New York: KPI.

Cohn, N. (1996) *Noah's Flood: The Genesis Story in Western Thought.* New Haven, CT, and London: Yale University Press.

Collins, B.J. (1997) 'Purifying a house: A ritual for the infernal deities (1.68).' In W.W. Hallo (ed) *The Context of Scripture. Volume I: Canonical Compositions from the Biblical World.* Leiden, New York and Cologne: Brill.

Collon, D. (1995) *Ancient Near Eastern Art.* Berkeley, CA: University of California Press.

Coogan, M.D. (1978) *Stories from Ancient Canaan.* Philadelphia, PA: The Westminster Press.

Cooper, J.S. (1996) 'Magic and m(is)use: Poetic promiscuity in Mesopotamian ritual.' In M.E. Vogelzang and H.L.J. Vanstiphout (eds) *Mesopotamian Poetic Language: Sumerian and Akkadian.* Groningen: STYX Publications.

Cross, F.M. (1973) *Canaanite Myth and Hebrew Epic: Essays in the History of the Religion of Israel.* Cambridge, MA: Harvard University Press.

Currid, J.D. (1997) *Ancient Egypt and the Old Testament.* Grand Rapids, MI: Baker Books.

Curtis, V.S. (1993) *The Legendary Past: Persian Myths.* Austin, TX: University of Texas Press.

Dalley, S. (1989) *Myths from Mesopotamia.* Oxford and New York: Oxford University Press.

Dani, A.H. (1986) 'Bahrain and the Indus civilisation.' In S.H.A. Al Khalifa and M. Rice (eds) *Bahrain through the Ages: The Archaeology.* London and New York: KPI.

Deighton, H.J. (1982) *The 'Weather-God' in Hittite Anatolia. An Examination of the Archaeological and Textual Sources.* Oxford: BAR international Series 143.

Dever, W.G. (1984) 'Asherah, consort of Yahweh? New evidence from Kuntillet 'Ajrud' *Bulletin of the American Schools of Oriental Research 255,* 28–29.

Dietrich, M. (1996) 'Aspects of the Babylonian impact on Ugaritic literature and religion.' In N. Wyatt, W.G.E. Watson and J.B. Lloyd (eds) *Ugarit, Religion and Culture: Proceedings of the International Colloquium on Ugarit, Religion and Culture. Edinburgh, July 1994.* Münster: Ugarit Verlag.

Doria, C. and Lenowitz, H. (eds) (1976) *Origins: Creation Texts from the Ancient Mediterranean.* Garden City, NY: Anchor Press/Doubleday.

Dresden, M.J. (1961) 'Mythology of ancient Iran.' In S.N. Kramer (ed) *Mythologies of the Ancient World.* Chicago, IL: Quadrangle Books.

Drysdale A. and Blake, G.H. (1985) *The Middle East and North Africa: A Political Geography.* New York and Oxford: Oxford University Press.

Dundes, A. (ed) (1988) *The Flood Myth.* Berkeley, CA, Los Angeles, CA, and London: University of California Press.

During Caspers, E.C.L. (1986) 'Animal designs and Gulf chronology.' In S.H.A. Al Khalifa and M. Rice (eds) *Bahrain through the Ages: The Archaeology.* London and New York: KPI.

Durkheim, E. (1968) *The Elementary Forms of the Religious Life.* New York: The Free Press.

Eickelman, D.F. (1998) *The Middle East and Central Asia: An Anthropological Approach.* Upper Saddle River, NJ: Prentice Hall.

Eliade, M. (1961) *The Sacred and the Profane.* New York: Harper and Row.

Emre, K. (1991) 'Cemeteries of second millennium B.C. in Central Asia.' In H.I.H. Prince Takahito Mikasa (ed) *Essays on Anatolian and Syrian Studies in the Second and First Millennium B.C.* Wiesbaden: Harrassowitz.

Faulkner, R.O. (trans) (1997) *The Ancient Egyptian Book of the Dead* (ed. C. Andrews). Austin, TX: University of Texas Press.

Feyerick, A. (ed) (1996) *Genesis: World of Myths and Patriarchs.* New York and London: New York University Press.

Foster, B.R. (1993) *Before the Muses: An Anthology of Akkadian Literature.* (Volumes 1 and 2.) Bethesda, MD: CDL Press.

Foster, B.R. (1995) *From Distant Days: Myths, Tales, and Poetry of Ancient Mesopotamia.* Bethesda, MD: CDL Press.

Frankfort, H. (1948) *Kingship and the Gods: A Study of Ancient Near Eastern Religion as the Integration of Society and Nature.* Chicago, IL: University of Chicago Press.

Frawley, D. (1993) *Gods, Sages and Kings: Vedic Secrets of Ancient Civilization.* Delhi: Motilal Banarsidass Publishers.

Frazer, J.G. (1955) *The Golden Bough: A Study in Magic and Religion.* Abridged edition. New York: St Martin Press.

Gaber, P. and Dever, W.G. (1998) 'The birth of Adonis?' *Archaeology Odyssey 1*, 2, 48–55, 61.

Gardner, J. and Maier, J.R. (1984) *Gilgamesh: Translated from the Sin-Legiunninni Version.* New York: Knopf.

Georges, R.A. (ed) (1968) *Studies on Mythology.* Homewood, IL: The Dorsey Press.

Gessel, B.H.L. van (1998) *Onomasticon of the Hittite Pantheon. Part I and II.* Leiden, New York and Cologne: Brill.

Gibson, J.C.L. (1978) *Canaanite Myths and Legends.* Edinburgh: T. and T. Clark.

Gimbutas, M. (1989) *The Language of the Goddess.* San Francisco, CA: Harper and Row.

Goodnick Westenholz, J. (1997) *Legends of the Kings of Akkade.* Winona Lake, IN: Eisenbrauns.

Gordon, C.H. (1961) 'Canaanite mythology.' In S.N. Kramer (ed) *Mythologies of the Ancient World.* Chicago, IL: Quadrangle Books.

Gordon, C.H. (1996) 'Mesopotamia: Land of myths.' In A. Feyerick (ed) *Genesis: World of Myths and Patriarchs.* New York and London: New York University Press.

Graves, R. and Patai, R. (1964) *Hebrew Myths: The Book of Genesis.* Garden City, NY: Doubleday.

Gray, J. (1964) *The KRT Text in the Literature of Ras Shamra.* Leiden: Brill.

Gunkel, H. (1997) *Genesis.* Macon, GA: Mercer University Press.

Gurney, O.R. (1977) *Some Aspects of Hittite Religion.* Oxford: Oxford University Press.

Gurney, O.R. (1990) *The Hittites.* London, New York: Penguin Books.

Güterbock, H.G. (1961) 'Hittite mythology.' In S.N. Kramer (ed) *Mythologies of the Ancient World.* Chicago, IL: Quadrangle Books.

Habel, N.C. (1988) 'The two flood stories in Genesis.' In A. Dundes (ed) *The Flood Myth.* Berkeley, CA, Los Angeles, CA, and London: University of California Press.

Hallo, W.W. (1996) *Origins: The Ancient Near Eastern Background of Some Modern Western Institutions.* Leiden, New York and Cologne: Brill.

Hallo, W.W. (1997) *The Context of Scripture. Volume 1. Canonical Compositions from the Biblical World.* Leiden, New York, Cologne: Brill.

Handy, L.K. (1994) *Among the Host of Heaven: The Syro-Palestinian Pantheon as Bureaucracy.* Winona Lake, IN: Eisenbrauns.

Harrison, J. (1903) *Prolegomena to the Study of Greek Religion.* Cambridge: Cambridge University Press.

Harrison, J. (1912) *Themis: A Study of the Social Origins of Greek Religion.* Cambridge: Cambridge University Press.

Heidel, A. (1946) *The Gilgamesh Epic and Old Testament Parallels.* Chicago, IL: The University of Chicago Press.

Heidel, A. (1951) *The Babylonian Genesis: The Story of Creation.* Chicago, IL: The University of Chicago Press.

Held, M. (1976) 'Two philological notes on the Enuma Elish.' In *Kramer Anniversary Volume (= Alter Orient und Altes Testament 25).* Neukirchen-Vluyn.

Hicks, D. (ed) (1999) *Ritual And Belief: Readings in the Anthropology of Religion.* Boston: McGraw-Hill College.

Hinnells, J.R. (1975) *Persian Mythology.* London: Hamlyn.

Hoffmeier, J.K. (1997) 'Historiography. King Lists (1.37).' In W.W. Hallo (ed) *The Context of Scripture. Volume I: Canonical Compositions from the Biblical World.* Leiden, New York and Cologne: Brill.

Hoffner, H.A. Jr. (1990) *Hittite Myths.* Atlanta, GA: Scholars Press.

Hooke, S.H. (1953) *Babylonian and Assyrian Religion.* London, New York: Hutchinson's University Library.

Hornung, E. (1982) *Conceptions of God in Ancient Egypt: The One and Many* (trans. by J. Baines). Ithaca, NY: Cornell University Press.

Hornung, E. (1992) *Idea into Image: Essays on Ancient Egyptian Thought* (trans. E. Bredeck). New York: Timken Publishers.

Hurwitz, S. (1992) *Lilith – The First Eve: Historical and Psychological Aspects of the Dark Feminine.* Einsiedeln, Switzerland: Daimon Verlag.

Ingold, T. (ed) (1988) *What is an Animal?* London: Unwin Hyman.

Ions, V. (1983) *Egyptian Mythology.* New York: Peter Bedrick Books.

Irving, T.B. (1985) *The Qur'an: The First American Version.* Brattleboro, VT: Amana Books.

Izre'el, S. (1992) 'The study of oral poetry: Reflections of a neophyte.' In M.E. Vogelzang and H.L.J. Vanstiphout (eds) *Mesopotamian Epic Literature: Oral or Aural?* Lewiston/Queenston/Lampeter: The Edwin Mellen Press.

Jacobsen, T. (1966) *The Sumerian King List.* (The Oriental Institute of the University of Chicago Assyriological Studies, No. 11.) Chicago, IL: The University of Chicago Press.

Jacobsen, T. (1970) *Toward the Image of Tammuz and Other Essays on Mesopotamian History and Culture'* W.L. Moran (ed). Cambridge, MA: Harvard University Press.

Jacobsen, T. (1976) *The Treasures of Darkness: A History of Mesopotamian Religion.* New Haven and London: Yale University Press.

Jacobsen, T. (1984) *The Harab Myth.* Malibu: Undena Publications. (Sources and Monographs on the Ancient Near East, Volume 2, Fascicle 3.)

Jacobsen, T. (1987) *The Harps That Once … Sumerian Poetry in Translation.* New Haven and London: Yale University Press.

The Jerusalem Bible (1968) Reader's Edition. Garden City, NY: Doubleday.

Joshi, P.J. (1986) 'India and Bahrain: A survey of culture interaction during the third and second millennia.' In S.H.A. Al Khalifa and M. Rice (ed) *Bahrain through the Ages: The Archaeology.* London and New York: KPI.

Jung, C.G. (1916) *Psychology of the Unconscious.* New York: Moffat Yard.

Jung, C.G. and Kerényi, C. (1963) *Essays on a Science of Mythology: The Myths of the Divine Child and the Divine Maiden.* New York: Harper and Row.

Kees, H. (1977) *Ancient Egypt: A Cultural Topography* (ed. T.G.H. James, trans. I.F.D. Morrow). Chicago, IL, and London: The University of Chicago Press.

Kilmer, A.D. (1972) 'The Mesopotamian concept of overpopulation and its solution as reflected in mythology.' *Orientalia 41*, 160–177.

KMT (1991) *A Modern Journal of Ancient Egypt.* Summer. San Francisco, CA: KMT Communications.

Kopalinski, W. (1990) *Slownik Symboli.* (*Dictionary of Symbols.*) Warsaw: Wiedza Powszechna.

Kotwal, F.M. and Boyd, J.W.(eds) (1982) *A Guide to the Zoroastrian Religion.* Chico, CA: Scholars Press.

Kramer, S.N. (1952) *Enmerkar and the Lord of Aratta. A Sumerian Epic Tale of Iraq and Iran.* Philadelphia, PA: Museum monographs, The University Museum, University of Pennsylvania.

Kramer, S.N. (1959) *History Begins at Sumer.* New York: Doubleday Anchor Books.

Kramer S.N. (ed) (1961) *Mythologies of the Ancient World*. Chicago, IL: Quadrangle Books.

Kramer, S.N. (1973) 'A Sumerian myth.' In J.B. Pritchard (ed) *The Ancient Near East. Volume I: An Anthology of Texts and Pictures*. Princeton, NJ: Princeton University Press.

Kramer, S.N. (1986) *In the World of Sumer: An Autobiography*. Detroit, MI: Wayne State University Press.

Kramer, S.N. and Maier, J. (1989) *Myths of Enki, the Crafty God*. New York and Oxford: Oxford University Press.

Lambert, W.G. and Millard, A.R. (1969) *Atra-hasis: The Babylonian Story of the Flood*. Oxford: Oxford University Press.

Leick, G. (1994) *Sex and Eroticism in Mesopotamian Literature*. London and New York: Routledge.

Lesko, L.H. (1991) 'Ancient Egyptian cosmogonics and cosmology.' In B.E. Shafer (ed) *Religion in Ancient Egypt: Gods, Myths, and Personal Practice*. Ithaca, NY, and London: Cornell University Press.

Lessa, W.A. and Vogt, E. (eds) (1979) *Reader in Comparative Religion: An Anthropological Approach*. New York: Harper and Row.

Lévi-Strauss, C. (1979) 'The structural study of myth.' In W.A. Lessa and E.Z. Vogt (eds) *Reader in Comparative Religion: An Anthropological Approach*. New York: Harper and Row.

Lichtheim, M. (1975) *Ancient Egyptian Literature. Volume I: The Old and Middle Kingdoms*. Berkeley, CA, Los Angeles, CA, and London: University of California Press.

Lichtheim, M. (1997a) 'The Great Hymn to the Aten (1.28). In the Tomb of Ay – West Wall, 13 Columns.' In W.W. Hallo (ed) *The Context of Scripture. Volume I: Canonical Compositions from the Biblical World*. Leiden, New York and Cologne: Brill.

Lichtheim, M. (1997b) 'The Great Hymn to Osiris (1.26) (On the Stela of Amenmose – Louvre C 286).' In W.W. Hallo (ed) *The Context of Scripture, Volume I: Canonical Compositions from the Biblical World*. Leiden, New York and Cologne: Brill.

Lichtheim, M. (1997c) 'Instructions. Merikare (1.35).' In W.W. Hallo (ed) *The Context of Scripture. Volume I: Canonical Compositions from the Biblical World*. Leiden, New York and Cologne: Brill.

Lichty, E.V. (1971) 'Demons and population control.' *Expedition 13*, 2, 22–26.

Lincoln, B. (1991) *Death, War, and Sacrifice: Studies in Ideology and Practice*. Chicago, IL: The University of Chicago Press.

Lippard, L.R. (1983) *Overlay. Contemporary Art and the Art of Prehistory*. New York: Pantheon Books.

Longrigg, S.H. (1967) *The Middle East: A Social Geography*. Chicago, IL: Aldine Publishing Company.

Loon, M.N. van (1985) *Anatolia in the Second Millennium B.C*. Leiden: Brill.

Lurker, M. (1984) *The Gods and Symbols of Ancient Egypt*. London and New York: Thames and Hudson.

Lyczkowska, K. and Szarzynska, K. (1981) *Mitologia Mezopotamii*. (Mythology of Mesopotamia.) Warsaw: Wydawnictwa Artystyczne i Filmowe.

Macqueen, J.G. (1996) *The Hittites and Their Contemporaries in Asia Minor*. New York: Thames and Hudson.

Mair, V.H. (1995) 'Mummies of the Tarim Basin.' *Archaeology*, March/April, 28–35.

Malandra, W.W. (1983) *An Introduction to Ancient Iranian Religion: Readings from the Avesta and Achaemenid Religion*. Minneapolis: University of Minnesota Press.

Malinowski, B. (1979) 'The role of magic and religion.' In W.A. Lessa and E.Z. Vogt (eds) *Reader in Comparative Religion: An Anthropological Approach*. New York: Harper and Row.

Mallory, J.P. (1996) *In Search of Indo-Europeans: Language, Archaeology and Myth*. London and New York: Thames and Hudson.

Manniche, L. (1987) *Sexual Life in Ancient Egypt.* London and New York: KPI.

Matthiae, P. (1980) *Ebla: An Empire Rediscovered.* London: Hodder and Stoughton.

Mayerson, P. (1971) *Classical Mythology in Literature, Art, and Music.* Glenview, IL: Scott, Foresman and Company.

Meeks, D. and Favard-Meeks, C. (1996) *Daily Life of the Egyptian Gods* (trans. G.M. Goshgarian). Ithaca and London: Cornell University Press.

Meier, S.A. (1991) 'Women and communication in the ancient near east.' *Journal of the American Oriental Society 111,* 540–547.

Meissner, B. (1925) *Babylonien und Assyrien II.* (Babylonia and Assyria II.) Heidelberg: Carl Winters.

Meshel, Z. (1979) 'Did Yahweh have a consort?' *Biblical Archaeology Review, 5,* 2, 24–35.

Meyers, C. (1988) *Discovering Eve: Ancient Israelite Women in Context.* Oxford: Oxford University Press.

Moran, W.L. (ed) (1970) *Toward the Image of Tammuz and Other Essays on Mesopotamian History and Culture. Thorkild Jacobsen.* Cambridge, MA: Harvard University Press.

Morenz, S. (1973) *Egyptian Religion* (trans. Ann E. Keep). Ithaca, NY: Cornell University Press.

Mughal, M.R. (1983) *The Dilmun Burial Complex at Sar: The 1980–82 Excavations in Bahrain.* State of Bahrain: Ministry of Information, Directorate of Archaeology and Museums.

Naccache, A.F.H. (1996) 'El's Abode in his land.' In N. Wyatt, W.G.E. Watson and J.B. Lloyd (eds) *Ugarit, Religion and Culture: Proceedings of the International Colloquium on Ugarit, Religion and Culture. Edinburgh, July 1994.* Münster: Ugarit Verlag.

Neusner, J. (1986) *Judaism, Christianity, and Zoroastrianism in Talmudic Babylonia.* Lanham, New York, London: University Press of America.

Nissen, H.J. (1986) 'The occurrence of Dilmun in the oldest texts of Mesopotamia.' In Al Khalifa, S.H.A. and M. Rice (eds) *Bahrain Through the Ages. The Archaeology.* London and New York: KPI.

Pardee, D. (1996) 'Marzihu, Kispu, and the Ugaritic funerary cult: A minimalist view.' In N. Wyatt, W.G.E. Watson and J.B. Lloyd (eds) *Ugarit, Religion And Culture: Proceedings of the International Colloquium on Ugarit, Religion and Culture. Edinburgh, July 1994.* Münster: Ugarit-Verlag.

Pardee, D. (1997) 'The Ba'lu myth (1.86).' In W.W. Hallo (ed) *The Context of Scripture. Volume I: Canonical Compositions from the Biblical World.* Leiden, New York and Cologne: Brill.

Parpola, S. (1997a) *State Archives of Assyria: Assyrian Prophecies.* Helsinki: Helsinki University Press.

Parpola, S. (1997b) 'The standard Babylonian Epic of Gilgamesh: cuneiform text, transliteration, glossary, indices and sign list.' In *State Archives of Assyria Cuneiform Texts, Volume I.* Helsinki: University of Helsinki: Department of Asian and African Studies.

Parrot, A. (1955) *The Flood and Noah's Ark.* New York: Philosophical Library.

Picard, B.L. (1993) *Tales of Ancient Persia.* Oxford, New York and Toronto: Oxford University Press.

Platt, R.H. (ed) (1980) *The Forgotten Books of Eden.* New York: Gramercy Books.

Popko, M. (1995) *Religions of Asia Minor.* Warsaw: Academic Publications.

Potts, D.T. (ed) (1983) *Dilmun.: New Studies in the Archaeology and Early History of Bahrain.* Berlin: D. Reimer Verlag.

Pritchard, J.B.(ed) (1973) *The Ancient Near East. Volume I: An Anthology of Texts and Pictures.* Princeton, NJ: Princeton University Press.

Pritchard, J.B.(ed) (1975) *The Ancient Near East. Volume II: A New Anthology of Texts and Pictures.* Princeton, NJ: Princeton University Press.

Puhvel, J. (1987) *Comparative Mythology.* Baltimore, MD: The Johns Hopkins University Press.

Quirke, S. (1992) *Ancient Egyptian Religion.* London: British Museum Press.

Rajaram, N.S. and Frawley, D. (1995) *Vedic 'Aryans' and the Origins of Civilization.* Quebec: W.H. Press.

Rao, S.R. (1986) 'Trade and cultural contacts between Bahrain and India in the third and second millennia B.C.' In S.H.A. Al Khalifa and M. Rice (eds) *Bahrain through the Ages: The Archaeology.* London and New York: KPI.

Redfield, R. (1965) *Peasant Society and Culture: An Anthropological Approach to Civilization.* Chicago, IL, and London: The University of Chicago Press.

Redford, D.B. (1987) *Akhenaten, the Heretic King.* Princeton, NJ: Princeton University Press.

Renfrew, C. (1987) *Archaeology and Language.* Cambridge: Cambridge University Press.

Rice, M. (1984) (ed) *Dilmun Discovered: The Early Years of Archaeology in Bahrain.* London and New York: The Longman Group.

Rice, M. (1985) *Search for the Paradise Land.* London and New York: Longman.

Rice, M. (1986) 'The island on the edge of the world.' In S.H.A. Al Khalifa and M. Rice (eds) *Bahrain through the Ages: The Archaeology.* London and New York: KPI.

Ritner, R.K. (1993) *The Mechanics of Ancient Egyptian Magical Practice.* Chicago, IL: Oriental Institute of the University Press.

Ritner, R.K. (1997a) 'The repulsing of the dragon (1.21) (Coffin Text 160).' In W.W. Hallo (ed) *The Context of Scripture. Volume I: Canonical Compositions from the Biblical World.* Leiden, New York and Cologne: Brill.

Ritner, R.K. (1997b) 'The Great Cairo Hymn of Praise to Amun-Re (1.25). P.Cairo 58038 (p.Bulaq 17).' In W.W. Hallo (ed) *The Context of Scripture. Volume I: Canonical Compositions from the Biblical World.* Leiden, New York and Cologne: Brill.

Ritner, R.K. (1997c) 'Book of the Dead 175 (1.18). "Rebellion, Death and Apocalypse."' In W.W. Hallo (ed) *The Context of Scripture. Volume I: Canonical Compositions from the Biblical World.* Leiden, New York and Cologne: Brill.

Roth, M.T. (1997) *Law Collections from Mesopotamia and Asia Minor.* Atlanta, GA: Scholars Press.

Sarna, N.M. (1996) 'Genesis I–II.' In A. Feyerick (ed) *Genesis: World of Myths and Patriarchs.* New York and London: New York University Press.

Schmandt-Besserat, D. (1992) *Before Writing: From Counting to Cuneiform.* Volume I. Austin, TX: University of Texas Press.

Shafer, B.E. (ed) (1991) *Religion in Ancient Egypt: Gods, Myths, and Personal Practice.* Ithaca, NY, and London: Cornell University Press.

Shaw, I. and Nicholson, P. (1995) *The Dictionary of Ancient Egypt.* London and New York: Harry N. Abrams.

Silverman, D.P. (1991) 'Divinity and deities in ancient Egypt.' In B.E. Shafer (ed) *Religion in Ancient Egypt: Gods, Myths, and Personal Practice.* Ithaca, NY, and London: Cornell University Press.

Silverman, D.P. (ed) (1997) *Ancient Egypt.* New York: Oxford University Press.

Singh, M. (1993) *The Sun: Symbol of Power and Life.* New York: Harry N. Abrams, and UNESCO.

Smith, M.S. (1994) *The Ugaritic Baal Cycle: Introduction with Text, Translation and Commentary of KTU 1.1–1.2., Volume 1.* Leiden and New York: Brill.

Soden, W. von (1994) *The Ancient Orient: An Introduction to the Study of the Ancient Near East.* Grand Rapids, MI: William B. Eerdmans Publishing Company.

Speiser, E.A (1955) *Ancient Near Eastern Texts Relating to the Old Testament.* Princeton, NJ: Princeton University Press.

Speiser, E.A. (1973) 'Akkadian myths and epics.' In J.B. Pritchard (ed) *The Ancient Near East. Volume I: An Anthology of Texts and Pictures.* Princeton, NJ: Princeton University Press.

Stark, R. and Bainbridge, W.S. (1987) *A Theory of Religion.* New York: Peter Lang.

Stiebing, W.H. Jr. (1993) *Uncovering the Past: A History of Archaeology.* Buffalo, NY: Prometheus Books.

Strensky, I. (1987) *Four Theories of Myth in Twentieth-Century History: Cassirer, Eliade, Lévi-Strauss and Malinowski.* Iowa City, IA: University of Iowa Press.

Strensky, I. (ed) (1992) *Malinowski and the Work of Myth.* Princeton, NJ: Princeton University Press.

Tigay, J.H. (1982) *The Evolution of the Gilgamesh Epic.* Philadelphia, PA: University of Pennsylvania Press.

Toynbee, A. (1956) *An Historian's Approach to Religion.* Oxford and New York: Oxford University Press.

Ullendorff, E. (1968) *Ethiopia and the Bible.* London: Oxford University Press.

Van Dijk, J. (1964) 'The cosmic motif in Sumerian thoughts.' *Acta Orientalia 28*, I, 1–59.

Vogelzang, M.E. and Vanstiphout, H.L.J. (ed) (1992) *Mesopotamian Epic Literature: Oral or Aural?* Lewiston/Queenston/Lampeter: The Edwin Mellen Press.

Vogelzang, M.E. and Vanstiphout, H.L.J. (ed) (1996) *Mesopotamian Poetic Language: Sumerian and Akkadian.* Groningen: STYX Publications.

Wallace, A.F.C. (1966) *Religion: An Anthropological View.* New York: Random House.

Wallace, H.N. (1985) *The Eden Narrative.* Atlanta, GA: Scholars Press.

Walls, N.H. (1992) *The Goddess Anat in Ugaritic Myth.* Atlanta, GA: Scholars Press.

Ward, W.A. (1994) 'Beetle in stone: The Egyptian scarab.' *Biblical Archaeologist 57*, 4, 186–202.

Wasilewska, E. (1991a) *The Search for the Sacred: the Archaeology of Religion and the Interpretation of Color Symbolism in Prehistoric Societies.* Ph.D. dissertation. Salt Lake City, UT: University of Utah.

Wasilewska, E. (1991b) 'Archaeology of religion: Colors as symbolic markers dividing sacred from profane.' *Journal of Prehistoric Religion 5*, 36–41.

Wasilewska, E. (1994) 'The search for the impossible: The archaeology of religion of prehistoric societies as an anthropological discipline.' *Journal of Prehistoric Religion 8*, 62–75.

Watterson, B. (1985) *The Gods of Ancient Egypt.* New York and Bicester: Facts On File Publications.

Weisgerber, G. (1986) 'Dilmun – A trading entrepôt: Evidence from historical and archaeological sources.' In S.H.A. Al Khalifa and M. Rice (eds) *Bahrain through the Ages: The Archaeology.* London and New York: KPI.

Widengren, G. (1951) *The King and the Tree of Life in the Ancient Near Eastern Religion.* Uppsala: Lundequistska Bokhandel. Leipzig: Harrassowitz.

Wiggins, S. (1996) 'Shapsh, lamp of the gods.' In N. Wyatt, W.G.E. Watson and J.B. Lloyd (eds) *Ugarit, Religion and Culture: Proceedings of the International Colloquium on Ugarit, Religion and Culture. Edinburgh, July 1994.* Münster: Ugarit Verlag.

Wilson, J.A. (1968) *The Culture of Ancient Egypt.* Chicago, IL, and London: The University of Chicago Press.

Zauzich, K. (1996) *Hieroglyphs without Mystery: An Introduction to Ancient Egyptian Writing* (trans. A.M. Roth). Austin, TX: University of Texas Press.

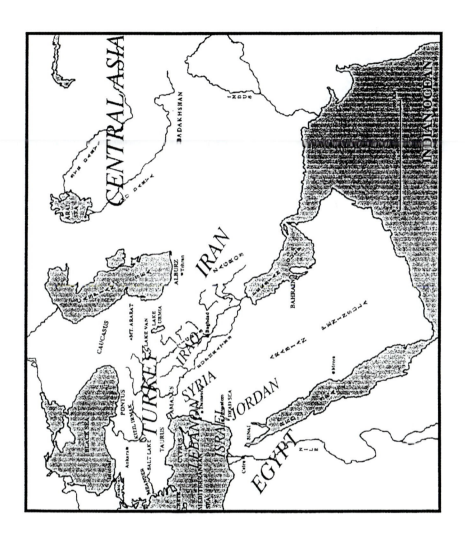

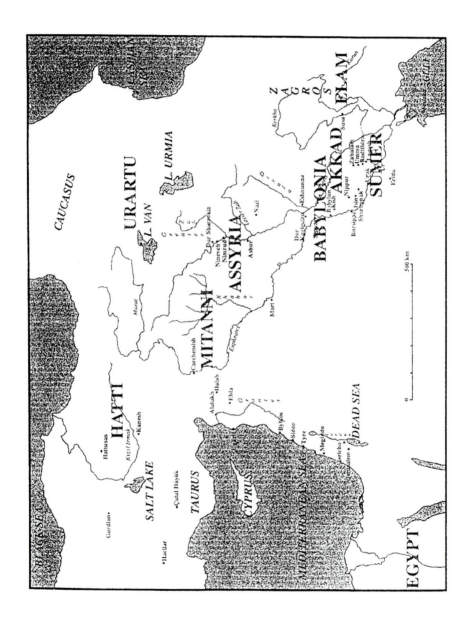

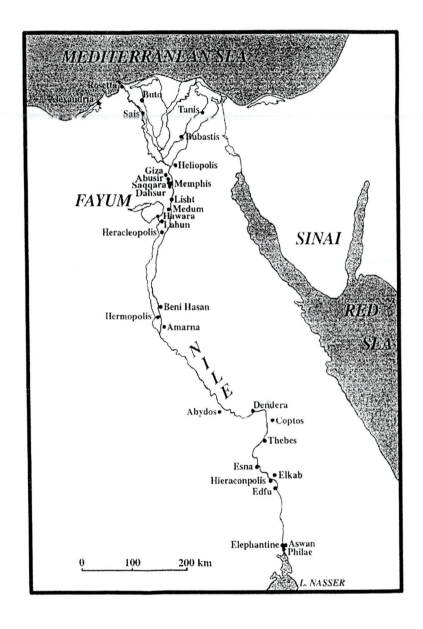

MEDITERRANEAN SEA

Rosetta
Alexandria
Buto
Sais
Tanis
Bubastis
Heliopolis
Giza
Abusir
Saqqara Memphis
Dahsur
FAYUM Lisht
Medum
Hawara
Lahun
Heracleopolis

SINAI

Beni Hasan
Hermopolis
Amarna

NILE

RED
SEA

Abydos Dendera
Coptos
Thebes
Esna
Elkab
Hieraconpolis
Edfu

Elephantine Aswan
Philae

0   100   200 km

L. NASSER

Appendix II: Chronological Outline of Middle Eastern History

DATE (B.C.) approximate	EGYPT	MESOPOTAMIA	ANATOLIA	SYRIA–PALESTINE	PERSIA
3500	Predynastic (cont.)	Early and Late Uruk Protoliterate			Proto-Elamite (e.g., Tall-i-Malyan)
	Early Dynastic (Dynasties I & II) around 3150–2700	Uruk Early Sumerian and Jemdet Nasr around 3200–2800			
	writing (hieroglyphic)	writing (Sumerian – cuneiform)			writing? (Proto-Elamite)
3000	Old Kingdom (Dynasties III to VI) around 2700–2190	Early Dynastic around 2800–2330			writing (cuneiform)
2500	Old Kingdom (cont.)	Early Dynastic (cont.)			
	First Intermediate Period (Dynasties VII to X and part of the XI) around 2200–2040	Akkadian Dynasty around 2330–2193			
		UR III around 2100–1955			
		Fall of Ur – around 2004			

DATE (B.C.) approximate	EGYPT	MESOPOTAMIA	ANATOLIA	SYRIA–PALESTINE	PERSIA
2000	Middle Kingdom (Dynasties XI to XII) around 2040–1785 Second Intermediate Period (Dynasties XIII to XVII) around 1785–1552 Hyksos rule	North – Old Assyrian around 1900–1750 South – Isin-Larsa Period around 2000–1763 Old Babylonian Period around 1950–1595 includes the First Dynasty of Babylon with Hammurabi – 1792–1750 1595 – Babylon captured by Mursilis I (Hittites)	Assyrian Colonies, e.g. Kültepe, Bogazköy, around 1940–1780 writing (cuneiform) Old Hittite Kingdom around 1700–1450 1595 – Babylon captured by Mursilis I	Canaanites Mari archives around 1810–1760 (annexed by Hammurabi) writing (cuneiform and linear alphabetic)	Old Elamite, e.g. Susa
1500	New Kingdom (Dynasties XVIII to XX) around 1552–1069 includes Amarna archives around 1350–1330	North – Mittani/Hurrian Kingdom around 1460–1330 North – Middle Assyrian around 1300–1100	Hittite Empire around 1420–1180	under Egyptian and Hittite control	Middle Elamite

DATE (B.C.) approximate	EGYPT	MESOPOTAMIA	ANATOLIA	SYRIA-PALESTINE	PERSIA
1500 (cont.)	around 1180 – the Sea People stopped by Ramesses III	South – Middle Babylonian around 1595–1000 includes the Kassite Dynasty around 1595–1158 destroyed in 1158 by the Elamites (Shutruk-nahhunte)	reign of Suppiluliumas around 1380–1334	around 1286 – battle at Qadesh between the Hittites and the Egyptians over control of this region	
			end of the Empire – arrival of the Sea People	numerous cities destroyed by the Sea People	1158 – Shutruk-nahhunte conquered Babylon
				Israelites and Philistines settled in southern Canaan	
1000	Assyrian invasion: 671 – Esarhaddon captured Memphis 663 – Ashurbanipal in Thebes Third Intermediate Period (Dynasties XXI to XXV) around 1069–702	North – Neo-Assyrian Period around 1000–612 Assyrian domination of the Middle East until 612	various independent kingdoms and principalities: Neo-Hittites (e.g. Carchemish), Urartians (e.g. Van), Phrygians (e.g. Gordion)	various independent. kingdoms and principalities: Aramaeans (e.g. Tell Half), Phoenicians (e.g. Sidon, Tyre), Israel and Judah (south)	Neo-Elamite (e.g. Susa), the Medes and the Persians

DATE (B.C.) approximate	EGYPT	MESOPOTAMIA	ANATOLIA	SYRIA–PALESTINE	PERSIA
1000 (cont.)	Saite Period (Dynasty XXVI) 664–525 Late Period (Dynasties XXVII to XXXI) 525–332; includes First Persian Domination (XXVII) – 525–404	612 – Fall of Nineveh (the end of the Assyrian empire) – combined forces of the Babylonians and Persians South – Neo-Babylonian Period around 1000–539 mostly under Assyrian control: includes Chaldean Dynasty (625–539) 597 and 586 – conquests of Jerusalem 539 – Cyrus' invasion of Babylon and the beginning of Persian domination	also invasions and/or settlements of the Cimmerians, Greeks, and the Medes small Indo-European kingdoms of Lycia and Lydia Persian wars	Assyrian domination 597 and 586 – conquests of Jerusalem by the Babylonians	the empire beginning with Cyrus the Great (550–530)

DATE (B.C.) approximate	EGYPT	MESOPOTAMIA	ANATOLIA	SYRIA–PALESTINE	PERSIA
500	Second Persian Domination (XXXI) 341–332 B.C.	Persian domination Achaemenid Empire 538–331	Persian wars and domination Greek colonies	Persian control	Achaemenid Empire
	332 – conquest (or liberation) by Alexander the Great	331 – Babylon captured by Alexander the Great			331 – Darius III defeated by Alexander the Great

HELLENISTIC PERIOD

323 – death of Alexander the Great and division of his empire among his generals

DATE (B.C.) approximate	EGYPT	MESOPOTAMIA	ANATOLIA	SYRIA–PALESTINE	PERSIA
	Ptolemaic Period 332–30 B.C. last ruler – Cleopatra VII	the Seleucids and the Parthians	small kingdoms, principalities, and colonies	small kingdoms and principalities conflict area between Seleucids and Parthians	the Seleucids and the Parthians

CHRISTIAN ERA/ROMAN DOMINATION
A.D. 1

BYZANTINE (EASTERN ROMAN) EMPIRE
A.D. 337

ISLAMIC ERA AND ARAB CONQUEST
A.D. 622

Subject Index

Author Index

Lightning Source UK Ltd.
Milton Keynes UK
UKOW051703151112

202146UK00005B/1/A